I0820253

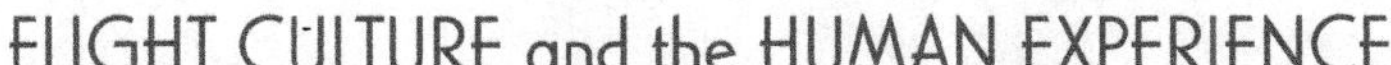

FLIGHT CULTURE and the HUMAN EXPERIENCE

THE WALTER PRESCOTT WEBB MEMORIAL LECTURES

Published for the University of Texas at Arlington
by Texas A&M University Press
College Station

FLIGHT CULTURE AND THE HUMAN EXPERIENCE

EDITED BY SCOTT W. PALMER

With Contributions by

Caroline E. Tapp
Patrick Luiz Sullivan de Oliveira
Johanna Rustler
Marc Alsina
Marc Dierikx
Rénald Fortier
Janet Bednarek
Michael W. Hankins

TEXAS A&M UNIVERSITY PRESS
College Station

First edition

♾ This paper meets the requirements of ANSI/
NISO Z39.48–1992 (Permanence of Paper).
Binding materials have been chosen for durability.

Library of Congress Cataloging-in-Publication Data
Names: Palmer, Scott W., 1967– editor | Tapp, Caroline E. writer of introduction
Title: Flight culture and the human experience / edited by Scott W. Palmer ; with contributions by Caroline E. Tapp, Patrick Luiz Sullivan de Oliveira, Johanna Rustler, Marc Alsina, Marc Dierikx, Rénald Fortier, Janet Bednarek, Michael W. Hankins.
Other titles: Walter Prescott Webb memorial lectures
Description: First edition. | College Station: Texas A&M University Press, [2025] | Series: The Walter Prescott Webb memorial lectures | Includes bibliographical references and index.
Identifiers: LCCN 2025028813 (print) | LCCN 2025028814 (ebook) | ISBN 9781648433078 hardcover | ISBN 9781648433085 ebook
Subjects: LCSH: Aeronautics—Social aspects | Aeronautics and civilization | Air travel—History
Classification: LCC TL553 .F55 2025 (print) | LCC TL553 (ebook) | DDC 387.7/42—dc23/eng/20250807
LC record available at https://lccn.loc.gov/2025028813
LC ebook record available at https://lccn.loc.gov/2025028814

CONTENTS

FLIGHT CULTURE and the HUMAN EXPERIENCE

INTRODUCTION

Caroline E. Tapp

I live on the flight path of Washington Dulles International Airport. It's not uncommon on a sunny day to experience a momentary eclipse as I find myself in the shadow of a 737 tracking northbound. If I'm lucky enough to be outside, I can decipher the airline by identifying the paint scheme and trademark designs. During this momentary suspension of time, I find myself musing about the comings and goings of each passenger above, the crew's home base, and whether anyone with a window seat is disappointed they won't catch a glimpse of the Washington Monument when they learn Reagan International is the airport *in* DC (we've all been there).

Instinctively looking up at the slightest sound of an engine overhead, I'm struck by the second nature of this ritual and its ingrained presence in my daily life. While not everyone has a steady stream of airliners gracing their neighborhood skies, I'd bet my frequent-flier miles that flight has entered your life in an equally ubiquitous manner. Whether through the movies we watch, the packages we receive, or the way we reach and understand the world around us, flight culture has become an intrinsic part of the human experience. As this volume shows, that experience transcends geographic borders and historical timelines and extends beyond technological understandings to ask complex and pointed questions about how various cultures interact with the realm of flight.

NEW AEROSPACE HISTORY TAKES FLIGHT

Flight Culture and the Human Experience marks yet another milestone in the expanding lens and scope of New Aerospace History. By centering the human experience of flight across the globe and providing complex analyses of how these experiences embed themselves in cultural understandings, each author presents a case for aviation's unique role in developing systemic structures that govern our understanding of technological development.

This volume builds on more than forty years of scholarly inquiry shaped by key observers and editors of collections of essays that have molded the field. In 1983, Joseph Corn's *Winged Gospel* compared American enthusiasm for aviation during the first half of the twentieth century to a secular religion that promoted the technology's power of democratization.[1] By the end of the decade, historian James R. Hansen identified such work as part of a larger conversation to be had about the way scholars, and historians in particular, study and discuss aviation. While aviation histories through the late 1980s intertwined important aspects of human relationships to technology, analysis still placed the technology itself at the center of the story. Noting that historians were not asking the "big" questions, the Smithsonian Institution Press aviation history advisory board commissioned a historiographical study on aviation history. "Something important is missing, they must feel—something that can help put together that which is loose and fragmentary; something that can make aviation history more meaningful in the overall record of human existence," Hansen noted.[2]

Immediately following Hansen's take on expanding the field, the early 1990s welcomed multiple new works, including Susan Ware's book on Amelia Earhart and feminism, Robert J. Jakeman's work on segregated flight training, and several examinations of aviation in the cultural imagination that furthered the types of questions scholars asked about flight.[3] Alongside the continuing growth of new social history in the United States, these studies fused previous technological understandings of flight with cultural issues shaping the field of aviation at large to enrich and expand the historiography. As former curator at the Smithsonian National Air and Space Museum, Dominick Pisano, noted in his overview for the Centennial of Flight Commission, "The combination of a new historiography [coupled] with increasing interest on the part of trained academic historians in aviation and space flight as legitimate topics in the history of technology have given historical treatment of the subject matter a new dimension."[4]

Just before the turn of the millennium, Roger Launius, then chief historian at NASA, coined the term "New Aviation History" to identify the field of scholarship that emerged following Hansen's 1989 call to create a meaningful record of aviation history and human experiences.[5] In the introduction to *The Airplane in American Culture* in 2003, Pisano convincingly articulated his belief that "nearly one hundred years after the invention of the airplane and with time to reevaluate its social cultural and political effects on our lives, the writing of the history of the subject has not progressed as far as it could or should."[6] As Launius suggested, New Aviation (subsequently, New Aerospace) History was the official response to this gap. Works including Deborah Douglas's *American Women and Flight Since 1940* (2004), A. Bowdoin Van Riper's *Imagining Flight* (2004), Margaret Weitekamp's *Right Stuff, Wrong Sex* (2004), and Scott W. Palmer's *Dictatorship of the Air* (2006) continued pushing for change in the field.[7]

In analyzing aviation from the perspective of cultural and social history, these new works revealed the human elements underlying histories of flight that had previously been told as stories of technology. Released in the same time frame, Bayla Singer's *Like Sex with Gods: An Unorthodox History of Flying* (2003) was yet another "exemplar of the 'New Aerospace History.'" Praising the work nearly two decades after its release, Jason Trew noted, "Not only does [Singer] show the interplay of psychological aspects of flight with its technical aspects, but she also embraces the playfulness of her approach."[8] New Aerospace History thus not only expanded methodologies but also included accessible and engaging writing styles to reach broader audiences.

This step toward inclusive engagement shines through three works published in 2013, Phil Tiemeyer's *Plane Queer*, Victoria Vantoch's *The Jet Sex*, and Jenifer Van Vleck's *Empire of the Air*.[9] In his review of the three monographs, Pisano's "New Directions for the History of Aviation" marked yet another expansion of the growing field. He explained how "the New Aerospace History is intrinsically committed to relating the subject to larger issues of society, politics, and culture, taking a more sophisticated view of the science, technology, and individual projects than historians previously held."[10] As Pisano argues, these three works represent a distinct shift away from technological determinism, or the idea that technology has a progressive quality that exists separate from or beyond the realm of human influence.

New Aerospace History has continued to push interdisciplinary boundaries by exploring how technological innovation and the daily experience of flight have become embedded within larger, systematic understandings of our world. In *Realizing the New Aerospace History*, a 2014 review of six books that "marked the best aspects of the genre," Roger Launius noted the extent to which these works have proven masterful at demonstrating how differing aspects of flight technology are central to comprehending society, culture, and politics at large. Echoing his original introduction from the 1999 volume *Innovation and the Development of Flight*, Launius described how these works "move beyond a fetish for the artifact to emphasize . . . whole technological systems . . . as an integral part of the human experience."[11] The shift in terminology from "New Aviation" to "New Aerospace" History by 2014 also represented an important recognition regarding the intertwining cultural systems that undergirded scholarly analysis of both aviation and spaceflight.

More recently, the field has continued to shift by reflecting the unique perspectives of those asking the questions. Jason Trew, for example, has encouraged historians of technology to focus more on the lived experience of "technology in use," while noting that aviation history is particularly well suited to do so. "Excitement over flight," he suggests, "should remain part of the historiographical toolkit, as both content for examination and the historian's own inspiration."[12] Themes such as sustainability and leadership have assumed a prominent role through works by mobility scholar Christopher Schaberg and transport and tourism scholar Stefan Gössling. Both have examined the cultural landscape of commercial aviation during the COVID-19 pandemic to highlight the economic importance and cultural significance of aviation.[13]

As the field continues to fill previous historiographical gaps by promoting inclusive investigations, works such as Anke Ortlepp's *Jim Crow Terminals*, Katherine Sharp Landdeck's *The Women with Silver Wings*, and Alan Meyer's forthcoming book *Flying While Black* are crucial to understanding the full scope and cultural landscape of aviation history.[14] Recent publications, including Michael Hankins's *Flying Camelot* and Randy Goguen's *From Yeomanettes to Fighter Jets*, underscore the importance of cultural analysis in military aviation history, a field that has historically emphasized technological and operational analysis over the influence of human factors.[15] Integrating with various fields has proven key to the success and reevaluation of histories involving aviation technology.

FLIGHT CULTURE AND THE HUMAN EXPERIENCE

This current volume opens novel and important pathways in New Aerospace History's continuing journey. Expanding upon public presentations delivered at the 55th Annual Webb Lecture Series (2021), it brings together the findings of seven established and emerging scholars to shed important new light onto the myriad ways aviation has contributed to the ideas, institutions, and identities that shape the contemporary human experience. Together, these seven essays reflect the value of comparative inquiry and the conscious effort by scholars to build upon Hansen's initial vision for a wider, more meaningful view of aviation history.[16]

While flight culture conjures images of the skies, Patrick Luiz Sullivan De Oliveira guides readers through the streets of Paris in 1848 in unraveling the story of Ernest Pétin, a French milliner turned airship designer. In the volume's opening chapter, "The Utopian Machine: Lighter-Than-Air Flight and Romantic Socialism in Nineteenth-Century France," De Oliveira reveals the complicated relationship between nineteenth-century socialist thought, utopian discourse, and a surprisingly widespread faith in lighter-than-air technology's ability to bring about new and improved worlds. De Oliveira argues that nineteenth-century romantic socialists, operating in a milieu promoted by the socialist press and social networks, "imagined dynamic and mobile societies" and embraced technologies that promoted movement. "Lighter-than-air flight," he suggests, "became one of their idealized emancipatory technologies." By analyzing how socialists and writers outside of the socialist press reacted to Pétin's design, De Oliveira demonstrates the extent to which flight captured the public imagination as a global technology and how enthusiasm for utopian ideals of flight lived on in the writings of Victor Hugo and others. Through this carefully crafted essay, De Oliveira shows that the ways in which flight is imagined or interpreted are just as important to the sociopolitical context as the technology itself.

The collection's second chapter, "The British Air Mechanic at War and Aircraft Innovation, 1914–18" by Johanna Rustler, examines the essential, though long overlooked, contributions made by air mechanics to the Royal Flying Corps, the Royal Naval Air Service, and the Royal Air Force (following the merger of the previous two in April 1918). Noting that the literature devoted to those who "served in support activities behind the lines" is limited, Rustler shows how the details of daily life and the difficulty of their work culminated from adaptation to both pressured environments and technical developments, leading air mechanics to emerge as a new category of skilled workers during World War I. Through an array of vivid anecdotes and examples, Rustler addresses a common gap in aviation history by showcasing the lives and experiences of air mechanics as crucial to the development of a professional air force. Her chapter sheds light on the role of support positions, interpersonal relationships, and the risk of all wartime activities that made up British flight culture during the First World War. Perhaps most importantly, she demonstrates how their stories reflect the human element within the development of the aviation industry at large.

Marc Alsina's contribution directs the reader's attention to flight culture in South America through a chapter devoted to "Gender, Race, and Heroic Aviation in Interwar Argentina, 1920–40," which tackles the important role aviation played in constructing national identity. Situating readers in the vibrant cosmopolitanism of interwar Argentina, the chapter begins with an examination of race, human biology, and culture in discourses surrounding aviation. By highlighting figures including Jorge Newberry, Capt. Pedro Zanni, and Eduardo Olivero, Alsina shows how "the *aviador* was transforming from an exceptional individual whom the common man should emulate, to an identity *of* the common man." In flipping the script to analyze women pilots, Argentine media outlets rejected *la mujer moderna*—the modern woman. Through media analysis of famed *aviadoras* Myriam Stefford and Carola Lorenzini, Alsina reminds readers of the limits of social change during the interwar period in Argentina. By juxtaposing the analysis of how Argentine people fixated on heroic aviation through conceptions of modern men and modern women, this chapter reveals the complex relationship between social thought, technological change, and the power of flight culture in shaping identity.

Marc Dierikx's chapter on "Civil Air Transport and the Colonial Context in the Interwar Period" continues the through-line of the time period while expanding the geographic scope. Beginning with a riveting passage from the diary of Dutch professor of cartography and future prime minister Willem Schermerhorn, concerning his ten-day journey to the Dutch East Indies, Dierikx immediately transports the reader into the anxiety of flying colonial air routes. Detailing the efforts of France, Britain, and the Netherlands to create air transportation routes within colonies in Africa and Asia, with vivid imagery of interwar era advertisements, Dierikx illuminates the myriad factors that influenced air travel during this period, including infrastructure, technology, geography, and of course, money. As airmail typically preceded passenger air transport, air travel between the colonies and home governments became an important step in maintaining diplomatic ties and reducing the distance, if only by appearance, between the two entities. The chapter serves as a well-researched reminder of aviation's central role in globalization and how the modern system of air transport was undergirded by the colonial air transport systems of the interwar era.

Expanding the theme of the interwar era with a biographical element, Rénald Fortier's chapter focuses on the unexpected (and in some circles, unwelcomed) winner of the United States' 1936 National Air Races, Frenchman Michel Détroyat. His story encompasses major milestones of the golden age of aviation, from the 1927 transatlantic flight of Charles Augustus Lindbergh to the acquisition of American combat aircraft by the French Air Force in 1938–40. Most notably, however, in addition to winning the Greve Trophy in 1936, Détroyat was the first foreign pilot to win the Thompson Trophy race. His victory spurred reactions from American spectators, including disapproval by Roscoe Turner, and conversations in the American air racing community regarding foreign participants that changed the course of the air racing world. The performance put French airplane manufacturers at center stage and left many questioning the role of investment, design, and risk in the aeronautical industry. Détroyat's arrest in 1944 on suspicion of cooperating with the German occupation authorities began the flier's fall from grace in the eyes of the French government and the aeronautical industry at large. Fortier reminds readers of how Détroyat's victories in the 1936 edition of the National Air Races marked the end of the golden age of air racing in France and how closely diplomacy, aerodynamics, and individual life stories are intertwined in the history of flight.

Approaching the midpoint of the twentieth century with the transition to the jet age of the 1950s, Janet Bednarek tackles the rise of US airports in her chapter "Chasing the Future: Why US Airports Seem Always Under Construction." Juxtaposing the glamour of the jet-set lifestyle with the dirty and crowded airports that facilitated an otherwise luxurious form of travel during this era, Bednarek's chapter reminds readers that the "pardon our progress" signs alerting travelers to continuous construction are part of a longer history made up of three important factors: the rapid growth and decline of airports from the 1950s through the early twenty-first century, a shift in the post-9/11 security regime that challenged previous conceptions of the consumer-oriented "AirMall" layout, and changing ideas about futuristic airports, including their design and features. Through careful analysis of the ebbs and flows of airports over seven decades, Bednarek's chapter is crucial to understanding the built landscape of aviation as integral to social, economic, and cultural analysis of the airline industry at large and aviation's role in the fabric of our lives.

Rounding out the volume is Michael W. Hankins's piece, "Selling the Fighter Pilot's Dream Machines: The F-15 and F-16 in the Public Eye." In peeling back the intricate layers of design, marketing, and behind-the-scenes conflicts in air force leadership, Hankins brings readers into the debates surrounding the development of the F-15 Eagle and F-16 Fighting Falcon. The chapter proves that, given the unique technological moment of the 1970s, these fighters could excel in specific tasks such as air-to-air combat as well as missions including bombing and ground support. Motivated by a desire to generate foreign sales, institutional concerns, and technological advancements, United States–based aerospace and defense company

General Dynamics touted the F-16 as a multirole or multimission fighter. These tensions regarding airframe capabilities, including the preferences of the "Fighter Mafia," played out in public marketing materials and manufacturer promotional materials. The cultural analysis of these fighters through marketing and promotion reveals technology as but one component in the larger history of US military aviation.

The intellectual journey provided by *Flight Culture and the Human Experience* is both profound and unique. Traveling from Africa, Asia, Europe, and North and South America, this edited volume serves as a metaphorical airliner traversing thousands of miles while the reader remains in the comfort of their seat. In a world where many are accustomed to the wonders and convenience of air travel, the historical analysis provided in the aforementioned chapters brings readers back to a time when flight was new while opening analytical paths for interpreting the future. The compilation of these works comfortably takes an esteemed position within the field of New Aerospace History.

This collection of essays speaks to the timelessness of flight and the effervescent glow of historic moments and provides critical layers for interpreting aviation technologies in relationship with the governments, people, and places impacted by their development. Next time you hear the distinct hum of a Cessna 172 or see that 737 cast a shadow on the world, I hope this volume is a reminder of the extent to which flight is a deeply embedded human experience. Whether on a personal, national, or global level, flight culture represents history in the making. This collection serves as your ticket to the past.

NOTES

1. Joseph Corn, *The Winged Gospel: America's Romance with Aviation, 1900–1950* (Oxford: Oxford University Press, 1983).
2. James R. Hansen, "Aviation History in the Wider View," *Technology and Culture* 30, no. 3 (1989): 644, https://doi.org/10.2307/3105965.
3. Susan Ware, *Still Missing: Amelia Earhart and the Search for Modern Feminism* (New York: W. W. Norton, 1993); Robert J. Jakeman, *The Divided Skies: Establishing Segregated Flight Training at Tuskegee, Alabama, 1934–1942* (Tuscaloosa: University of Alabama Press, 1992); Peter Fritzsche, *German Aviation and the Popular Imagination* (Cambridge: Harvard University Press, 1992); Robert Wohl, *A Passion for Wings: Aviation and the Western Imagination, 1908–1918* (New Haven: Yale University Press, 1994).

4. Dominick A. Pisano, "The Social and Cultural History of Aviation and Spaceflight, Part I," US Centennial of Flight Commission, accessed February 2, 2024, http://www.centennialofflight.net/essay/Social/SH-OV2.htm.
5. Roger D. Launius, ed., *Innovation and the Development of Flight* (College Station: Texas A&M University Press, 1999), 14. See also Roger D. Launius, "The Historical Dimensions of Space Exploration: Reflections and Possibilities," *Space Policy* 16 (2000): 23–38.
6. Dominick A. Pisano, ed., *The Airplane in American Culture* (Ann Arbor: University of Michigan Press, 2003), 6.
7. Deborah G. Douglas, Amy E. Foster, Alan D. Meyer, and Lucy B. Young, *American Women and Flight Since 1940*, 1st ed. (Lexington: University Press of Kentucky, 2004); Bowdoin Van Riper, *Imagining Flight: Aviation and the Popular Culture* (College Station: Texas A&M University Press, 2004); Margaret Weitekamp, *Right Stuff, Wrong Sex: America's First Women in Space Program* (Baltimore: Johns Hopkins University Press, 2004); Scott W. Palmer, *Dictatorship of the Air: Aviation Culture and the Fate of Modern Russia* (New York: Cambridge University Press, 2006).
8. Jason M. Trew, *The Icarus Solution: The Lure of Logic and Airmindedness* (Maxwell Air Force Base: Air University Press, 2022), 18.
9. See Phil Tiemeyer, *Plane Queer: Labor, Sexuality, and AIDS in the History of Male Flight Attendants* (Berkeley: University of California Press, 2013); Victoria Vantoch, *The Jet Sex: Airline Stewardesses and the Making of an American Icon* (Philadelphia: University of Pennsylvania Press, 2013); Jenifer Van Vleck, *Empire of the Air: Aviation and the American Ascendancy* (Cambridge: Harvard University Press, 2013).
10. Dominick A. Pisano, "New Directions for the History of Aviation," *American Studies* 53, no. 3 (2014): 66.
11. Roger D. Launius, review of *Realizing the New Aerospace History*, by Alexander C. T. Geppert, Matthew H. Hersch, David P. D. Munns, Kendrick Oliver, Phil Tiemeyer, Peter J. Westwick, and William Deverell, *Historical Studies in the Natural Sciences* 44, no. 2 (2014): 187–95, https://doi.org/10.1525/hsns.2014.44.2.187.
12. Trew, *Icarus Solution*, 18.
13. For work by Christopher Schaberg, see *The Textual Life of Airports* (New York: Continuum International, 2011); and *Grounded: Perpetual Flight . . . and Then the Pandemic* (Minneapolis: University of Minnesota Press, 2020). For Stefan Gössling's article on sustainability, see "Risks, Resilience, and Pathways to Sustainable Aviation: A COVID-19 Perspective," *Journal of Air Transport Management* 89 (2020), 101933, ISSN 0969–6997, https://doi.org/10.1016/j.jairtraman.2020.101933.
14. Anke Ortlepp, *Jim Crow Terminals: The Desegregation of American Airports* (Athens: University of Georgia Press, 2017); Katherine Sharp Landdeck, *The Women with Silver Wings: The Inspiring True Story of the Women Airforce Service Pilots of World War II* (New York: Crown, 2020); Alan Meyer, *Flying While Black: The Slow Pace of Racial Integration in the Airline Industry*, forthcoming.
15. Michael W. Hankins, *Flying Camelot: The F-15, the F-16, and the Weaponization of Fighter Pilot Nostalgia* (Ithaca: Cornell University Press, 2021); Randy Carol Goguen, *From Yeomanettes to Fighter Jets: A Century of Women in the U.S. Navy* (Annapolis: Naval Institute Press, 2024).

16. This volume is the result of the 55th annual Webb Lecture Series, presented in 2021. For more information, visit "55th Webb Lecture Series (2021)," Department of History and Geography, University of Texas at Arlington, https://www.uta.edu/academics/schools-colleges/liberal-arts/departments/history/research-outreach/webb-lecture-series/past-lectures/55th-annual.

THE UTOPIAN MACHINE

Lighter-Than-Air Flight and Romantic Socialism in Nineteenth-Century France

Patrick Luiz Sullivan De Oliveira

Visitors to Paris in early 1848 would have encountered a city bursting with political effervescence. Faith in the July Monarchy, whose liberal constitutionalism served mainly the interests of propertied elites, had run out, and the language of republicanism, socialism, and dissent was in the air. People had found a way around the ban on public assemblies by organizing banquets that were little more than disguised political meetings. Tensions were escalating, and all that was needed was a match to light the fuse—something that would come soon enough when the government tried to outlaw the banquets in February and the city broke into revolution.

But everyday life continued alongside this emancipatory energy. If one walked around central Paris in mid-1848, where the Centre Pompidou currently stands, one would encounter narrow streets, small shops, and overcrowded residences. This was still a few years before Baron Haussmann tore apart old buildings and pierced the wide boulevards that made the city into the Paris we know today, before the glitz replaced the grime of these working-class neighborhoods. This area had been devastated by the 1832 and 1849 cholera epidemics and was the epicenter of the 1832 June Rebellion, which Victor Hugo depicted in *Les Misérables*. It was also the center of insurgency and repression during the 1834 revolt protesting the July Monarchy's restrictive laws on association—a repression seared into visual form by Daumier's haunting *Rue Transnonain, April 15, 1834*, which depicts the aftermath of troops invading a house and gunning down the men, women, and children who lived there (fig. 1.1).[1]

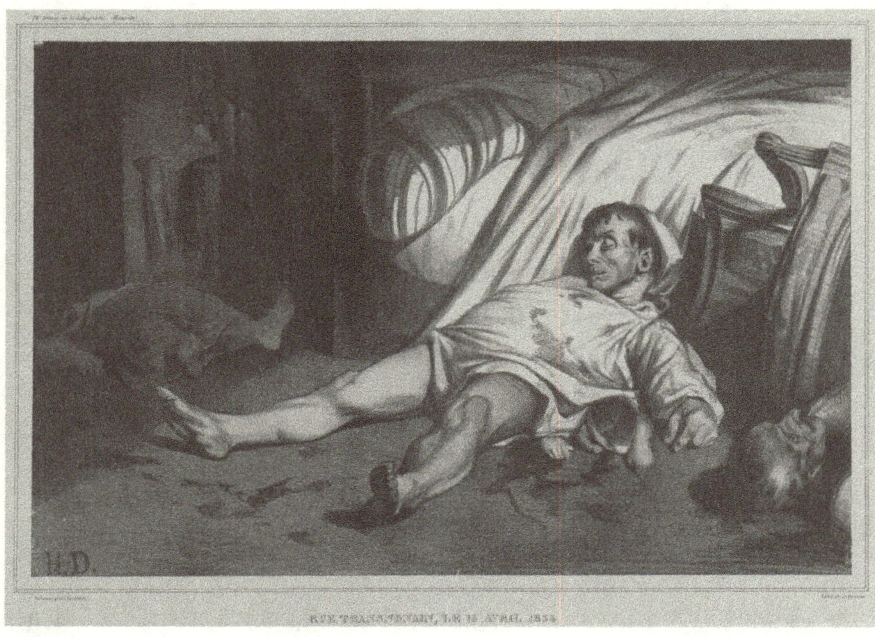

Figure 1.1. Honoré Daumier, *Rue Transnonain, le 15 avril 1834*, 1834. Courtesy of the Cleveland Museum of Art.

If one walked a few blocks south from the site of this massacre, one would have observed a vibrant community of small shops that relied on the foot traffic created by Les Halles, the city's main food market. At 34 Rue Rambuteau was a small shop named *Au Franc Picard*—the name indicating the shopkeeper's humble roots in Picardy. The owner, Ernest Pétin, was tall and blond and possessed a large forehead and blue eyes that projected the image of a dreamer (fig. 1.2). A milliner, he specialized in cotton bonnets. But those were not the only things displayed at his shop window. Strollers, if uninterested in fashion, might have breezed past those. What would have caught their attention was a strange apparatus: a sixty-centimeter wooden frame featuring inclined planes, propellers, rudders, parachutes, and four red spheres (fig. 1.3). A label read, "Balloon steering, Pétin system."[2] The strangely designed airship, which Pétin called a *locomotive aérostatique* (or aerostatic locomotive), was about to become the talk of the town and transform the milliner into a minor technological celebrity (fig. 1.3).

Why did Pétin, an artisan who specialized in making hats, also fancy himself an airship designer? And why did Parisians become enthralled by the grandiose plans of this marginal figure? To answer this question, we

Figure 1.2. Anonymous, *Portrait of Ernest Pétin*, ca. 1861. Courtesy of Musée Carnavalet.

must immerse ourselves in the rich universe of early socialist thought and its complex relationship to technology.[3] Methodologically speaking, that means taking nineteenth-century utopian discourses of science and technology in their own terms, not imposing our own contemporary conceptions of what constitute appropriate scientific and technological methods and findings onto the past.[4] In doing so, we can understand how romantic socialists embraced lighter-than-air flight as a transformative technology, using it to dream of new and improved worlds.

NAVIGATION AÉRIENNE SYSTÈME PETIN.

DESCRIPTION

DE LA

LOCOMOTIVE AÉROSTATIQUE PÉTIN

A DOUBLE POINT DE SUSPENSION STABLE.

Depuis la magnifique découverte de Montgolfier, qui est arrivé à donner le moyen de monter, de se soutenir ou de descendre dans l'atmosphère, bien des tentatives ont été faites pour trouver le moyen de se diriger volontairement dans tel ou tel sens, parallèlement à la surface de la terre. Mais tous les efforts ont été infructueux jusqu'ici, parce que les inventeurs ont trop négligé d'aider leur imagination par l'observation des lois de la nature, sans lesquelles nul ne peut rien produire en ce monde. M. Pétin a commencé par étudier avec soin toutes les lois de la locomotion dans l'eau, à la surface de la terre solide, à la surface des fleuves et des mers, enfin dans le milieu aérien.

Il a constaté que les corps animés ou inanimés ne se meuvent jamais à moins de la combinaison de l'action de la pesanteur avec la résistance du milieu ambiant. La volonté intervient dans la locomotion des êtres animés, de manière à placer les corps inertes en eux-mêmes, de telle sorte que la pesanteur les fasse agir ou que la résistance du milieu les arrête; dans tous les cas, un point d'appui est nécessaire pour déterminer la direction des mouvements. Le point d'appui est solide dans la locomotion terrestre, il est fluide dans la navigation fluviale ou maritime. Peut-il exister dans la navigation aérienne? Évidemment oui.

Lorsque le ballon, plus léger que l'air, monte dans l'atmosphère, l'air s'oppose à son ascension; cette résistance de l'air sera point d'appui. Si le ballon, plus lourd que l'air, vient à descendre, il y a résistance dont on peut se servir également pour point de direction.

M. Pétin concentre la résistance, lors de l'ascension du ballon, en se servant d'une sorte de parachute cônique, dont l'entonnoir est tourné vers le zénith; dans la descente, le cône est tourné vers la terre. Sur ce point d'appui est posé le levier qui se trouve formé de plusieurs ballons placés de part et d'autre et reliés entre eux d'une manière rigide par une carcasse, une charpente convenable. Remarquons en passant que cette multiplication des ballons fait disparaître toutes les chances de chute dangereuse, de naufrage aérien, car la rupture ou l'explosion de l'un des appareils ne nuira point absolument à la marche de l'ensemble; elle permet de soulever de grands fardeaux sans augmenter, outre mesure, les dimensions d'un ballon. Mais achevons la description de la locomotive.

Les ballons font monter la machine; de chaque côté du point central aux extrémités du levier, sont deux appareils, des sortes d'ailes qui peuvent se replier sur elles-mêmes. Sur ces ailes agit la résistance de l'air qui s'oppose à l'ascension dans une certaine mesure. Si l'on vient à diminuer les ailes d'une certaine dimension, la force ascensionnelle devient plus grande de ce côté et immédiatement la locomotive se meut comme si elle était placée sur un plan incliné invisible.

Pour mettre ces ailes en mouvement, il y a au milieu du cône central, dont nous avons parlé, une hélice mise en mouvement par la résistance de l'air, lorsque l'aérostat vient à se mouvoir. A cette hélice, on emprunte la force qui développe ou fait replier les ailes de suspension, et en outre qui conduit d'autres hélices de traction, qui aident à la marche, et servent à tourner à droite et à gauche, à donner par conséquent les mouvements latéraux.

L'hélice peut être mise en mouvement par l'aéronaute, et alors elle agit contre l'air atmosphérique, dans lequel elle se visse en quelque sorte, soit pour monter, soit pour descendre.

On peut ainsi s'élever ou s'abaisser sans jeter de lest ou sans perdre de gaz, seul moyen à employer pour produire l'ascension ou la descension, et sans lequel toute locomotion éloignée et longue est impossible, à cause des déperditions continuelles des forces de l'appareil.

Nous avons voulu, dans cette description rapide, nous borner à exposer succinctement les divers organes auxquels a recours M. Pétin, pour résoudre un problème de la plus haute importance industrielle. Nous pensons que le plus bel éloge que nous puissions faire de cet appareil, c'est d'en faire comprendre la possibilité, pour nous parfaitement démontrée.

L'avenir de la navigation aérienne est certainement dans les idées qu'il a développées et coordonnées.

B....

Cet appareil est composé de quatre ballons de 30 mètres chacun, reliés entre eux par une carcasse convenable; ils portent un plan de 120 m. de long sur 27 de large; il peut transporter 500 hommes avec des vitesses de 10, 20, 30 et même 50 lieues à l'heure.

S'adresser, pour de plus amples renseignements, à L'INVENTEUR, rue de Rambuteau, 34, à Paris.

Imp. de Pollet, rue St-Denis, 331, au coin du pass. du Caire.

Figure 1.3. Pamphlet describing Pétin's aerostatic locomotive. *Navigation aérienne. Système Pétin*, ca. 1848. Courtesy of Bibliothèque Historique de la Ville de Paris.

A bonnet maker and shopkeeper by day, Pétin had grander aspirations during his sparse free time. He left us no autobiographical writings, but it would not be unreasonable to suspect that his personal fulfillment and overall sense of self stemmed from more than just a deep pride in his own specialized craftsmanship. Given the utopian dreams that he believed he could make real by inventing a new machine, he was not unlike the eccentric workers whose mentality Jacques Rancière explored in *The Nights of Labor*—one of those who were "doubly and irremediably excluded for living as workers did and speaking as bourgeois people did."[5] As such, Pétin's never-completed airship and other similar projects were the substantiation of a resistance to the political, social, and economic conditions of the time. They were imagined as solutions to an emerging economic system that consolidated capital in the hands of a few and devalued the work of artisans. The prospect of lighter-than-air flight as a transformative technology that would bring about a new world became especially seductive once the political door for social revolution, which found itself briefly ajar in 1848, was slammed shut in the face of Pétin and his brethren after French authorities brutally squashed the working-class revolution in June.[6] But even that dream was short-lived, for the utopian aspirations for lighter-than-air flight dissipated as romantic socialism experienced its downfall in the second half of the nineteenth century.

LATE EIGHTEENTH-CENTURY BALLOONOMANIA

It would be useful to situate ourselves in the longer history of lighter-than-air flight before we go further with Pétin and the *locomotive aérostatique*.[7] There was much enthusiasm after the Montgolfier brothers conducted the first hot-air balloon ascent in the South of France on June 4, 1783. On August 27, thousands of Parisians gathered at the Champs de Mars to watch the ascent of a hydrogen balloon. Among them was Benjamin Franklin, who, after hearing someone mock the apparatus for being useless, apparently quipped, "What is the use of a newborn babe?"[8] Despite skepticism by people like the man to whom Franklin replied, in the years preceding the French Revolution, the balloon became a centerpiece of the European scientific landscape, sparking vivid debates on how to put it to use. Things became so intense that contemporaries claimed they were living in the midst of balloonomania, something that was encouraged by a series of firsts. On September 19, the first living beings—a sheep, a duck, and a rooster—went aloft aboard a hot-air balloon that ascended before the king and queen in Versailles. The first manned hot-air balloon flight took place just two months later on November 21, followed by a hydrogen one on December 1 (fig. 1.4). Then on January 7, 1785, two aeronauts, a Frenchman and an American, flew across the English Channel. During this period, ascents in Paris drew as much as half of the city's population, and the balloon made its way into plays, illustrations, clothing, furniture, and more (fig. 1.5).

Figure 1.4. Print depicting Jacques Charles and Nicolas-Louis Robert conducting the first human flight aboard a hydrogen balloon from the Jardin des Tuileries on December 1, 1783. *Départ de M. M. Charles & Robert, du Jardin des Tuileries dans leur Machine Aërostatique, le 1er Décembre 1783*, 1783. Courtesy of Musée Carnavalet.

Figure 1.5. A fan decorated with images of Charles and Robert's first ascent from the Jardin des Tuileries, ca. 1783. Courtesy of Musée Carnavalet.

But these early triumphs were followed by catastrophe when, on June 15, 1785, two aeronauts also attempting to cross the channel by air fell to their deaths after their hybrid hot-air and hydrogen balloon caught fire. While this tragic event did not bring the public's balloonomania to an end, the continuing inability to steer balloons dampened enthusiasm among the scientific establishment. The Académie des Sciences, the bastion of French science, had initially been very interested in the technology, but by 1785, it had pretty much gotten over it. Thus, the balloon entered the nineteenth century having lost much of its stature as a revolutionary technology. It had not "grown up," and it seemed destined to be nothing more than an amusing plaything.

A GARDEN OF UTOPIAS

Although lighter-than-air flight was all but dead among respectable men of science at the turn of the nineteenth century, by the 1830s, transformations in the political, economic, and social realms had created an imaginative space where the practical utilities of flight became inseparable from the invention of a new world.

The late eighteenth and early nineteenth centuries witnessed the creation of new political communities in the United States, France, Haiti, and Latin America. Those who lived through that tumultuous moment developed a new understanding of historical time that recognized a clear rupture between the "old regime" (a term only invented following its demise) and the new, which offered not only the potential of political emancipation but also the notion of forward-looking progress.[9] Even though the First French Republic did not endure, republicanism had established itself as a viable movement and started developing its own rhetoric and traditions. The initial splash of the Age of Revolutions had passed, but its ripples lived on.[10]

Meanwhile, a slower but nonetheless transformative event was taking place. The concept of an "industrial revolution" has been the subject of controversy among historians, who have debated when, how, and even if it ever happened.[11] Regardless, it is undeniable that urban centers in the first half of the nineteenth century experienced major transformations—both in labor relations and in living conditions. While one would be hard-pressed to identify anything close to large-scale industrialization in France during the first half of the nineteenth century, the country still experienced remarkable transformations in the modes of production and a growing concentration of capital in the hands of merchants who commissioned work from laborers who, until only recently, had enjoyed a greater degree of parity and independence. But the skilled artisan in the first half of the nineteenth century was still a figure to be reckoned with; he would not be peacefully subsumed into the logic of liberal capitalism. As such, modern working-class consciousness did not appear ex nihilo in industrial factories but started to take shape in this milieu that was experiencing the birth pains of a new kind of socioeconomic order.[12] The 1830s saw the first major organized labor revolts, such as the silk weaver revolts in Lyon and the Swing Riots in England.[13]

The early nineteenth century was also a period of remarkable urban growth. In Paris, the population grew from about 550,000 in 1801 to 785,000 in 1831 to slightly over 1 million in 1846.[14] Growth was especially prominent in neighborhoods on the Right Bank, where Pétin's shop was located.[15] The two quartiers neighboring his store—Marchés and Lombards—had densities of about 136,000 and 120,000 residents per square kilometer (by comparison, Manhattan's density in 2018 was an estimated 27,826 per square kilometer).[16] Contemporary observers noticed that squalid living conditions and tenuous employment contributed to the formation of a new class—the so-called *misérables* that gave Hugo's novel its title. For many, the health condition of the social body was intrinsically connected to that of the biological body. The cholera epidemic that killed approximately 20,000 Parisians in 1832 was taken to be a clear sign of the need for reform.

All these factors contributed to the coalescence of the so-called social question, a capacious category of inquiry that permitted intellectuals to articulate the need to resolve a universal problem that was, paradoxically, both timeless and urgent. Encompassing the realms of economics, morality, hygiene, and more, the "social question" provided grounds for the radical rethinking of society, for, as Holly Case explains, just about all of its articulations were based on the premise that there "was a tension or contradiction between the spirit of the time and the conditions of the time."[17] As such, the political, social, and intellectual conditions in urban centers across Europe were ripe for the emergence of utopian thought. Paris, in particular, became an epicenter for the configuration of utopian movements, spawning a rich line of system-makers who creatively sought to synthesize new scientific developments with their eccentric interpretations of Christianity—men whom the historian Frank Manuel has labeled "the prophets of Paris."[18] We can also call them romantic socialists.

Advancements in printing technology and the liberalization of the press laws that followed the July Revolution in 1830 opened space for the discussion of socialist ideas, and in this new context, the ideas of thinkers like Charles Fourier, Claude Henri de Saint-Simon, and Étienne Cabet spread widely.[19] Here is not the place to discuss the specific elements and developments of Fourierism, Saint-Simonianism, and Icarianism, especially given that their idiosyncrasies were further complicated by the fact that they featured sectarian divisions within themselves—some emphasizing the importance of practical social and political change, others emphasizing a more millenarian disposition.[20] That said, the various currents of Fourierism, Saint-Simonianism, and Icarianism shared certain elective affinities. As Manuel explains, early modern utopians imagined ahistorical communities situated within isolated environments, such as islands. But this all changed after the French Revolution, with utopias becoming something more akin to "euchronias," communities that could come to life in the future. In addition, Fourierism, Saint-Simonianism, and Icarianism all engaged explicitly with the period's major scientific and industrial developments. Whereas their antecedents tended to construct static and isolated communities, nineteenth-century utopians imagined dynamic and mobile societies that required networks of movement, exchange, and communication.[21] These were critical shifts, for it meant that utopia was no longer a *good-place/no-place*, as coined by Thomas More's 1516 book, but a *good-place/*

future-place. To quote Saint-Simon, "Poetic imagination has put the Golden Age in the cradle of the human race, amid the ignorance and brutishness of primitive times; it is rather the Iron Age which should be put there. The Golden Age of the human race is not behind us but before us; it lies in the perfection of the social order. Our ancestors never saw it; our children will one day arrive there; it is for us to clear the way."[22]

The romantic socialists saw the French Revolution as embodying this ambition, but they were also traumatized by the mass unrest that marked the Age of Revolutions (Saint-Simon was born in 1760, Fourier in 1772, and Cabet in 1788). Having either witnessed or heard about violent paroxysms in France, the United States, Haiti, and Latin America, they sought a reformist path toward radical change. For them, revolution and the violence it could engender were not viable options; instead, they wanted to find a way to peacefully reform and order a world put asunder. Relatedly, they saw growing tensions between classes as being central to the era's general malaise. But they rejected the notion that these straining tensions implied insurmountable antagonism. Instead, they sought pathways toward class reconciliation. Even Cabet, the most egalitarian of the three, rejected the path of open conflict when the time came to commit (he sought conciliation in 1848, and in the June Days, the workers he had so diligently courted were massacred in the streets of Paris by the bourgeois forces of order).[23] Contrary to Enlightenment thinkers who were inclined to theorize a natural equality among men and edged toward a blank-slate view of human nature, the romantic utopians believed that humans were a diverse lot and that human nature was only slightly malleable.[24] For Saint-Simon, Fourier, and Cabet, individual self-realization would come through the development of social arrangements that harmonized the diversity of interests and aptitudes found in each individual and across humanity.

Because they abhorred revolution and favored planned reform, all three movements emphasized the importance of controlling and rationally organizing commerce and exchange. As mentioned previously, industrialization was still very much restricted to minor pockets of the economy, so the worker's "villain" was not yet the factory owner who controlled the means of production but the merchant who could easily be seen as a hoarder and price gouger.[25] Because of this, romantic socialists were some of the most enthusiastic embracers of technologies of mobility—especially the railroad. The way they saw it, more possibilities for exchange meant less likelihood of merchant monopolies.

The romantic socialists have had the unfortunate distinction of serving as naive counterparts to Karl Marx and Friedrich Engels's so-called scientific socialism. Marx occasionally dispensed a positive comment toward these early movements, and both he and Engels recognized them as forerunners to the ideology they were busy developing. But the two were acerbically critical of the romantic socialists' flights of fantasy and pursuit of social reform and class conciliation (as Engels put it, "To the crude conditions of capitalist production and the crude class conditions corresponded crude theories").[26] Marx's later followers were even less generous, framing these movements as an embarrassing prelude to "true" socialism. Given that Fourier wrote that humans would eventually develop a tail that would serve as an eclectic tool (the *archibras*), one has to admit that ridicule came easily. But as Jonathan Beecher argues in his biography of Fourier, "There is a close connection between the 'madness' of his cosmogony and the insight of his social criticism."[27] Fourier's nearly boundless imagination was what allowed him to foresee the psychological boredom of work as a critical issue in industrial society. Furthermore, eccentricity allowed for eclecticism, with the movements being much more open to outsiders than the more mainstream conservative and liberal ideologies. This helps explain why workers outside of the circuits of power—including Ernest Pétin—drew from them in imagining their own futures.

The romantic socialists also blurred the lines that rationalist Enlightenment thought had established between the natural and the artificial. The historian John Tresch has persuasively shown that post-Napoleonic Paris was the European hotspot for the development of a strain of "mechanical romanticism" that ignored a strict division between organicism and mechanicism.[28] Unlike the British romantics, this French vein did not reactionarily position itself on the side of the natural against the mechanical. Instead, it believed that the forces of science and technology allowed for the artful synthesis of the mechanical and the organic for the purposes of human emancipation. Mechanical romantics were especially interested in technologies that gave off the impression of being alive, like steam and electricity, and sought to achieve harmony and unity across different fields—the scientific, social, and political.

Victor Meunier, for example, a prolific writer whose mission to popularize science was shaped by his militant socialism, placed high hopes on the attainment of social harmony through scientific enlightenment.[29] "Science pervades all things moral, political, and economic, as it invades religion," he wrote in 1851. "After taking hold of dogma, it takes hold of morals, education, work, and consequently the government. It is the Church and the State. Social unity is restored; dualism gives way to harmony."[30] Meunier elaborated on this in an article for *La Démocratie pacifique*, the most prominent Fourierist newspaper. As he explained, socialism was defined by two goals: the emancipation of the working class and the redirection of human forces away from conflict and toward harmony. These two aspirations, he argued, were shaped by direct experience of progress in science. How could mankind continue seeing "Earth as a place of exile and expiation," as it did in the Middle Ages, when it now had in its hands steam engines, railroads, balloons, daguerreotypes, and more?[31] Meunier's scientific teleology implied the achievement of a socialist future through science and technology. This profession of faith in science and technology was par for the course among the romantic socialists; lighter-than-air flight became one of their idealized emancipatory technologies.

THE BALLOON IN THE GARDEN

The balloon and ideas about lighter-than-air flight, which had been marginalized by respectable circles of science since the turn of the nineteenth century, found a new home within this complex and rich milieu. According to the historian Luc Robène, by the 1830s, the solution to conquering the air was defined by the figure of an isolated artisan working alone in his workshop.[32] But Robène's characterization of this as an "isolated" practice is suspect. Men like Pétin might have worked on their designs in solitude under dim candlelight, but their plans were inseparable from the rich intellectual environment in which they were embedded—an environment that was shaped by the socialist press and social networks where they could discuss their ideas. Furthermore, these artisans were often inspired by public encounters with spectacular balloon ascents. As *Le Siècle* reported in 1850, "Today it seems like the public's fever for balloon ascents has passed on to the brain of inventors."[33]

Early socialist ideologies, advancements in science and technology, and encounters with balloon ascents all stimulated people. As one contemporary put it, if ballooning had fallen into discredit amid the circles of official science, there were now "men strengthened in their confidence on the power of the human mind guided by the study of nature [who] pursued with a kind of fury a science that for them seemed to contain the seeds of an incommensurable future."[34] With no official support and little money of their own, the men behind mid-century projects to steer balloons usually relied on subscriptions to finance their experiments. To draw public attention, these subscriptions were defined by bombastic rhetoric, their authors not only promising that they had found the solution to flight but also claiming that, much like the utopian ideologies that surrounded them, flight would fundamentally change social relations.

As mentioned earlier, one of the main distinctions between early modern utopias and nineteenth-century ones was that the former tended to be located in space, the latter in time. Ideas about flight also changed with this crucial shift. In utopian writing before the nineteenth century, flight was a form of locomotion that allowed the protagonist to reach a new world. Take Cyrano de Bergerac's *Histoire comique des États et Empires de la Lune* (1655), where the protagonist flies to the moon and discovers a new civilization, which, in a manner typical to the "extraordinary voyages" genre, serves as a distorted mirror to satirize Cyrano's own society. But the balloon's invention in 1783 had shown human flight to be possible and instigated people's imaginations regarding its transformative possibilities. Air travel stopped being imagined as just a kind of portal into a new world and started to be thought of as a constitutive technology for social reform. Flight was more than just a way to *get to* utopia; it would help *make* utopia. For instance, in 1839 Cabet published *Voyage en Icarie*, a novel-manifesto depicting an idyllic, centrally planned society where the abolition of private property meant that a worker and his family could reside in a single home, children could go to school instead of work, and the family did not have to worry about being taken advantage of by unscrupulous merchants. In this utopia, steerable balloons were the fastest, most pleasant, and safest mode of transportation, and the government provided savants with all the necessary resources to develop them.[35]

The socialist press devoted considerable attention to developments in transportation technology, in particular the railroad. *La Démocratie pacifique* excitedly covered railroad innovations in England and France. It also expressed a growing concern about the financial class taking over the expansion of the rail network. The shadow cast by these developments was so large that it even found its way into unrelated articles, including a study about Paris's birds published by the naturalist Alphonse Toussenel. A rabid anti-Semite, Toussenel claimed that the "homicidal locomotive" was an "instrument of oppression in the hands of the Jews, who forcefully fill[ed] valleys, pierce[d] mountains, and destroy[ed] the work of God everywhere."

For Toussenel, the balloon offered a utopian alternative to the fictional Jewish conspiracy and real environmental destruction. He argued that while "the moralists of antiquity condemned Icarus's presumptuousness," in fact, he should be mourned and celebrated together with Prometheus, for if the desire to fly was lodged in man's mind, then it was because God had willed it so.[36]

Articles about lighter-than-air flight also appeared frequently in *La Démocratie pacifique*. A. Ysabeau, for instance, made a call for extensive studies of the atmosphere to uncover wind patterns that could be used to transport balloons across Europe and, eventually, the Atlantic. In his view, the atmosphere would one day surpass the ocean as the "great common route of humankind," for the aeronaut would not have to disembark in a port where he would be subject to both fiscal and intellectual borders, as was the case with the sailor. And while many Frenchmen argued that flight was a particular French calling (especially later on with the increase of nationalism after the 1870–71 Franco-Prussian War), Ysabeau reflected Fourierist ideology and claimed that "in science, there are no nations."[37]

La Démocratie pacifique also kept readers abreast of balloon ascents and other aeronautical experiments. These accounts were often accompanied by unanswered calls for the government or "the spirit of association" to finance more research in the field.[38] Marginalized from the circles of official science, those who aspired to find a solution to flight had to elaborate their ideas and seek support for their initiatives in more open (and therefore less disciplined) forums by publishing their own pamphlets, books, and articles in the popular press.[39] This helps explain why, starting in the early 1840s, the annual occurrence of the expression "navigation aérienne" in the corpus of French books digitized by Google experienced remarkable growth (fig. 1.6).

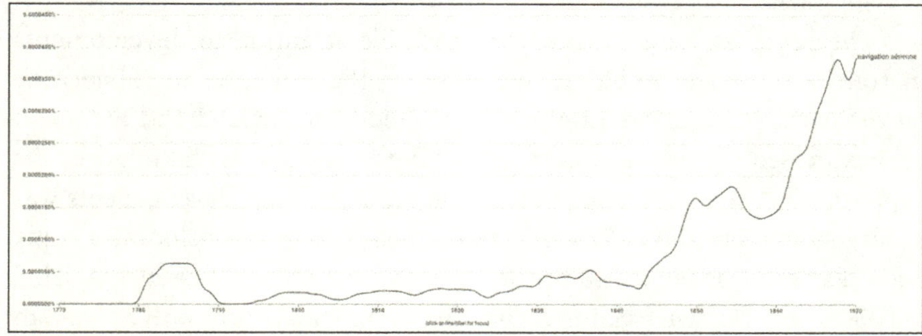

Figure 1.6. "Navigation aérienne." Google Books Ngram Viewer, https://books.google.com/ngrams.

PÉTIN'S *LOCOMOTIVE AÉROSTATIQUE*

It is within this context that Ernest Pétin's work and the enthusiastic public reception of his *locomotive aérostatique* must be understood. Although the machine's curious design underwent several changes throughout the years, every version of the project was massive. An early description claimed the *locomotive* would be made up of four 30-meter-wide balloons connected to a 120-meter-long and 27-meter-wide frame, which could transport five hundred people at speeds up to fifty *lieues* per hour (about two hundred kilometers per hour).[40] A latter description claimed that the *locomotive* was made up of a 70-meter-long and 10-meter-wide frame, which sustained sixteen inclined planes, four propellers, two steam engines, and two 54-meter-long carriages. Attached to the frame were three 20-meter-wide silk hydrogen balloons, with a lift of 15,090 kilograms (about 6.5 percent of what the *Hindenburg*-class Zeppelins were capable of).[41]

Pétin fashioned a totalizing method to arrive at this design—in other words, he believed that the only way to arrive at the solution to flight was to address all problems simultaneously and that all the answers could be found in nature, much like how Fourier approached his own study of society. A pamphlet describing the airship explained how "Pétin started off by carefully studying all the laws of locomotion in water, on the surface of solid earth, on the surface of rivers and seas, and finally in the aerial milieu."[42] The unifying element in all these modes of locomotion, Pétin argued, was the point d'appui, or the fulcrum, like the resistance water offers a sailboat. Finding the point d'appui had become an obsession among those searching for a solution to flight since the balloon's early days—so much so that in 1841 an airship designer called it "*the aeronauts' philosopher stone.*"[43] In fact, the point d'appui was also the explanation for the steerable balloons in Cabet's *Voyage en Icarie.*

The milliner believed that the atmosphere worked as a natural point d'appui, for it offered resistance whenever a balloon ascended or descended. Seeking to enhance that resistance, he included a reversible parachute at the center of a long lever. Each extremity of the lever featured a set of inclined planes that could fold upon themselves. Pétin imagined that having the parachute enhance the fulcrum while the inclined planes served as counterpoise would produce a differential in the equilibrium and transform the upward movement into an oblique one. The propellers would make the machine ascend and descend without wasting gas or ballast. He expected that the airship would move forward in a vertical zigzag motion thanks to the force exerted by the air on the inclined planes.[44] One can imagine Pétin seeking to create a kind of self-reliant system that worked by harnessing and organizing the forces of nature—a mechanical analogue to Fourier's phalanstery.

Pétin calculated that he needed 100,000 francs to build his *locomotive aérostatique*. Observing the lack of government support for aeronautical research, he decided that the way to go about it was to open a national subscription.[45] He embarked upon a publicity campaign, first presenting his project in Fourierist salons all over Paris. *La Démocratie pacifique* then started covering the initiative, presenting its readers with detailed descriptions of the machine and discussing its feasibility. Pétin's analogical and totalizing method resonated with the Fourierists. Toussenel, for one, believed that mankind was at the cusp of witnessing a metamorphosis analogous to the caterpillar becoming a butterfly "because aerial locomotion was the first condition to achieving the unity and fraternity of peoples, the supreme goal of science."[46]

Just shortly before Pétin's airship became a celebrity artifact, Victor Meunier wrote a series of articles discussing the prospects of "aerial locomotion" for *Le Travail affranchi*, a socialist newspaper that promoted the reorganization of labor driven by workers' interests.[47] Meunier prophesized that the conquest of the air would mean "no more borders, no more mountain ranges, no more rivers, no more precipices, no more obstacles of any kind" and that "the atmosphere [was] the route through which these fraternal relationships [would] be established, which [would] then transform the five parts of the world, the provinces, and the states into the departments of a single nation that [would] be named HUMANITY." He compared "aerial locomotion" directly with the railroad, claiming that while the latter was a national technology, the former was a global one.

Meunier's vision for flight was informed by all the major principles of the romantic socialist Weltanschauung. The world, as Meunier saw it, featured populations that were spread apart and had to depend on themselves for survival, often at the mercy of infertile soils and having to take up occupations that were antithetical to their nature. But Meunier argued that "aerial locomotion would put an end to this anomaly." He explained,

> Destined to play its part in the universal concert of peoples, each nation has received its share of a particular skill; its climate and soil are linked to its vocation. Once products can travel from one antipode to the other without great expense, each people will apply themselves to the special function that their attractions attribute

> them. With the globe administered as one unit, we will ask of each climate only that which it is suitable for. At that time, to cite one example, Spain will give up becoming an industrial nature and turn its efforts to agriculture. The aerial locomotives regularly serving all parts of the world will transport succulent fruits from the tropics to the north, and products from the manufacturing peoples to the south. Through universal exchange, every place on earth will enjoy the works of the entire universe and achieve extreme wellbeing and splendor.[48]

This was a global vision thoroughly shaped by Fourierism—first because it would create a direct path between producer and consumer, thereby eliminating the possibility of merchant monopolies, but just as important, because it would allow the peoples of earth to conduct labor in accordance with their characters, which were defined by a specific combination of passions. In short, a phalanstery on a global scale.

Meunier went beyond simply championing Pétin's aerostatic locomotive. The writer argued that for there to be progress, there needed to be financial support and infrastructure for scientific research and technological experiments. He wrote, "One of the first things that the new regime should do is to politely ask the savants and the industrialists to solve, as quickly as possible, the problem of aerial locomotion and to give them the means to do so."[49] He even drafted a decree that would set a deadline for the solution to the problem of flight, provide a provisional credit to finance the research, and establish a commission to guide the initiative.[50]

Meunier was hardly alone in his enthusiasm for Pétin's project. The most sustained engagement with the *locomotive aérostatique* was a thirty-two-page-long pamphlet by Perreymond, the pseudonym of a commentator allied with Victor Prosper Considerant, who wrote primarily on matters of urban planning and proposals to transform Paris into an organic entity that promoted social harmony.[51] Perreymond's pamphlet introduced readers to Pétin's project by situating it within the global ambitions of romantic socialists. As he explained, sea exploration had allowed humans to uncover uncharted territories, but at the current stage humanity found itself in, it was "no longer a question of discovering, but of being able to quickly visit them."[52] Aeronautics would provide the path to that, and the "aerial ship" that would unite Europe to the "plains of the Sahara," the "elevated plateaus of Tibet," the "deep valleys of Peru," and the "islands of Oceania" was to become "the most formidable instrument of the joint action of humanity."[53]

Perreymond's exposition reveals that romantic socialists were not immune to the imperialist biases that informed then-contemporary European thinking. Flight would serve as an "impetus for western civilization," whose scientific mastery over nature "would be felt in all latitudes," thus awakening the people of Africa and Asia "from their age-old lethargy" and promoting unity across humankind.

Perreymond also explicitly tied Pétin's project to Fourierist methods. He explained how Pétin had been faithful to the analogical premises of Fourier's theory—a "theory full of charm and poetry, like any profound idea about the natural laws of creation."[54] The airship's analogue in nature had supposedly been the butterfly's wing movements, although Perreymond's explanation for how butterflies fly was certainly different from what we now know about their mechanics. Some copies of the pamphlet also came with a short text briefly elaborating on some of the more eccentric elements of Fourierist geography. In short, flight would allow man to "acquire a full awareness of the roundness of the Globe" and its great divisions: the Orient and the Occident. Each had its own particular functions, and therefore different "physical and moral histories," but together they formed a totality, which supposedly was geologically represented by a large mountain range that united the two—the earth's "dorsal spine."[55] Romantic socialists were drawn to the prospects of flight not only because it could transform the world but also because the aerial perspective shared elective affinities with their own ways of making sense of human history and experience. As the Icarian *Le Populaire* put it in responding to a reader's letter in 1845, "Like an aeronaut who ascends aboard a balloon and who soon sees nothing but the great masses, by elevating ourselves through our thought to great philosophical heights we no longer see individuals but only Humanity."[56]

Discussions of Pétin's design were not limited to the socialist press. Théophile Gautier, a writer who usually did not have much to say about technology, felt the need to extend himself beyond the art and theater columns that he wrote for *La Presse*, France's first penny press newspaper that tried to stay apolitical in order to reach a broader readership. According to Gautier, while other men were preoccupied with frivolous political questions (like whether France should be a republic or a monarchy), Pétin had realized that "the face of the world [would] be changed by the great innovations of modern industry." Thus, he argued, what use would borders, customs duty, passports, and other "forms of ancient barbarism that we call civilization" be once travel by balloon became just as common as travel by rail? How would war be possible once frequent travel enabled people from different countries to develop relationships "like friends who live[d on] the same street?"[57] A similar sentiment was expressed in a song written by the dramatist Anicet Bourgeois to try to rally people to give money to Pétin's subscription:

If the immortal work is achieved
Liberty will no longer have any barriers.
No more exiles, slaves, borders;
No more fighting: men will come together.
Humanity will spread its word
In huge concerts from high in the sky.[58]

Other songs were published during the period, such as Victor Rabineau's *À M. Pétin. La navigation aérienne* and Hippolyte Demanet's humorous *Madame Godichon au premier voyage du navire aérien de M. Pétin.*[59] These cultural products typically cost only ten centimes, and even those who could not afford one were likely to come across the songs through *goguettes*—working-class singing societies. Meanwhile, those with more disposable income could see a satire mocking the complexity of Pétin's project at the Théâtre des Variétés, which specialized in vaudevilles (fig. 1.7).[60] All of this indicated the extent to which Pétin's project had entered the popular imagination.

Finally, there were those who came from humbler backgrounds than Gauthier but nevertheless managed to describe Pétin's project in even more lyrical terms. François Barrillot, a printer from Lyon, had no formal education but acquired sophisticated literary skills through his métier and published poetry in the local press. In 1840, he moved to Paris, where Béranger, France's most famous *chansonnier*, found him a job at the Imprimerie Royale. Barrillot worked there from 1844 to 1849, when he was fired for being too vocal about his socialist politics and had to search for work at other presses. During those years, much like Rancière's workers, Barrillot would labor during the day and write at night, his poetry drawing from contemporary social issues and becoming increasingly politicized.[61]

In 1849, Barrillot published a twenty-five-centime poem titled *Icare vengé par Pétin*, which framed the pursuit of flight as a struggle between human reason and the tyrannical forces of religion and monarchy.[62] If in antiquity, Icarus was unjustly punished by Apollo, whose rays melted the wax holding together the inventor's wings, now the light of science was ridding the world of gods and kings. Barrillot posited that the "fantastic dreams of our naïve forefathers" were about to "come true in an even more

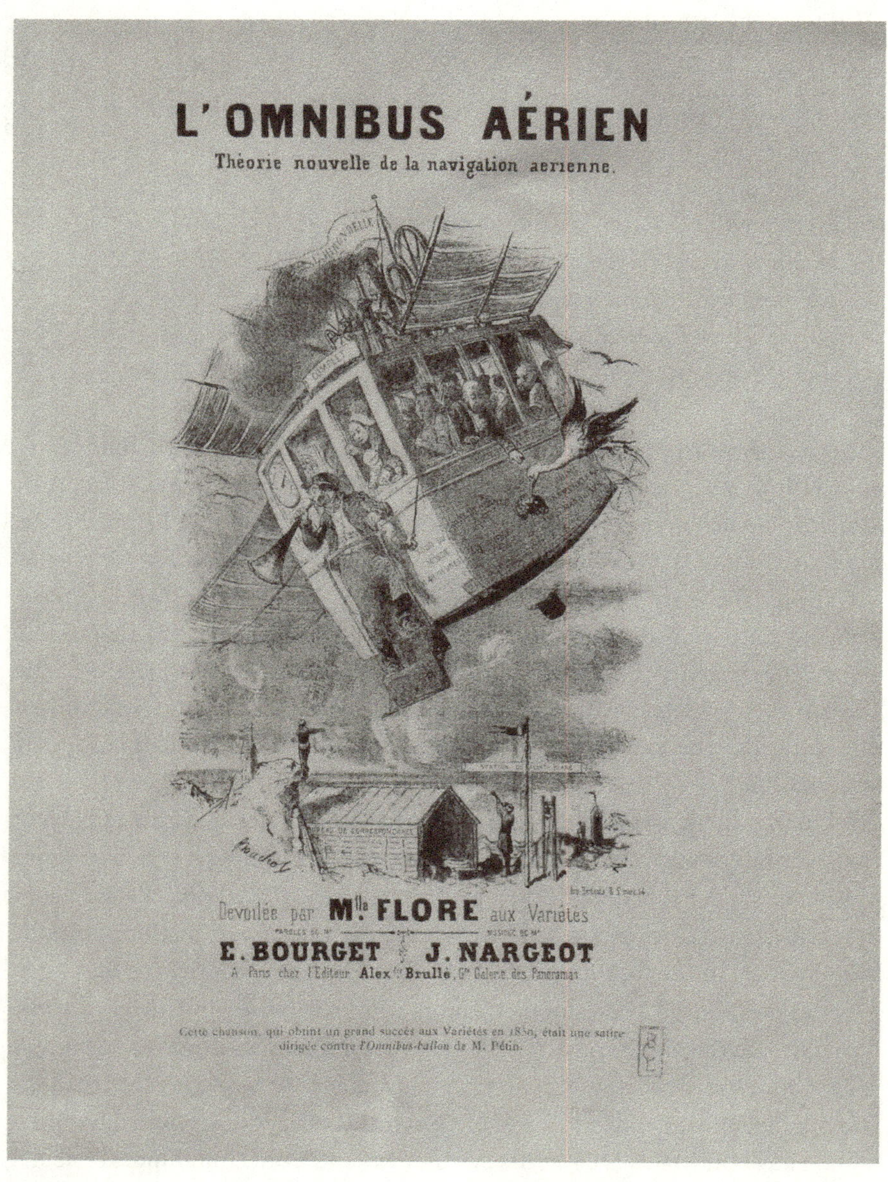

Figure 1.7. Cover of E. Bourget and J. Nargeot's *L'Omnibus aérien. Théorie nouvelle de la navigation aérienne*, a song that mocked the convoluted explanation for Pétin's *locomotive aérostatique*. Paris, ca. 1851. Courtesy of the Bella C. Landauer Collection of Aeronautical Sheet Music, Smithsonian Institution.

beautiful, more poetic, / Truer, more attractive, more marvelous way," with Pétin's "celestial skiff" avenging Icarus and "sowing peace, love, freedom" all over the world. For Barrillot, Pétin's airship was to be a grandiose messenger for the new republic that had replaced the July Monarchy in February 1848, spreading its ideals across the world. Or, as he put it, France, a "virgin with a star-studded brow who had married a kingly people / Give the world the Universal Republic!" Obviously, these were the ideals of the Second Republic as it had been imagined by the social democrats—one founded not only on political but also social rights—and they would lose power after the brutal June Days.

Many Parisians shared the enthusiasm of Meunier, Gauthier, and Barrillot. Pétin secured a room at the Palais-National (the rechristened Palais-Royal), where every day at 2 p.m. he offered free lectures about his system. These became so popular that authorities eventually granted him the palace's largest room.[63] He also opened a construction yard at 46 Rue Marbeuf (at the corner of the Champs-Élysées) and charged visitors fifty centimes to see the work in progress. He built at least three of the balloons that were to be part of the system; these were put at the disposition of the aeronaut Jean-Eugène Poitevin, who made audacious ascents featuring multiple horses (purportedly to test the balloon's lift, but also to make money).[64]

Although it caused much hubbub among Parisians, Pétin's project was never completed. On September 18, 1851, the artisan announced in *La Presse* that he would have to conduct the demonstration of his invention abroad. He claimed that while he had received government permission to demonstrate his airship, the space he was granted to work on it was not large enough.[65] In search of new subscribers, he left for England, followed by the United States and then Mexico, where people did not show the same interest as the Parisians had (a Mexican newspaper called him "a liar, a poseur of the first order").[66] But Pétin probably never turned a personal profit from his subscriptions, for he was an earnest believer in his project.[67] He died destitute in 1878, living through his final years on the charity of a brother who prohibited him from busying himself with balloons.[68]

UTOPIA DEFLATED

The era of the Second Republic was an exciting period for both utopian ideologies and utopian imaginings of flight. In February 1848, when the people revolted against the July Monarchy and the barricades went up in Paris, many believed they were at the threshold of a new world. However, that dream was short-lived. The new republic did not resolve France's internal contradictions. If workers and bourgeoisie had been united at the barricades in February, four months later they found themselves divided. The bourgeoisie's vision of revolution was circumscribed by political rights. They saw themselves threatened by radical social reform, something that would not do for the workers, who also aspired to economic emancipation. On June 22, after hearing that the government was planning to shut down the National Workshops created to deal with the unemployment crisis, workers took to the streets of Paris. The barricades were up for five days, but by June 26, the National Guard had squashed the uprising, leaving thousands dead and injured and deporting thousands of others to Algeria.

As indicated by Pétin's activities, the utopian aspirations for flight to contribute to the achievement of a kind of universal Second Republic persevered even after the tragic June Days. Many others also imagined how aeronautics could serve their cause. For instance, in 1849 A.-J. Francallet, fearing a Russian invasion led by Tsar Nicholas I, a "sworn enemy of all liberal institutions," proposed an aeronautical design that would succeed where Napoléon had failed—protecting France from external invasions.[69] Meanwhile, in 1851, Prosper Meller Jeune imagined designs that included another airship that operated through inclined planes and a *chemin de fer aérostatique*, similar to a modern-day cable car.[70] One could argue that with the prospect of revolutionary change through politics having been washed away with working-class blood, those who dreamed about better days displaced their hopes to technology.

But late 1851 proved to be a watershed moment. An opportunistic Louis-Napoléon Bonaparte (the first Napoléon's nephew) outwitted a divided legislature and solidified his power, culminating in the establishment of the repressive Second Empire. A yearslong brutal crackdown on left-wing politics followed. The regime instituted censorship and repression on a scale that had not been seen in decades, driving most moderate and radical socialists into exile. The garden of utopias that had previously flourished in Paris quickly withered.

France's experience with lighter-than-air flight offers a remarkable parallel to the sociopolitical story. The most public effort to find a solution for navigating the airs during the Second Empire was Henri Giffard's. Born in 1825, Giffard trained as an engineer and worked with locomotives. With the steam revolution in full force, he thought the technology could be useful in providing the force to move balloons across the air. Unlike Pétin, Giffard was wealthy enough not to require a public subscription, and he constructed a steam-powered airship with help from Paris's most famous aeronaut and balloon manufacturer, Eugène Godard. He ascended aboard it on September 24, 1852. The three-horsepower engine powered a three-blade propeller that moved the forty-four-meter-long machine at a speed of two to three meters per second. He managed to fly about twenty-seven kilometers, but the journey was essentially driven by the wind, since the dirigible's engine could not overcome even a light breeze.[71] Even so, Giffard received positive attention from the press, made some design adjustments, and conducted another experiment in 1855. But after that, he did not follow through on any more attempts to steer lighter-than-air machines. This might be explained by the fact that the 1855 experiment ended in a bang when the dirigible's envelope exploded.

Giffard's experiments were certainly more successful than Pétin's, but paradoxically, the public commentary featured little utopian enthusiasm. Much of this had to do with the fact that the romantic socialists failed to give birth to a new world, but it was also a reflection of the situation in France after Louis-Napoléon's coup d'état. As mentioned, the new regime did not provide an environment conducive to utopian imaginings. Public disillusionment with lighter-than-air flight was also further aggravated by high-profile failures. In the mid-1860s, a man named E. Delamarne made headlines claiming to have found the solution to the problem of aerial navigation. He made a couple of public demonstrations in 1865 and 1866, but they were pathetic failures. Describing the second experiment, a reporter wrote how "the balloon looked like a giant potato wearing a dressing gown, swinging with the grace of an elephant dancing on a rope."[72] Whether Delamarne believed in his project like Pétin or was merely a swindler is beside the point; in the tribunal of public opinion, he came off as the latter.

Crowds continued to gather to watch balloon ascents, especially when they featured animals, parachutes, or fireworks. But by the 1860s, lighter-than-air flight no longer inspired much faith in the triumph of man over the winds—let alone in utopian progress. We can see this clearly in the entry for "AÉROSTATION" in the 1860 edition of the *Dictionnaire des inventions et découvertes anciennes et modernes*, which stated that "the art of aerial navigation had not progressed at all" since the balloon's invention and that the technology was only good to entertain idlers during public spectacles.[73] According to the entry, which was especially critical of Pétin's design, it was clear that "*in the present state of our mechanical resources*, the steering of aerostats should be regarded as a problem of impossible solution."[74]

By the 1860s, many Parisians had become disenchanted with the prospects of an aeronaut deliberately choosing what path to take as he soared above their boulevards, just as many had become disenchanted with those ideologies that Karl Marx and Friedrich Engels had disparaged as "utopian socialism." But the anticipatory imaginings of the romantic socialists left their traces, including in the writings of France's most famous writer: Victor Hugo. The image of lighter-than-air-flight as an emancipatory technology featured prominently in his searing indictment of Louis-Napoléon's coup d'état, the 1852 pamphlet *Napoléon le Petit*. Toward the end, after hundreds of pages excoriating the actions of the *grand* Napoléon's nephew, Hugo turned a hopeful eye toward the future. "Have faith," he wrote. "The future, we repeat, is the Republic for all. Let us add: the future is peace with all." Hugo explained that it would be a mistake to fall into the trap to just "abuse and dishonor the century in which we live[d]," which in fact was "the greatest of all centuries." Following a list of social, technological, and cultural progress achieved since the French Revolution, he arrived at the last major thing the century had yet to achieve: "discover the means of steering through a mass of air a bubble of lighter air"—in other words, steer a balloon. Hugo argued that people were on the verge of doing so and that as soon as that happened, "borders [would] vanish, barriers [would be] swept away, everything that resemble[d] a Great Wall of China around commerce, around industry, around nationalities, around progress, [would] crumble." For Hugo, Louis-Napoléon's coup represented a new low for France, so to keep hope alive, he turned his attention upward and toward the future. With the achievement of human flight, there would be "no more hatreds, no more interests tearing one another apart, no more wars; a new sort of life, made of harmony and enlightenment, [would] spread and appease the world; the fraternity of peoples [would] traverse spaces and communes in the eternal blue, men [would] mingle with one another in the skies."[75] Although Pétin's project is not directly referenced, the utopian airship of the humble milliner is undeniably present in one of the nineteenth century's classic works of political dissent.

Hugo's political vision of liberal republicanism was further radicalized during his exile, acquiring a texture richly influenced by the thought of romantic socialists—the Fourierists, Saint-Simonians, and Icarians he encountered and whose works he read.[76] In fact, during this period, Hugo refined his idiosyncratic teleology of history, which culminated in a Europe united through peaceful social transformation.[77] Hugo's philosophy of history is most evident in *La Légende des siècles*, an epic poem that he began working on while in exile. Written between 1855 and 1876, *La Légende des siècles* seeks to present a progressive history of humanity's rise from darkness into light. As Hugo put it in the preface, the work would trace "the blossoming of the human race from century to century, man rising from darkness to the ideal, the paradisiacal transfiguration of earthly hell, the slow and supreme hatching of freedom."[78]

The epic's climax is a two-part poem titled "Vingtième Siècle (Pleine Mer—Plein Ciel)." The poem juxtaposes the image of the steamship in "Pleine Mer" to the airship, or what Hugo calls the "*aéroscaphe*," in "Plein Ciel."[79] Hugo labeled the steamship in "Pleine Mer" "Leviathan," the biblical sea monster. His description was influenced by the construction of the British Great Eastern, the largest steamship of its time. While the Great Eastern was not a warship, the Leviathan in Hugo's poem is; he mobilized it as a technological symbol of the murderous nineteenth century—a century of wars and imperialism. It is an ugly beast, "a large dead sperm whale with an iron carcass" featuring "dreadful rusty cannons." The framing makes sense, for the steamship was one of the quintessential technologies of violent imperialism, as seen by how it was used by the British during the Opium Wars of the mid-nineteenth century.

If the Leviathan in "Pleine Mer" represented the horrors of nineteenth-century technology—of, as Hugo put it, "*l'ancien monde*"—the *aéroscaphe* in "Plein Ciel" represented the promises of a hopeful twentieth century. Hugo would have been familiar with Pétin's project. He was interested in aeronautics, and his description of the *aéroscaphe* harkens back to the *locomotive aérostatique*. Hugo's poetic airship features a large frame suspended by four inflatable globes, and its point d'appui is the air itself, just as Pétin described. "Plein Ciel" also expressed much of the utopian hopes that Pétin and his enthusiasts had for flying machines; it is a patchwork influenced by texts like Barrillot's poem, Gautier's description, and other aeronautical sources from the preceding century.[80] It begins,

Far in the depths, beyond the nights, beyond the swell,
In a space between the clouds, which allows us to see
The heavenly joy above the seas,
A dim and faint dot appears; in the wind,
This point moves through space; it is alive;
It goes off, down and up; it does what it desires;
It approaches, it takes shape, it arrives; it is a sphere;

It is an indescribable and surprising vessel,
A globe like the world, and also like the eagle;
It is a ship on the move. Where? In the sublime ether!

Hugo explained that this "impossible vessel" is the materialization of mankind's audacity and an instantiation of its deliverance. But, he asked, as man takes up to the sky, is it still appropriate to call him man? Has he not become angel? Not quite, Hugo answered. He remains man, "but not the fumbling man, / Not the fallen Adam!" Man has entered a new age, an age without warfare or borders. Where does the *aéroscaphe* carry man? Hugo wonders,

To the divine and pure future, to virtue,
To the science we see glisten
To the death of plagues, to the generous oblivion,
To abundance, to calm, to laughter, to the happy man.

And . . .

It carries man to man and spirit to spirit.
It civilizes, O glory! It ruins, it withers
All that dreadful past we find frightening,
It abolishes the law of iron, the law of blood,
The swords, the shackles, the slavery, as it moves
Through the sky like a marching band.

According to Hugo, the airship, whose age was to come in the twentieth century, would finally bring to fruition the ideals of the French Revolution. It would render *liberté*, *egalité*, and *fraternité* possible on a global scale. The *aéroscaphe* would figuratively and literally unburden humanity of the weight and oppression of the old regime and help inaugurate a new age of universalism and peace.

Today the poem might seem hopelessly naive, but Hugo was on to something. For instance, the advent of mass air travel in the second half of the twentieth century became one of the constitutive elements of a shared European identity built on the ideal of unfettered mobility, an identity that has helped sustain the European Union.[81] But the solution to flight did not usher in the universal utopias dreamed of by Hugo and the romantic socialists. They underestimated the extensive infrastructure and bureaucracy necessary to allow for air travel on a mass scale, just as they underestimated the nation-state's ability to retain control over its borders and its people. Even more troubling was their inability to imagine that greater mobility might exacerbate global social inequalities rather than erase them, and how flight could become an engine of destruction. Utopianism—technological utopianism—is funny that way. It opens up radical possibilities for change, but it can also cloud our vision.

NOTES

1. The best study on the social and political ties developed within the working-class neighborhoods of central Paris is Maurizio Gribaudi, *Paris, ville ouvrière: Une histoire occultée (1789–1848)* (Paris: La Découverte, 2014). On the 1832 and 1849 cholera epidemics, see Catherine J. Kudlick, *Cholera in Post-Revolutionary Paris: A Cultural History* (Berkeley: University of California Press, 1996). On the 1834 revolt, see Jill Harsin, *Barricades: The War of the Streets in Revolutionary Paris, 1830–1848* (New York: Palgrave, 2002), 84–105. Alexandre Ledru-Rollin, a young radical lawyer who would go on to become one the leading figures of the Second Republic, published a popular pamphlet featuring interviews with survivors of the Rue Transnonain massacre titled *Mémoire sur les événements de la Rue Transonain dans les journées des 13 et 14 avril 1834* (Paris: Guillaumin, 1834).
2. "Direction des ballons, système Pétin." Unless otherwise indicated, all translations from French are my own. On Pétin's shop and background, see Gaston Tissandier, *La navigation aérienne, l'aviation et la direction des aérostats dans les temps anciens et modernes* (Paris: Librairie Hachette, 1886), 200–201; and J. Lecornu, *La navigation aérienne: Histoire documentaire et anecdotique* (Paris: Librairie Nony, 1903), 170–71. See also E. Pétin, business card, n.d., folder 25, box 23, Tissandier Collection, Library of Congress (TC-LoC).
3. François Jarrige, ed., *Dompter Prométhée: Technologies et socialismes à l'âge romantique (1820–1870)* (Besançon: Presses Universitaires de Franche-Comté, 2016).
4. Here I take inspiration from Jonathan Beecher's seminal biography, *Charles Fourier: The Visionary and His World* (Berkeley: University of California Press, 1986). I also draw from Frank E. Manuel in adopting an ecumenical definition of "utopian thought" insomuch as it does not need to manifest itself in a fully developed treatise or literary tract but simply "evoke a vision of the life of man in an earthly paradise that would be radically different from the existing order and would presume to render its inhabitants happier in some significant sense of that ambiguous yet unavoidable word." Manuel, ed., "Toward a Psychological History of Utopias," in *Utopians and Utopian Thought* (Boston: Beacon, 1965), 70.
5. Jacques Rancière, *The Nights of Labor: The Workers' Dream in Nineteenth-Century France*, trans. John Drury (Philadelphia: Temple University Press, 1989), ix.
6. Karl Marx's *The Class Struggles in France, 1848–1850* remains one of the most enlightening accounts of the events that transpired in France from the late 1840s to the early

1850s. Worthy analyses since then include John M. Merriman, *The Agony of the Republic: The Repression of the Left in Revolutionary France, 1848–1851* (New Haven: Yale University Press, 1972); Mark Traugott, *Armies of the Poor: Determinants of Working-Class Participation in the Parisian Insurrection of June 1848* (Princeton: Princeton University Press, 1985); Maurice Agulhon, *1848 ou l'apprentissage de la République (1848–1852)* (Paris: Éditions du Seuil, 2002); Maurizio Gribaudi and Michèle Riot-Sarcey, *1848, la révolution oubliée* (Paris: La Découverte, 2008); and Samuel Hayat, *Quand la République était révolutionnaire. Citoyenneté et representation en 1848* (Paris: Éditions du Seuil, 2014).

7. The historiography on ballooning in the late eighteenth century is vast. The following summary is based on Charles Coulston Gillispie, *The Montgolfier Brothers and the Invention of Aviation, 1783–1784* (Princeton: Princeton University Press, 1983); Luc Robène, *L'Homme à la conquête de l'air: Des aristocrates éclairés aux sportifs bourgeois*, vol. 1 (Paris: L'Harmattan, 1998); Marie Thébaud-Sorger, *L'aérostation au temps des Lumières* (Rennes: Presses Universitaires de Rennes, 2009); Michael R. Lynn, *The Sublime Invention: Ballooning in Europe, 1783–1820* (London: Pickering and Chatto, 2010); Mi Gyung Kim, *The Imagined Empire: Balloon Enlightenments in Revolutionary Europe* (Pittsburgh: University of Pittsburgh Press, 2016).
8. Seymour L. Chapin, "A Legendary Bon Mot? Franklin's 'What Is the Good of a Newborn Baby?,'" *Proceedings of the American Philosophical Society* 129, no. 3 (1985): 278–90.
9. Reinhart Koselleck, *Futures Past: On the Semantics of Historical Time*, trans. Keith Tribe (New York: Columbia University Press, 2004); Ambrogio A. Caiani, "Re-inventing the *Ancien Régime* in Post-Napoleonic Europe," *European History Quarterly* 47, no. 3 (2017): 437–60; William Max Nelson, *The Time of Enlightenment: Constructing the Future in France, 1750 to Year One* (Toronto: University of Toronto Press, 2021).
10. Pamela M. Pilbeam, *Republicanism in Nineteenth-Century France, 1814–1871* (London: Macmillan, 1995).
11. The historiography here is vast, but good starting points include David Landes, *The Unbound Prometheus: Technological Change in Western Europe from 1750 to the Present* (Cambridge: Cambridge University Press, 1969); R. M. Hartwell, "Was There an Industrial Revolution?," *Social Science History* 14, no. 4 (1990): 567–76; Joel Mokyr, ed., *The British Industrial Revolution: An Economic Perspective*, 2nd ed. (New York: Routledge, 1999); Kenneth Pomeranz, *The Great Divergence: China, Europe, and the Making of the Modern World Economy* (Princeton: Princeton University Press, 2000); Jeff Horn, *The Path Not Taken: French Industrialization in the Age of Revolution, 1750–1830* (Cambridge: MIT Press, 2006); and Jan de Vries, *The Industrious Revolution: Consumer Behavior and the Household Economy, 1650 to the Present* (Cambridge: Cambridge University Press, 2008).
12. See William H. Sewell Jr., *Work and Revolution in France: The Language of Labor from the Old Regime to 1848* (New York: Cambridge University Press, 1980).
13. E. J. Hobsbawm and George Rudé, *Captain Swing* (New York: Pantheon, 1968); Fernand Rude, *Les Révoltes des canuts, novembre 1831–1834* (Paris: La Découverte, 2007).

14. Louis Chevalier, *Laboring Classes and Dangerous Classes in Paris During the First Half of the Nineteenth Century*, trans. Frank Jellinek (New York: Howard Fertig, 1973), 183. Chevalier provides exact numbers, but they are obviously unreliable.
15. Chevalier, *Laboring Classes*, 189–93.
16. Chevalier, *Laboring Classes*, 194.
17. Holly Case, "The 'Social Question,' 1820–1920," *Modern Intellectual History* 13, no. 3 (2016): 758.
18. Frank E. Manuel, *The Prophets of Paris* (Cambridge: Harvard University Press, 1962).
19. Thomas Bouchet, Vincent Bourdeau, Edward Castleton, Ludovic Frobert, and François Jarrige, eds., *Quand les socialistes inventaient l'avenir: Presse, théories, et expériences, 1825–1860* (Paris: La Découverte, 2015).
20. See Pamela Pilbeam, *Saint-Simonians in Nineteenth-Century France: From Free Love to Algeria* (Basingstoke: Palgrave Macmillan, 2014); Christopher H. Johnson, *Utopian Communism in France: Cabet and the Icarians, 1839–1851* (Ithaca: Cornell University Press 1974), 16.
21. Manuel, "Toward a Psychological History," 79–82.
22. Claude Henri de Saint-Simon, "European Community," in *French Utopias: An Anthology of Ideal Societies*, ed. Frank E. Manuel (New York: Schocken, 1971), 275.
23. Johnson, *Utopian Communism in France*, 260–87.
24. Beecher, *Charles Fourier*, 73.
25. As Beecher explains, Fourier's critique of society traced the roots of poverty to the realm of exchange, not production. This was not surprising, given that the merchant manufacturer was still the prominent figure in the capitalist economy. Beecher, *Charles Fourier*, 199–200.
26. Friedrich Engels, *Socialism: Utopian and Scientific*, trans. Edward Aveling (London: Swan Sonnenschein, 1892), 11.
27. Beecher, *Charles Fourier*, 12.
28. John Tresch, *The Romantic Machine: Utopian Science and Technology After Napoleon* (Chicago: University of Chicago Press, 2012).
29. Catherine Glaser, "Journalisme et critique scientifiques: L'exemple de Victor Meunier," *Romantisme*, no. 65 (1989): 27–36.
30. Victor Meunier, "La Science et la contre-révolution," in *Science et Démocratie*, première, 30 (Paris: Germer Baillière, 1865), article originally published in June 1851.
31. Victor Meunier, "C'est la Destinée," *La Démocratie pacifique*, October 22, 1849.
32. Robène, *L'Homme à la conquête*, 332.
33. Untitled press clipping, *Le Siècle*, September 27, 1850, folder Pétin, box SFNAé P2, Centre de Documentation du Musée de l'Air et de l'Espace (CD-MAE).
34. Albert de la Fizilière, "Locomotion aérienne, système de M. Petin," *Journal des faits*, October 25, 1850, folder Pétin, box SFNAé P2, CD-MAE.
35. Cabet, *Voyage en Icarie, roman philosophique et social*, 2nd ed. (Paris: J. Mallet, 1842), 71–73.
36. Alphonse Toussenel, "Les oiseaux de Paris," *La Démocratie pacifique*, October 27, 1844.
37. A. Ysabeau, "Des Aërostats," *La Démocratie pacifique*, December 26, 1843.

38. Anon., "Ascension aérostatique," *La Démocratie pacifique*, April 25, 1844.
39. As J.-M. Demongeot—a parish priest in northeast France with a side hustle of researching a solution for flight—explained in his own tract, all the members of the Académie des Sciences he got in touch with (Arago, Pouillet, Poncelet) discouraged him from pursuing aeronautical research because developments in terrestrial transportation based on the steam engine meant aeronautics would not be that useful. And while he initially thought he should follow their advice, he realized after often encountering news reports of aeronautical experiments that he should publicize his ideas to society. J.-M. Demongeot, *Navigation aérienne ou direction des aerostats dans l'air* (Wassy: Lerrouge-Prignot, 1847), 1.
40. Ernest Pétin, "Souscription nationale pour arriver à la realization de la navigation aérienne par le système Pétin," 1849, folder 11, box 9, TC-LoC.
41. Eugène Nus, "Navigation aérienne. Système Pétin," *La Démocratie pacifique*, July 20, 1851.
42. "Description de la locomotive aérostatique Pétin à double point de suspension stable," ca. 1848, Actualités 125, Bibliothèque Historique de la Ville de Paris (hereafter BHVP).
43. A. J. Sanson, *Navigation dans l'air. Le point d'appui aérien applicable à l'aérostation* (Paris: Ledoyen, 1841), 13.
44. For efforts at detailed descriptions of how Pétin's system worked, see Reverchon, *Rapport sur un nouveau système de direction aériennece (système Pétin)* (Paris: Deutreville, 1849); and Ch. De Chabannes, *Navigation aérienne. Notice explicative du système Pétin* (Paris: Imprimerie de Paul Dupont, 1851).
45. Ernest Pétin, "Souscription nationale pour arriver à la realization de la navigation aérienne par le système Pétin," 1849, folder 11, box 9, TC-LoC.
46. Alphonse Toussenel, "Le monde des oiseaux," *La Démocratie pacifique*, August 4, 1850.
47. *Le Travail affranchi* was started by members of the short-lived Luxembourg Commission. The Second Republic's provisional government created the Commission to placate workers who were suffering with the labor crisis and demanded a Ministry of Labor to address their problems. The Commission became a thriving site of working-class politicization and developed several proposals for social reform (such as the creation of worker cooperatives). Its dissolution in May 1848 was a clear sign that the new regime was heading toward a more conservative direction than those who were instrumental in ushering it in expected.
48. Victor Meunier, "Locomotion Aérienne," *Le Travail affranchi*, February 11, 1849.
49. Meunier, "Locomotion Aérienne," February 18, 1849.
50. Meunier, "Locomotion Aérienne," February 18, 1849.
51. On Perreymond, see Nicholas Papayanis, *Planning Paris Before Haussmann* (Baltimore: Johns Hopkins University Press, 2004), 176–200; and Lloyd Jenkins, "Utopianism and Urban Change in Perreymond's Plans for the Rebuilding of Paris," *Journal of Historical Geography* 32, no. 2 (2006): 336–51.
52. Perreymond, *Navigation aérienne.—Système-Petin. Notions élémentaires sur l'aéronautique et sur les sciences accessoires à cet art* (Paris: Librairie Nouvelle, 1851), 5.
53. Perreymond, *Navigation aérienne*, 7.
54. Perreymond, *Navigation aérienne*, 30.

55. Perreymond, *Navigation aérienne*, 35–36 (annexed pamphlet, "Du Globe Terrestre").
56. "Correspondance," *Le Populaire de 1841, Journal de la reorganization sociale et politique*, May 11, 1845.
57. Théophile Gautier, "Locomotion aérienne. Système de M. Petin," *La Presse*, July 4, 1850.
58. A. Bourgeois, *Navigation aérienne de M. Petin: Appel national* (Paris: Cassanet, 1850).
59. Victor Rabineau, *À M. Pétin. La navigation aérienne* (Paris: Chez Durand, 1851); Hippolyte Demanet, *Madame Godichon au premier voyage du navire aérien de M. Pétin* (Paris: Typ. Beaulé et Comp., 1851).
60. E. Bourget and J. Nargeot, *L'Omnibus aérien. Théorie nouvelle de la navigation aérienne* (Paris: Alexandre Brullé, ca. 1850).
61. Eugène Baillet, *De quelques ouvriers-poètes: Biographies et souvenirs* (Paris: Labbé, 1898), 59–69.
62. F. Barrillot, *Icare vengé par Pétin* (Paris: Durand, 1851).
63. Anon., "Nouvelles de Paris," *La Presse*, July 22, 1850.
64. Unidentified press clipping, September 14, 1851, folder 25, box 23, TC-LoC.
65. Petin, "Au Rédacteur," *La Presse*, September 19, 1851.
66. Quoted in Tom D. Crouch, *The Eagle Aloft: Two Centuries of the Balloon in America* (Washington, DC: Smithsonian Institution Press, 1983), 218–20.
67. According to one article, "he alienated a 120,000-franc house, his only asset" and "d[id] not eat, d[id] not drink, [d]id not sleep. He only dream[t] to gift his century with a new element of grandeur and social activity." Unidentified press clipping, "De la direction des aérostats. Pétin," folder 25, box 23, TC-LoC.
68. Abel Hureau de Villeneuve, "Ernest Pétin," *L'Aéronaute*, August 1878, 255–60.
69. A.-J. Francallet, *Moyens de diriger les aérostats et de les faire servir à la défense de nos frontiers* (Paris: L. Matthias, 1849).
70. Prosper Meller Jeune, *Des Aérostats. Navigation aérienne; chemin de fer aérostatique; aérostats captifs* (Bordeaux: Gounouilhou, 1851).
71. Robène, *L'Homme à la conquête*, 352–53; Philippe Foubert, *Eugène Godard: Une vie en ballon, 1827–1890* (Paris: Bernard Giovanangeli, 2014), 62–63; O. Chanute, *Aerial Navigation* (New York: Railroad and Engineering Journal, 1891), 7–8; "Le risque et l'invention," *La Presse*, September 26, 1852.
72. Untitled press clipping, May 11, 1866, Actualités 125, BHVP.
73. Marquis de Jouffroy, *Dictionnaire des inventions et découvertes anciennes et modernes, dans les sciences, les arts et l'industrie, avec les principales applications aux besoins de la société, et l'exposition tant de leurs procédes que des perfectionnements ou ils sont parvenus à l'époque actuelle*, vol. 1 (Paris: J.-P. Migne, 1860), 39–40.
74. Jouffroy, *Dictionnaire des inventions*, 141.
75. Victor Hugo, *Napoléon le Petit* (Paris: J. Hetzel, 1870 [1852]), 259–62.
76. Paul Berret, *La philosophie de Victor Hugo en 1854–1859 et deux mythes de la* Légende des siècles (Paris: Henry Paulin, 1910), 24, 36–54.
77. Edward Ousselin, "Victor Hugo's European Utopia," *Nineteenth-Century French Studies* 34, no. 1 (2005): 32–43.
78. Victor Hugo, *La Légende des siècles*, vol. 1 (Paris: Michel Lévy Frères—Hetzel, 1859), xvii.

79. Victor Hugo, *La Légende des siècles*, vol. 2 (Paris: Michel Lévy Frères—Hetzel, 1859), 205–48.
80. Berret, *La philosophie de Victor Hugo*, 110–33.
81. On mobility as an important factor in connecting Europe, see Richard Ivan Jobs, *Backpack Ambassadors: How Youth Travel Integrated Europe* (Chicago: University of Chicago Press, 2017).

2

THE BRITISH AIR MECHANIC AT WAR AND AIRCRAFT INNOVATION, 1914–18

Johanna Rustler

Several archetypes dominate popular representations of the British fighting man in the First World War. One is an exhausted figure in a muddied uniform entrenched at the Western Front. Another is the daring aviator in a clean uniform, white silk scarf, leather flying hat, and gloves. The air mechanic blackened by aviation's spirit in overalls stained with grease and covered with lice is not among these enduring images. Indeed, he is hardly mentioned in postwar writings and appears eternally muted in cinematic adaptations of the war in the air—a silent figure in the background. Ironically, the air mechanic played a far more significant role in this period of military aviation's innovative beginnings than has previously been acknowledged.[1]

Air mechanics serving in the Royal Flying Corps (RFC), the Royal Naval Air Service (RNAS), and from April 1918, the Royal Air Force (RAF), following the amalgamation of the RFC and RNAS, were noncommissioned officers responsible for a pilot's mechanical safety and the airworthiness of aircraft. These responsibilities included repairing damages, rearming guns, refilling tanks, and maintaining, overhauling, and improving fuselages, propellers, and engines. The RFC, founded in April 1912, was the airborne force of the British Army; the RNAS, formed in July 1914, was the equivalent air arm of the Royal Navy. Both aerial branches were initially engaged in support and reconnaissance activities before merging in April 1918 to become the RAF.[2]

Within the personnel structure of the new air force, the air mechanic was the most junior rank, lower and inferior to flight sergeants and corporals. The mechanics were, among others, designated as riggers, fitters, armorers, gear mechanics, sailmakers, and black-, copper-, and tinsmiths.

This research focuses specifically on the ranks of air mechanic riggers and fitters.[3] The rigger was responsible for joining, assembling, and welding mechanical components until an aircraft was in flying condition. The fitter was responsible for dismantling, repairing, and removing engines, wings, gears, and fuselages. Both roles were directly linked to the most critical and expensive part of an aircraft: the engine. Depending on skill and experience, the tasks of the air mechanic in the RNAS were divided into three ranks: first, which represented the most skilled and highest paid position, then first acting, then second class. The RAF utilized a system similar to the RFC: first, second, and third class air mechanic.[4]

Mechanics experimented with aeronautical engineering at a time when it was still in its infancy. To date, their contributions to aviation history have not received enough attention from scholars. Their everyday lives and learning procedures during the First World War (1914–18), as well as their innovations, contributed greatly to the development of the airplane. Their discoveries led to essential improvements and new equipment; these, in turn, are fundamental to understanding how critical features of military aviation developed. Discoveries as seemingly mundane as figuring out the optimum operating temperature for a particular engine and solving problems arising from production faults and other mechanical problems, as well as innovations such as the development of the bomb rack, the air speed indicator, and the interrupter gear, are among the many notable contributions made by air mechanics.

This chapter focuses on mechanics rather than engineers or pilots. It concentrates first on the challenges that British air mechanic fitters and riggers faced in the First World War and then looks more closely at the men who filled these roles, highlighting, in particular, their existing skills and training. In exploring how these challenges were overcome using innovative means, the chapter demonstrates that air mechanics learned on the spot, benefiting from trial-and-error experimentation in the stressful situation of a combat environment.

Secondary literature on workers, who engaged in dirty, mundane labor or on tasks that may appear uninteresting, is, perhaps unsurprisingly, limited. The personal experiences of those who served in support activities behind the lines have attracted little scholarly interest. In contrast to the exploits of renowned fighter aces, who flew the planes and won medals or badges for their daring stunts and enemy "kills," the mechanics' work was not considered glamorous or daring in the popular imagination. Existing literature contains few references to car mechanics or railway engineers; they are never the focus and are usually discussed in their supporting roles. Among the few studies that focus on technical developments and logistics, Michael Donne's *Leader of the Skies—Rolls-Royce: The First Seventy-Five Years* emphasizes the engineers who designed and developed new aircraft at Rolls-Royce and the All British (Engine) Company's production facilities.[5] Donne describes the airplane's transition from being used for general reconnaissance, photographic, and mapping duties to becoming weaponized machines capable of conducting offensive airborne operations. Readers are shown how technical challenges emerged and how the new, unheralded combat role obliged everyone associated with military aircraft production to start virtually from scratch in designing new airframes. In providing essential insight into the work of engineers, Donne's study inaugurated discussion of the people behind the machines, but there is more to the story.

Peter Dye, in *The Bridge to Airpower*, draws attention to the Southern Aircraft Repair Depot, the RFC's central logistics headquarters, which contained a department in which air mechanics were taught the trade of repairing aircraft; eventually, it became the largest aircraft repair station in Britain.[6] Dye emphasizes the importance of logistical organization and the exploitation of national resources in the creation of new materials to advance technological developments, including aeronautics. By providing details of the logistic communications that took place between repair depots and the fighting fronts regarding the shipment of aircraft and spare parts, he advances the discussion of background workers, though his work is confined to the history of military aviation and its logistical support. This chapter, by contrast, sheds light on the lives and distribution of these men rather than the resources they utilized in undertaking their jobs.

Original sources on First World War mechanics are relatively few and far between. The massive, multivolume study of the air forces in the First World War published in 1922 by H. A. Jones and Sir Walter Raleigh provides some documentary evidence. However, despite the collection's vast size (one volume is over three thousand pages long), it provides insights into only a small part of the air mechanic's world: training.[7] After the First World War, pilots of various ranks published memoirs or books to share their wartime experiences. Among these, Air Chief Marshal Sir Philip Joubert de la Ferté was one of the very few to dedicate a publication to the ground crews. While his work is largely anecdotal and lacks source material, it does tell the stories of the "forgotten ones" within the air forces, such as carpenters and painters, blacksmiths and coppersmiths, riggers and fitters.[8] This chapter draws from accounts, testimonies, and words of the air mechanics and other ground crew members found in memoirs or firsthand archival sources.

During the emergence of the RFC, RNAS, and RAF, the mechanics' contribution was critical to the development of a professional air force. In fulfilling their roles, air mechanics contrived innovations and developments that added to the refinement of aircraft and good practices that underpinned the way British military aviation evolved. Those original service personnel developed their skills through thorough study and practical learning to assimilate aviation's peculiarities and challenges.

THE TRINITY: THE INTERCONNECTION OF GROUND AND AIR CREW

At the beginning of the war, a clear objective within the RFC, RNAS, and RAF was forging the close personal link between pilot, fitter, and rigger. The three men who serviced and flew each machine were also known as a "trinity" and were bound together by ties of mutual trust, since the pilot was dependent on the operational status of the aircraft.[9] This ternary structure did not function when there was distrust or lack of respect within the group.[10] Pilots and air mechanics were uniquely interdependent. Each member of the trinity recognized the common bond, especially during practice flights in single-seat fighter squadrons, when air mechanics were not able to fly in the machines they looked after, unlike their counterparts in two-seater squadrons.[11] The celebrated RNAS and RAF flying ace Leonard Henry Rochford eloquently expresses in the introduction to his memoir the mutual respect felt in this instance between the pilots and their ground crews:

> Although the narrative is almost entirely devoted to my own and other pilots' activities in the squadron I feel compelled to take this opportunity to express appreciation of the quite magnificent work done by our ground staff of all ranks. In No. 3 Naval/203 RAF it was the inviolable practice to leave maintenance responsibility entirely to the Technical Officers, Warrant and Chief Petty Officers and their skilled mechanics. Pilots were only expected to report troubles. Thereafter the matter was left to the "professionals." Without them we pilots could have achieved nothing. At all times their morale was high and despite often having to work day and night—frequently under the most trying conditions—to keep the

> machines serviceable, the standard of maintenance of aeroplanes, engines, guns and transport was always exceptionally high. It is with the greatest pleasure that I now pay this tribute to their invaluable efforts.[12]

This statement shows that valuable appreciation by a pilot toward the professionals, who took over the mechanical work once pilots finished their flying tasks. In comparison, the private papers of the historian Sir Arthur Wynn Bryant—an RAF pilot during the war and author of multiple acclaimed biographies and historical accounts of modern war—demonstrate that, for him, being an air mechanic was a position of distaste, disregard, and contempt.[13] During the war, Bryant lost his wings and was grounded because, at the frequently performed eye test, it was noticed that his eyesight had deteriorated; he was therefore reassigned to administrative work censoring servicemen's letters. As his correspondence demonstrates, he disliked the ground crew, especially air mechanics, and he condemned any officer who socialized with noncommissioned officers.[14] In letters to his mother, Bryant complained:

> The British mechanic is not amenable to discipline—also dirty jobs like tinkering with engines do not tend towards spirit-de-corps, that the men being free from danger do not realise the need for discipline and that the non-commissioned officers are mostly riff-raff promoted not for strengths of character but for mechanical proficiency. [. . .] The men do not respect [their superiors]; in many cases I know of the officers having sat drinking and joking with mechanics in local cafés of very bad repute, and then indulging in unseemly squabbles with the same mechanics, and attempting to use their superior position to run them in. It makes one ill.[15]

Bryant's disdainful attitude shows that, contrary to Rochford's assessment, an air mechanic's contribution was occasionally dismissed as less significant than that of pilots. Like soldiers, air mechanics still had to drill, exercise, and respect their superiors and comrades, but technical aptitude was recognized and widely considered to be the most important commodity for the war effort.[16] These two examples suggest the diversity of opinions on air mechanics even by contemporaries and might explain the scarcity of stories on air mechanics written by pilots, observers, or engineers within the air forces.

BACKGROUND: WHO WERE THE AIR MECHANICS?

The men who were deployed as first and second class air mechanics were usually members of the skilled working classes who had served apprenticeships and were employed as tradesmen in workshops.[17] The RFC, RNAS, and RAF represented attractive options for potential air mechanic recruits. It was considerably safer than being entrenched as an infantryman or stationed as a cavalryman on the front lines.[18] Also, there was the attraction of aviation, a new kind of engineering that seemed to herald the future and hold the promise of a potential career in an emerging technology. Because of the airborne weapon's unknown and unproven fighting values, the War Office was reluctant to pump large amounts of money into the RFC's development. The RFC, therefore, found itself in a desperate position, facing acute shortages of both men and funding.[19] In addition to attracting skilled tradesmen through advertising campaigns and responding to the conscription of recruits into other forces, the RFC and RNAS called for boys, who were less expensive to employ, to join the ground crews as apprentices.[20] Candidates aged fifteen-and-a-half to sixteen were invited to take the entrance examination.[21] Many of the boys who responded had experienced the impact of the war on British society.[22] The "boy mechanic," as the apprentice was known, was the lowest mechanical rank within the RFC, RNAS, and RAF and therefore the cheapest to employ. Entry requirements were stricter for those who wanted to join the naval wing under the age of eighteen; applicants had to provide proof of good character, a certificate of birth or baptism, and a letter of consent from their parents.[23]

Harold Marsh is an example of a skilled RNAS boy mechanic. He had been employed as a car mechanic at his uncle's taxi firm in North London when motorized vehicles were coming into general use. He enlisted with the RNAS at the age of sixteen and received his basic training at RAF Withnoe in Southern England; his final promotion was to first class air mechanic fitter.[24] Another example is James McCudden, who joined the RFC before the war started in 1913 as an air mechanic and went on observational flights. After 1916, he became a successful and well-known fighter pilot.[25] Men like Marsh and McCudden are typical of the recruits who became air mechanics. Marsh and McCudden were born in 1900 and 1895, respectively, and showed an interest and had experience in machinery at an early age before joining the air forces as air mechanics. However, McCudden's experience after he received his training was anything but typical; he was one of the few air mechanics allowed to accompany pilots on test flights and was subsequently deployed as an observer before earning renown as a fighter ace.[26]

The typical air mechanic was generally between the ages of twenty-two and thirty-eight, was from a working-class background, and had a primary school education and prior training in a skilled trade such as blacksmithing, mechanics, or rigging. Many air mechanics had previous experience working on motorcars and motorbikes.[27] Even though 20-horsepower lorry, 20-horsepower motorcar, and even smaller motorcycle engines were quite different from 160-horsepower aircraft engines, the gap was usually covered quickly.[28] Importantly, the men were required to be good at reading and had to have neat handwriting. Reading and editing manuals, writing reports, filing for spares, and cataloging maintenance were central tasks of the rigging and fitting jobs.

ENTRY REQUIREMENTS AND WAGES—THE SELECTION PROCESS

To join the army, the navy, or the air force, every man had to pass an entrance examination tailored to the specific role for which they were applying. Aspiring air mechanics first had to pass the British Army's medical and physical examination, followed by a series of rigorous entrance exams testing their mechanical skills, knowledge, and attitude toward the war effort.[29] While the physical requirements were not officially listed, age, height, and chest expansion were defined. The target age group was between eighteen and thirty, and the candidates had to have a minimum height of five feet two inches (158 cm) and an average two-inch (5.1 cm) chest expansion.[30] Any basic engineering or mechanical skills were identified during the oral examination.[31]

A senior engineer commander undertook the interview component of the assessment, which amounted to a screening test that encouraged the candidate to talk about his past and future plans.[32] The practical test varied depending on the supervising examiner, usually a technical sergeant major, who evaluated the candidate's skills with a metal file and drill.[33] As aircraft had been manufactured as individual experimental models with minimal, if any, production runs, authorities at the beginning of the war had an imprecise idea of whom to recruit and what necessary skills they should possess.[34] The testing method perfectly illustrated the authorities' confusion about the competencies they expected from candidates. Air Mechanic S. Burdett described it as absurd: "The test was farcical, but extremely hard work. Taking a block of steel, about four inches long, and two inches square, the [sergeant major] in charge took a file, filed a deep inch in one corner, and said, 'There you are, file that up square again.' So about an hour later, after expending a lot of energy, and losing a lot of sweat, I handed it over, and became [. . .] what was then called 2nd A.M."[35] Marsh's examination was also based on filing, answering some questions, and drawing a diagram of a gearbox. He excelled in mathematics and physics, which enabled him to understand complicated workshop manuals.[36] Because of his advanced knowledge (he was previously employed as a motor mechanic), once he was eighteen years old, he was put in charge of twenty-two men on 165 machines.

Potential recruits, inspired by the contemporary curiosity with aviation, considered the new service with keen interest. Innately talented air mechanics often taught themselves in any way possible as well as learning from their teachers and superiors, cultivating skills such as wire splicing, as air mechanic G. Clarke did before he applied.[37] Experienced mechanics found it relatively easy to get into the RFC, RNAS, and RAF. If a candidate mentioned during his interview that he owned a motorcycle and did his own repairs, he was immediately accepted for the entrance examination.[38] Once the exam was passed, recruiting and special aeronautical engineering training was given at the Royal Aircraft Establishment Farnborough, RNAS Eastchurch, and later at RAF Cranwell in Lincolnshire. After training, most air mechanics were deployed in provisional repair shops, on RNAS ships, and to aircraft repair depots.[39]

Rank and daily pay rates were based on the results of these exams; the relative generosity of RFC, RNAS, and RAF remuneration further added to the attraction of the service. Rates of pay were comparatively favorable, especially for skilled and semiskilled personnel, and a meritocratic ethos permeated the service, which meant the competent and skilled could advance through the ranks along a clear career path.[40] The pay rates were based on skill, which meant that in the RFC, a boy mechanic and a third class air mechanic, which were the lowest ranks in technical trades, were categorized as least skilled or unskilled and earned one shilling per day. A second class air mechanic was categorized as semiskilled and received two shillings per day. A first class air mechanic, the most highly skilled, earned four shillings to five shillings per day. It was similar in the RNAS and the same in the RAF after the amalgamation. The daily payment for corporals and sergeants was raised to five shillings and six shillings, respectively.[41] These rates of pay were relatively generous when compared to infantry foot guards, where a private earned one shilling and one penny daily and a corporal one shilling and nine pence.[42] The air forces were notably meritocratic, and if a trainee was interested in his trade and successful, he was able to progress through the ranks to more difficult and more important work.[43] The private papers of William Henry Gough show the progression through the RNAS air mechanic ranks. Gough joined the service on December 31, 1916, as an air mechanic second class; became an acting air mechanic first class a year later; was promoted to air mechanic first class on December 31, 1918; and was demobilized on February 6, 1919.[44] The entrance examination was vital for the air forces to keep the mechanical level at a high standard and to educate mechanics in a new, evolving technology.

THE AIR MECHANIC'S TRAINING REGIME

RFC recruits were given three months of technical training, most often at the Southern Aircraft Repair Depot and Royal Aircraft Establishment in Farnborough and after 1917 at the No. 1 School of Technical Training at RAF Halton in Buckinghamshire.[45] Naval air mechanics were trained for six months at the Naval Flying School in Eastchurch on the Isle of Sheppey or the maritime air station on the Isle of Grain, both in Kent. The training was demanding and exhausting; the syllabus was divided into three different schedules, each lasting two weeks and concentrating on drills, lectures, and technical instruction.[46] After training, the most skilled air mechanics would be posted into their units and subsequently deployed overseas, where the RFC, RNAS, and RAF were operating.[47] However, the air mechanic had to be itinerant and prepared for rapid deployment. Aircraft sorties were still comparatively short. Average combat endurance during the war was one-and-a-half to two hours long, so air bases were located close to the front to optimize their operational capability.[48] Because of the risk of air bases being captured and supply lines being cut, air mechanics had to be able to pack up their provisional hangars and workshop lorries, get all aircraft airborne, and leave as quickly as possible. Pulling out was often practiced with the goal of dismantling hangars and tools, moving thirty miles, and rebuilding hangars within four hours.[49]

While in the depots and shops, the air mechanic was under the constant supervision of a senior air mechanic or sergeant major, who submitted regular progress reports to headquarters.[50] Pilots placed their trust and lives in the air mechanic's ability to keep the machines in good order. If a plane was faulty, not well overturned, or not efficiently refueled, it might crash because of an air mechanic's mistake or—many pilots' worst nightmare—catch fire once it became active, an eventuality that could result in the pilot being trapped in the cage of the fuselage and burned alive.[51] Central to the mechanic's trade and owing to the high risk of engine failure, when an engine came into the depot for a major overhaul or repair, the semiskilled workshop personnel observed the skilled men at their work. They were able to ask questions and take notes and were sometimes allowed to assist. Fitter and First Class Air Mechanic General S. Burdett wrote in his diary, "I think that the engines that we worked on must have been dismantled, and reassembled so many times, that they almost fell apart, but at least we learned how they worked, and how to handle them."[52] As already mentioned, most of these men were proficient, if not advanced, motorcycle or automobile mechanics before the war; therefore, they were familiar with the general upkeep, repair, and maintenance of engines.[53] These were transferable skills, and consistent mechanical principles easily adapted to the more powerful aircraft engines that allowed men competent along these lines to work efficiently and independently quite quickly.

THE AIR MECHANIC'S DEPLOYMENT, WORK, AND RESPONSIBILITIES

There were three types of aircraft repair and maintenance facilities: the provisional repair shops at the front for essential repairs and restoring damaged machines; workshops and repair shops that were built across France and Britain in permanent locations; and the aircraft depots, where more extensive work and major repairs were carried out, located in Britain.[54] Of these, the provisional repair shops were the most vital to operational flying. There, air mechanics and other ground crew carried out refueling, rearming, and most urgent and temporary repairs; determined whether an aircraft was salvageable or not; and decided which parts of a machine needed to be taken apart or sent to one of the other repair facilities.[55] After a machine returned from combat or reconnaissance duties, the pilot was debriefed to ascertain the aircraft's performance. If there was an issue, it was investigated, resolved, and tested, and then the plane was refueled and rearmed. If the damage was extensive and exceeded the provisional repair shop's capacity, it would be loaded onto a military transporter and sent to an aircraft depot.[56]

The provisional repair shops were individually called "flights." Each flight consisted of four officer fliers—pilots—with an airplane allocated to each; seven sergeants—usually observers or subpilots; and thirty-two air mechanics.[57] An air mechanic's basic tool kit consisted of pliers, a screwdriver, an adjustable wrench, copper wire, and adhesive tape. This kit had to be carried in a mechanic's pockets at all times and meant he was prepared for most mechanical challenges.[58] The flight was also equipped with a motorcyclist, two transport trucks, two Crossley tenders, a workshop truck, and an equipment truck and was therefore self-supporting if detached.[59] In addition to repairs, the air mechanic carried out daily engine inspections and regular maintenance and applied minor adjustments. The main work was done from the workshop trucks, which were usually positioned close to the air base. These vehicles were equipped with lathes, drills, and forges, and after 1916, they were fitted with lighting powered by an independent gasoline-driven generator.[60] Air Mechanic W. J. Smyrk from No. 60 Squadron recalled this setup:

> Normal battle damage to airframes, requiring wing patching, strut replacement, etc., would be repaired in the flights. The equipment store in Headquarters Flight carried a considerable range of spares; I think it would have been possible to build a complete machine from them. A set of planes was stocked for each flight, but not unpacked until needed. The Equipment Officer was responsible for running the store and was assisted by technical stores sergeant, a sergeant, a corporal and two airmen. The headquarters stores' [trucks] were available for moving all the gear. Each flight carried two spare engines, making six in all for the squadron. We were expected to keep at least four of them completely serviceable, which meant they were going through the station workshop all the time. Of course, in France they were only temporary workshops made up from the workshop [trucks] allocated to each flight, including the Headquarters. I used to park the four [trucks] in a square and work in the centre; the sailmakers made a huge tent which completely covered the enclosed area. Each [truck] had a ten-horsepower motor, driving a generator, together with a little hand-operated shaping machine that we managed to "scrounge" in France.[61]

At provisional repair shops, such as Smyrk described, the air mechanics' main task was keeping aircraft in the air and operational; this was not easy. Maintaining the flightworthiness of an aircraft required itinerant practicality; this called for a degree of swapping and borrowing components, spares, and other items of equipment that placed exceptional demands upon the air mechanic. They had to be familiar with the intimate details of every aircraft they worked on—how to strip it down, reassemble it, service it, maintain it, and preserve its operational status. In the absence of spare parts, the pressure to keep an aircraft flightworthy, and therefore ensure the safety of the pilot, required innovation. At the outset of the war, aircraft manufacturers only produced complete machines—not spare parts.[62] When spares were not available, they had to be exchanged with other types of aircraft or cannibalized from unrepairable machines. Air mechanics struggled for the duration of the war to obtain appropriate spare parts.[63] As aircraft maintenance and repair became more demanding and manufacturers adapted to the ground crew's requests, factory-produced standard components became more freely available.[64] Later in the war, specific spare part schedules were recorded in the workshops and centrally registered for each aircraft employed by the RFC, RNAS, and RAF. Spares were ordered fortnightly by telegram and prioritized over all other requests.[65] According to the *Report on Aircraft Salvage and Repair Depot*, 15 percent of all-metal fittings, including wiring plates, joint sockets, and bolts, could be recovered from salvaged engines and reused.[66]

After only eighteen to thirty hours of flying time, engines had to be replaced or routinely overhauled.[67] All moving parts, linkages, fuel supply systems, cables, pipes, fixtures, and fittings had to be thoroughly checked. Machines had to be rearmed, refueled, and replenished; faulty parts repaired and replaced; and wear and tear fixed.[68] Because of time constraints, it was often easier to replace the whole engine than to perform diagnostics and repairs on an engine situated in the fuselage. Every operational squadron possessed three to four spare engines in case of unexpected overhauls, wreckage and failures, or damage sustained. The fuselage, constructed predominantly of wood and fabric, had a lifespan of 150 flying hours, after which it was either sent away for use by training squadrons or scrapped.[69] Replacement fuselages and engines were flown directly to reception parks or were sent via ship, rail, or motor vehicles in waterproof crates to designated sites where they were then assembled by air mechanics.[70]

Each engine had its unique peculiarities, which an experienced air mechanic was expected to know. For example, the Clerget engine had the habit of developing frost in its lubrication system. The RAF 4E engine overheated regularly. The Le Rhône engine was generally manufactured with inferior materials and consequently experienced a multitude of serious problems.[71] Sir Henry Robert Moore Brooke-Popham, later air chief marshal, who was a pilot, wing commander, and senior staff officer during the war, praised the Hispano Suiza engine but added wryly that "like other engines the Hispano has its faults—faults in design, faults in manufacture, and faults arising in use."[72] Air mechanics conducted troubleshooting experiments on faulty engines to find practical solutions and develop strategies to prevent additional problems from arising.[73] Because mass-produced aircraft engines were a new and relatively unproven technology, it was not unusual that they encountered performance-related problems. This was, however, a perpetual issue; as engine performance improved, new operational problems were discovered, requiring mechanics to constantly adapt. Records of an engine's idiosyncrasies, failures, and their subsequent solutions were kept in a logbook by every squadron. This way, an individual and type profile was created that proved invaluable to engineering researchers and developers. The work done on every part had to be entered in the workshop logbook, dated, and signed by the sergeant major or superintendent—"the greatest care and attention to the minutest detail [was] absolutely necessary"—and the book had to be forwarded to RFC headquarters at the Southern Aircraft Repair Depot in Farnborough each week.[74] The difficulty of the work performed by these air mechanics is noticeable through the notebooks and logbooks kept, registering all the work they performed on one engine after a flight to keep it functional.

THE DANGERS OF BEING AN AIR MECHANIC

The career life expectancy of a fighter pilot in 1916 amounted to no more than forty to sixty hours of active flying time.[75] However, while not as high as among pilots, casualties and injuries among air mechanics were common as well. According to the database of the RAF People Index, an online resource compiled from the military records of the AIR75 Series in the National Archives and other RFC, RNAS, and RAF databases and documents, air mechanics accounted for more than 25 percent of all aviation-related deaths.[76] While pilot fatalities were more likely to occur within a narrow band of incidence, the causes of death among air mechanics were more varied. Significant debilitating injury was an ever-present threat. New power-driven machinery and equipment were tools with which many men were unfamiliar, and serious injuries were frequent, especially in stressful situations.[77] Frostbite during winter and metal burns in summer could hinder air mechanics from performing basic motor repairs. Severe head injuries could occur when swinging the propellers—which, at the beginning of the war, had to be undertaken manually—clockwise or counterclockwise, depending on the engine.[78] When the blades were swung and the engine engaged, some unfortunate air mechanics were not quick enough when moving away from the aircraft and were killed.[79] In addition to workshop or airfield injuries, there were added combat risks. Sometimes pilots took on air mechanics as copilots for extra insurance in the event of in-flight mechanical emergencies or forced emergency landings due to mechanical failures, exposing them to further dangers.

Because of the value of the engine, by the end of the war, air mechanics were being employed frequently in perilous attempts to rescue airplanes that had crashed or made forced landings in no-man's-land or even enemy-occupied territory in order to salvage still-serviceable parts.[80] According to the historian Peter Liddle, these recovery teams were able to retrieve more than 95 percent of all crashed aircraft that were salvageable.[81] A technical sergeant major ran each team and would lead the party with the aim of trying to attach a rope to the aircraft and then drag it to the safety of the Allied trenches.[82] This operation invariably drew substantial attention and fire from the enemy, which, in turn, often damaged the fuselage, leaving it unsalvageable. However, the all-important engines were relatively well protected and could be successfully rescued.[83] This was an especially hazardous activity that cost the lives of many air mechanics. According to the diary of squadron leader Hugh Nelson—who led a salvage team himself—the casualty rates among these groups were high; on average, one-third of the men in each team were injured.[84] Statistically, in comparison to pilots in the air or infantrymen in the trenches, air mechanics were less likely to get injured or die, except when deployed in salvage teams or participating in trial flights with faulty machines. However, their tasks were still usually strenuous, exhausting, and occasionally highly dangerous to perform.

INNOVATION: HOW DID AIR MECHANICS LEARN?

The air mechanics were an essential, integral component of a functioning military air force. The RFC, RNAS, and RAF focused on resource development under war conditions and produced a cohort of invaluable, skilled practitioners, whose input and advantage to the wartime and subsequent peacetime economies were immense. Their work was vital for sustaining a functional air force; their mechanical success or failure usually resulted from investigative experiments and alterations or trial-and-error research. Depots and repair shops were hubs of innovation in which air mechanics were able to freely discuss these trials while exchanging and sharing their knowledge.

Air Chief Marshal Sir Henry Robert Moore Brooke-Popham attested to the innovation that took place in the repair shops: "We would continually be finding some essential or desirable alteration to aeroplanes or engines. But if this was introduced during the process of manufacture, delay and output would be caused, because the factories concerned being laid out on a production basis could not make and change rapidly. We got over this to some extent by making modifications at our own depots in Britain or in France."[85] These depots were the vital link between headquarters and the front lines. When mechanical innovations that improved aircraft or engine performance were discovered or devised, changing the production process of engines to implement these modifications would have drastically decreased the factories' production capacity. Therefore, carrying out known modifications and improvements was left to air mechanics at the depots and repair shops. The depots proved themselves indispensable. As such, they grew in size and capacity throughout the war; new depots were being established right up to the end of the conflict.[86]

As knowledge of aviation was still limited to the basic theories involving flight technology, even qualified air mechanics learned on the job.[87] The practical problems they faced required careful formulation and solutions. One of the characteristics of the forces' pioneering stance was the ability to adapt new knowledge and distribute it among those who needed to know it and could apply it to improve the collective efficiency of the organization. Learning through trial and error or practical application was common among mechanics.[88] The continuous introduction of new machines challenged the air mechanics, who were often unacquainted with the new types of engines and were therefore unable to correctly overhaul them after they emerged from the factories.[89] The constant pressure to adapt and respond to technical developments, however, encouraged competence and resilience. These qualities became defining characteristics of the air mechanic.

Air mechanics emerged as a new category of skilled worker. Contrary to the trends typically observed in industrial manufacturing, air mechanics responded to advances in aviation design by becoming more skilled.[90] Compared to other existing military structures, such as the infantry, a whole new organizational system formed around the lower ranks of the RFC, RNAS, and RAF, encompassing the technical specifications required to maintain and keep a military air force functional and airborne. Individual disciplines became more specialized, and air mechanics developed expertise in areas that only a few years prior had not existed.[91] Since airplane types were constantly modified and updated, from late 1916 onward, aircraft types were typically obsolete within a year of their initial deployment. Because of the rapidity of technological change, some aircraft types were, soon after their introduction, declared "cannon fodder" and therefore out-of-date.[92] The air mechanic's adaptability highlights the uniqueness of the aviation sphere in these early times. The ground crews had to be versatile and resilient to embrace new developments, which became an ongoing feature of the (not-yet-fully-formed) military aviation domain. Central to that adaptability was a culture of learning by doing and trial and error, which also became standard practice within the ground crew's day-to-day regime; the importance of this feature was widely recognized by pilots, superior officers, and the sergeant majors who supervised the workshops.[93]

At the beginning of the war, military aviation existed in only a rudimentary sense. Aircraft at that point were little more than fuselages made from chemically treated canvas and wood built around simple engines. By 1918, vastly superior all-metal airplanes had appeared and entered service.[94] By the end of the war, a comparatively sophisticated service had been created. Not only was it much larger—for every aircraft in service in 1914, there were more than ninety in service when the war ended—but also its equipment was significantly more advanced and possessed far superior performance capabilities.[95] Engineers, designers, and technicians constructed the bridge between these two points. However, air mechanics contributed to critical innovations; their discoveries in the repair workshops and depots allowed technical advances in aircraft and engine design to occur far more efficiently.[96] These improvements emerged from a culture of innovation born out of trial and error and the need to find practical solutions for the unforeseen problems created by enhanced performance.

Air mechanics experimented with older aircraft to cope with the frequent paucity of spare components. Rather than sending obsolescent aircraft back to headquarters for training purposes, they dismantled and stored parts that fit or could be adapted to fit other models.[97] Because the process of the air mechanic's improvement relied heavily on learning by doing, the outcomes of experimental trial and error were often comparatively minor refinements and fortuitous discoveries resulting in innovations that proved to be vital for the war in the air. There were variations of how and to what extent knowledge was incorporated into these problem-solving procedures. Teaching practical skills frequently involved the rationalization of ad hoc adjustments and empirical techniques as well as formal theories. Technical innovations continued to be based on experimentation in addition to relying on theoretical models of artifact functioning.[98] Machines were repaired and examined by air mechanics, who improved them in ways that engineering companies could not. Air mechanics were in direct and constant contact with the machines, were familiar with the faults and idiosyncrasies of individual aircraft, and were therefore able to provide feedback to engineers that helped them develop improved models.[99]

Seasonal variations rigorously tested the air mechanic's adaptability. For example, in the summer months, engines tended to run hot and therefore with reduced power.[100] This meant that the air mechanic had to use the cooler hours during the day—most often in the late evening, at night, or early morning—to clean plugs and reset magnets. Working hours were long and often influenced by weather conditions and the severity of the machine's problems. The ground crew was responsible for ensuring an aircraft's readiness and often worked night shifts to finish their tasks in time for takeoff the following morning. Consequently, the men got into the habit of sleeping in cockpits and under wings in the hangars, even in the winter months.[101] Cold weather, naturally, brought different problems. Metal components and air mechanics' hands functioned poorly in freezing conditions, which meant that performing detailed and precise work often required double the time it took in warmer months. Water-cooled engines required built-in radiators to keep the water from freezing. However, this development was not consistently successful, and even the radiator had to be carefully thawed before use.[102] The rotary engine was lubricated with castor oil, which reacted strangely to the cold, transforming from a liquid state into a sticky gum-like consistency that blocked all openings in the engine and had to be heated before use.[103] The only means of heating oils was through a coke brazier, which was a significant fire hazard in an enclosed wooden hangar containing wooden and fabric fuselages.[104] Engines misfired mid-flight, and oils froze at high altitudes, resulting in crashes on the frozen or muddied landing surfaces of the air bases.[105] Beardmore engines were difficult to start in cold weather because the gasoline blend could not mix properly.[106] To solve this problem, Air Mechanic Robert Davidson, who joined the No. 18 Squadron of the Royal Flying Corps in late 1915 and served subsequently in France, decided to block the air intake with his hands to reduce the oxygen absorption into the mixture. This simple trick enabled the machine to take off, despite drenching his hands in fuel; it quickly became standard air mechanics' practice. Davidson's "hands on" solution was widely repeated in the Second World War, with the air mechanic's hat replacing his hands.[107] Many of the ad hoc modifications, adjustments, and experiments made by ground crews throughout the RFC, RNAS, and RAF at the time ultimately influenced the rapidly evolving designs of airframes and engines.

CIRCULATION OF INFORMATION, INVENTION, AND INNOVATION

When problems occurred, such as a mechanical failure or engine defect, air mechanics would have to find solutions. They were generally expected to follow the "make do and mend principle." Whether an attempted solution was successful or failed, it would be minutely recorded in logbooks or workshop journals held by the sergeant major. He would then circulate and distribute this to other repair depots and squadrons overseas. Air mechanics in various locations would test successful solutions, and if further testing demonstrated their validity, the adjustments would be made compulsory for all machines of the same model.[108] The operational pace was determined by the length of time it took air mechanics to work on individual aircraft.[109] For example, it took 135 hours to take apart, clean, and pack an RE8 airplane into boxes for the parts to be used as spares.[110] The same procedure took 100 hours for the slow and stable BE2c but 210 hours for the Sopwith TF2 Salamander bomber.[111] Aircraft designs often worked to the mechanics' disadvantage. For example, in most aircraft types, if a radiator needed replacing, the fuel tank had to be removed first, but this required the removal of an aircraft's engine, which in turn had to be preceded by removing the top wing. While the actual repair on the radiator took no more than ten to twenty minutes, dismantling the aircraft to get to the radiator (and then reassembling it all) required up to a week.[112]

An example of this process and the operational pace is documented in the private papers of Robert Davidson.[113] When a Farman Experimental 2b (FE2b) monoplane broke its wing in a forced landing sixty miles from the air base near Peronne in Northern France, Davidson flew immediately to the landing site with a pilot to assess the machine. He examined the problem, experimented a bit, recorded his actions in the No. 18 Squadron FE2b logbook, and sent this off to headquarters to be investigated and subsequently distributed to the Southern Aircraft Repair Depot.[114] As he described in his report, he had established a method of replacing the twelve-foot-long top section without dismantling the wing:

> This involved supporting the aeroplane with trestles under the front and the rear of the nacelle, one under the tail and one under each wing tip. As the upper tail booms were fastened to each end of the rear spar of the top centre section, you will realise that when this wing section was removed the balance of the plane was very precarious until the new section was in position. Fitting the new engine was straightforward, except that, being short of manpower I had to borrow four German prisoners-of-war and, as a result of the language difficulties, I thought (at one time) the engine was going to topple over, so we manhandled it into position. We finished the repairs in about one-and-a-half days and the plane flew back to the squadron.[115]

Davidson's account shows to what extent air mechanics had to think on their feet and how familiar they had to be with the aircraft and their work.

Another example is found in the papers of RFC First Class Air Mechanic A. E. Herbert. Herbert trained at Farnborough and was subsequently stationed at the Central Flying School in Upavon in Southwest England. Competitions were often organized at the Upavon School to encourage innovation and experimentation and allow air mechanics to share and experience the effects of their work.[116] Herbert was part of a group of air mechanics that introduced height and speed flying competitions at the Southern Aircraft Repair Depot. To determine which aircraft flew the fastest, the men developed an instrument that was able to measure the speed of an aircraft relative to the air. An airspeed indicator had been initially developed for measuring the speed of a boat traveling across water, but Herbert attached it to the back of an Airco DH9 single-engine biplane bomber. The device was a simple L-shaped tube filled with liquid that reacted to the air stream and displayed the airspeed to the pilot in knots.[117] This innovation was then further developed at the Southern Aircraft Repair Depot; it became a standard measuring instrument that every aircraft routinely possessed, called the velometer.[118]

As aircraft were transformed into weapon platforms, air mechanics were frequently employed to fit machine guns, such as the Lewis or Vickers models, onto the fuselage.[119] The interrupter gear, also called a synchronization gear, fastened to the armament of a tractor aircraft—a machine where the propeller is attached at the front of the fuselage—to enable bullets to fire through the rotating blades.[120] The gear had to be precisely set and constantly retimed to maintain firing accuracy. The process of ensuring the correct timing of a bullet passing between the rotating blades of the propeller rather than into the blades was a skill that required time, considerable labor, and many spare propeller blades. Indeed, the interrupter gear was a source of constant concern throughout the war because it frequently misfired or overheated. One air mechanic from No. 43 Squadron in Saint-Pol-du-Mer in Northern France, E. A. Gray, recalled replacing a propeller with seven holes in one blade and four in another.[121] Another essential tool for pilots to practice their shooting accuracy was the camera gun, which, instead of firing a bullet, took a picture. The rings of a gunsight were built into the camera lens. When the gun was fired at a target, the resulting pictures showed the degree of accuracy.[122] Stanley Burdett, an air mechanic at No. 11 Training Squadron, RFC Spittlegate near Grantham in the East Midlands of England, recalled in his memoirs placing a camera gun on the fuselage fitting and using this to help program the interrupter gear and thus save propeller blades. Burdett's experiment of fitting the interrupter gear with the help of the camera gun immediately became regular practice. For his efforts, Burdett was promoted to first class air mechanic.[123]

First Class Air Mechanic W. Teasdale, who joined the RNAS in early 1915, likewise contributed significantly to the development of military aviation by devising improvements in aerial bombing. Teasdale was one of the few air mechanics who accompanied pilots on test flights.[124] While working on a Wright Seaplane aboard the HMS *Ark Royal*, the first ship designed and built to serve as an aircraft carrier, Teasdale took his place in the observer's sea only to realize that because a large amount of equipment, bombs, and guns were stowed underneath, he was forced to sit cross-legged. He subsequently began to experiment with attachments on the fuselage that could store bombs on the outside of the aircraft. In September 1915, he modified handheld bombs and attached an angle iron bracket onto the bottom of the fuselage, which could carry six of the modified bombs. These were held in place with a split pin attached to a cable connected to an easily accessible handle in the cockpit. He reported his findings to his sergeant major, who passed his idea up the communication chain. In due course, the bomb rack became one of the most critical pieces of equipment on military aircraft.[125]

Air mechanics in the First World War operated in settings where conditions could be highly challenging, with new technology being pushed to the limits of its performance in a hostile military environment. In the early years of the war, military aviation was still in its infancy. By the end of the conflict, however, the RAF had grown to 137 times the size of the RFC and RNAS combined; expenditures had multiplied two hundredfold; and the number of aircraft had increased to over ninety times the 1914 baseline.[126]

As hostile as the environment was, it was also a hub of innovation; pilots, air crews, and ground crews all played their part in a collective effort. Nevertheless, it was also an arena in which they could respond to the challenges they encountered. As a result, the collective air mechanics' experience and their inventions and innovations were incorporated into future aircraft design, expanding operational capacity, refining aircraft performance and weapons capabilities, and keeping pilots in the air.

CONCLUSION

A focus on the men in the lower ranks and their stories within the forces' systems offers new perspectives on the development of aviation. It demonstrates that the RFC, RNAS, and RAF were, inevitably, microcosms of the society from which their personnel were drawn and were built upon the relationships between all its members, including pilots, fitters, and riggers, who formed a team that underpinned the air forces' ability to function efficiently. Significantly, these developed into personal relationships based on mutual trust and respect that transcended social boundaries and had to work in life-and-death situations. In the heat of battle and under the stress of war, a meritocratic organization emerged, serving as a guidepost for future social development and emancipation. There were, of course, exceptions, but generally, the spirit of cooperation and mutual endeavor defined the character of the men and the organization they were part of. Air mechanics benefited from an environment in which merit and skill were valued.

Despite air mechanics' relative anonymity, their contributions in the form of innovations, technical developments, and the improved performance of aircraft and engines, in addition to the procedures surrounding aviation generally, were undoubtedly significant. Their intimate relationships with the aircraft, the engines, and the mechanical infrastructure gave them unique insight into the problems and challenges arising from their use. They had no option other than to find solutions for issues that otherwise might ground the machines and exclude them from the war effort. Under constant pressure, they devised solutions and recorded and distributed them among other air mechanics and collectively paved the way for greater technical developments, which were then incorporated as standard design features of new aircraft. The repair shops, where most air mechanics were based, became centers of technical excellence, hubs of innovation and modification. The air mechanic's credo of learning by doing became a ubiquitous feature of the military aviation landscape. Practical solutions to engineering problems not previously encountered drove the fledgling industry onward. The novel, pioneering, and essential expansion of the aeronautical experience continuously pushed aircraft performance boundaries forward. Air mechanics' requirement to assimilate information and pass on new knowledge represented a key cycle in the learning dynamic.

Although air mechanics were not exposed to as many of the direct threats that pilots, infantry, and cavalry faced, wartime life was nevertheless dangerous for them. There were risks associated with handling heavy machinery and the moving parts of powerful, high-performance engines and machines. Injuries were not uncommon, and many air mechanics were killed in accidents as they worked on the aircraft to maintain, repair, or simply start them. In the case of salvage teams, the danger was explicit. The air mechanics were exposed directly to enemy fire and demonstrated courage and tenacity in fulfilling their roles under great duress. Despite the challenges and risks, they often worked around the clock and were frequently deprived of sleep and rest to ensure their aircraft were ready for action.

Most air mechanics came from working-class backgrounds and entered the service with an elementary education. When they entered the service, a few of them had never seen or worked on an aircraft engine before, yet they became proficient, accomplished, and innovative contributors not only to engine maintenance but, importantly, to the engine's future technical refinement. These men's contributions opened doors to new developments in military aviation that may otherwise have remained closed. Some men who entered the service became experts and passed on their expertise to others who followed after them. In this way, they became valuable human resources and instigated a process of refinement that benefited not only the RFC, RNAS, and RAF but also the aviation industry as a whole.

NOTES

1. This chapter focuses exclusively on male air mechanics, since there are only a few archival sources that mention female air mechanics employed by the RFC, RNAS, or RAF. Most of the women employed by the RFC, RNAS, and RAF worked as dopers in dope shops, where fabric, which was going to cover the wings, was chemically treated to become waterproof with glue, boiled oil, or oak varnish.
2. H. A. Jones and Walter Raleigh, *The War in the Air: Being the Story of the Part Played in the Great War by the Royal Air Force*, vols. 1–6 (Oxford: Clarendon, 1931).
3. Jones and Raleigh, *War in the Air*, 288.

4. Jones and Raleigh, *War in the Air*, 288–89.
5. Michael Donne, *Leader of the Skies—Rolls-Royce: The First Seventy-Five Years* (London: F. Muller, 1981).
6. Peter Dye, *The Bridge to Airpower: Logistics Support for Royal Flying Corps Operations on the Western Front, 1914–18* (Annapolis: Naval Institute Press, 2015); Farnborough Air Sciences Trust (hereafter FAST), Graham Rood, "A Brief History of Farnborough Aviation Site Part 2: The Great War 1914–18," *Aviation Science and Development at Farnborough History and Learning Briefings*, 2011, https://airsciences.org.uk/FAST_Briefings_02_History_Part2.pdf.
7. Jones and Raleigh, *War in the Air*, 288.
8. Philip Joubert De La Ferté, *The Forgotten Ones: The Story of the Ground Crews* (London: Hutchinson, 1961).
9. Joubert De La Ferté, *Forgotten Ones*, 56.
10. Joubert De La Ferté, *Forgotten Ones*, 56.
11. Royal Air Force Museum (hereafter RAFM), *AM3 Frederick Louis Bernard Burns*, DC73 104/7; Joubert De La Ferté, *Forgotten Ones*, 56.
12. Leonard H. Rochford, *I Chose the Sky* (London: Grub Street, 2015), 8.
13. Liddell Hart Centre for Military Archives (hereafter LHCMA), *Bryant B12 AB RFC/RAF 1918*, August–December 1918.
14. LHCMA, *Bryant*.
15. LHCMA, *Bryant*.
16. FAST, *RAF Circular No. 43*, May 10, 1915.
17. Imperial War Museum (hereafter IWM), *Harold Marsh*, Oral History 12099, 1991.
18. IWM, *Harold Marsh*.
19. Anon., "Grantham and the War, Mechanics Wanted for Air Service—Royal Flying Corps Needs," *The Grantham Journal*, August 25, 1917, 4.
20. David French, *Economic and Strategic Planning for War 1905–1915* (London: Allen and Unwin, 1982), 45; Joubert De La Ferté, *Forgotten Ones*, 117–18.
21. Joubert De La Ferté, *Forgotten Ones*, 117–18.
22. Joubert De La Ferté, *Forgotten Ones*, 117–18.
23. Fred J. Adkin, *From the Ground Up: A History of RAF Ground Crew* (Shrewsbury: Airlife, 1983), 43.
24. IWM, *Harold Marsh*.
25. James McCudden, *Flying Fury: Five Years in the Royal Flying Corps* (Folkestone: Bailey and Swinfen, 1973).
26. McCudden, *Flying Fury*.
27. RAFM, *Frederick Louis Bernard Burns*; IWM, *Harold Marsh*; IWM, *RFC Air Mechanic's Notebook*, Documents 9549, 1917–18.
28. RAFM, *Frederick Louis Bernard Burns*.
29. RAFM, *Frederick Louis Bernard Burns*, 36.
30. Adkin, *From the Ground Up*, 27.
31. Joubert De La Ferté, *Forgotten Ones*, 36.
32. Joubert De La Ferté, *Forgotten Ones*, 36.
33. Adkin, *From the Ground Up*, 36; Joubert De La Ferté, *Forgotten Ones*, 36; IWM, *Private Papers of S. Burdett BEM*, Documents 11996; IWM, *Harold Marsh*.

34. Jones and Raleigh, *War in the Air*, 288.
35. IWM, *S. Burdett BEM*.
36. IWM, *Harold Marsh*.
37. Adkin, *From the Ground Up*.
38. RAFM, *Frederick Louis Bernard Burns*.
39. IWM, *Private Papers of Wing Commander S. E. Townson*, Documents 7134; IWM, *Private Papers of A. E. Herbert*, Documents 11049.
40. Jones and Raleigh, *War in the Air*, 288.
41. Anon., "Flying Corps Expansion—an Effort to Raise 10,000 Men," *Nottingham Evening Post*, January 28, 1916, 9; Joubert De La Ferté, *Forgotten Ones*, 36.
42. IWM, *S. E. Townson*.
43. IWM, *S. E. Townson*; Adkin, *From the Ground Up*, 32.
44. IWM, *Private Papers of W. H. Gough*, Documents 720.
45. IWM, *S. E. Townson*.
46. Adkin, *From the Ground Up*, 31.
47. IWM, *S. Burdett BEM*.
48. The National Archives (hereafter TNA), *Life of Engines During September 1916. Summary of Causes of Failure of Engines Sent to Engine Repair Shops During February 1917*, 1917, AIR1 29/15/1/142.
49. Adkin, *From the Ground Up*, 57.
50. RAFM, *A Mech 3 John Roscoe*, X003 380/007/002/021, 1918–19.
51. IWM, *Australia and the War*, LBY EX 377.
52. IWM, *S. Burdett BEM*.
53. RAFM, *Frederick Louis Bernard Burns*.
54. FAST, *Report No. AERO 2150A*.
55. IWM, *Australia and the War*; Adkin, *From the Ground Up*, 61.
56. IWM, *Australia and the War*; Adkin, *From the Ground Up*, 61.
57. Adkin, *From the Ground Up*, 57.
58. Joubert De La Ferté, *Forgotten Ones*, 33.
59. Adkin, *From the Ground Up*, 57.
60. IWM, *Private Papers of Group Captain H. Nelson CBE*, Documents 3938.
61. W. J. Smyrk, "No. 253: RFC An Interview with Mr. W. Smyrk," *The 1914–1918 Journal* (1970), 55–68, in Dye, *Bridge to Airpower*.
62. Dye, *Bridge to Airpower*, 98–99.
63. TNA, *93rd Meeting* (June 12, 1917), AIR1 1144/207/28.
64. TNA, *93rd Meeting*.
65. Dye, *Bridge to Airpower*, 98–99.
66. TNA, *Report on Aircraft Salvage and Repair Depot*, AIR1 2423/305/18/29.
67. TNA, *Life of Engines*.
68. TNA, *Life of Engines*.
69. TNA, *Assistant Director of Aeronautical Equipment*, AIR1 911/204/5/832.
70. RAFM, *Preparatory Measures to Be Taken by Armies and Corps Before Undertaking Offensive Operations on a Large Scale*, MFC76 1/26, November 24, 1916; IWM, *S. E. Townson*.

71. Aiden J. Williams, "The RFC/RAF Engine Repair Shops: Pont de l'Arche France," *Cross and Cockade Great Britain Journal* 17 (1986), 155.
72. TNA, *Miscellaneous Technical Correspondence*, AIR1 1411/204/28/43.
73. Williams, "RFC/RAF Engine Repair Shops," 155.
74. General Staff: War Office, *Training Manual, Royal Flying Corps, Part I* (London: His Majesty's Stationery Office, 1914), 10–16.
75. Chris McNab, *The World War I Aviator's Pocket Manual* (Oxford: Casemate, 2018), 8.
76. Royal Flying Corps, "People Index," accessed May 4, 2018, http://www.airhistory.org.uk/rfc/people_index.html.
77. IWM, *S. Burdett BEM*.
78. IWM, *Private Papers of J. W. Larrett*, Documents 11115.
79. IWM, *S. Burdett BEM*; Rochford, *I Chose the Sky*, 14.
80. Peter H. Liddle, *The Airman's War, 1914–18* (London: Blandford, 1987), 99.
81. Trevor Henshaw, *The Sky Their Battlefield* (London: Grub Street, 1995), 132.
82. Dye, *Bridge to Airpower*, 69.
83. Smyrk, "No. 253," 55–68.
84. IWM, *H. Nelson CBE*.
85. TNA, *Air Cdre Brooke-Popham: The Development of Aeroplane Co-Operation with the Army During the War*, AIR69 31.
86. Dye, *Bridge to Airpower*, 49.
87. Donne, *Leader of the Skies*, 8.
88. Donne, *Leader of the Skies*, 3; Jamie Barber, "The Informally Trained Mechanic: Skill Acquisition in the Workplace," *Journal of Vocational Education Training* 55, no. 2 (2003): 133.
89. Donne, *Leader of the Skies*.
90. IWM, *S. E. Townson*.
91. IWM, *S. E. Townson*.
92. John Howard Morrow, *The Great War in the Air: Military Aviation from 1909 to 1921* (Washington, DC: Smithsonian Institution Press, 1993), xv, 204.
93. FAST, *RAF Circular No. 43*.
94. General Staff: War Office, *Training Manual*, 11–12; TNA, *Report on Aircraft Salvage*.
95. General Staff: War Office, *Training Manual*, 11–12; TNA, *Report on Aircraft Salvage*.
96. Donne, *Leader of the Skies*, 8.
97. RAFM, *Frederick Louis Bernard Burns*.
98. TNA, *RFC Work Summaries 1916*, AIR1 759/204/4/164–170.
99. Donne, *Leader of the Skies*.
100. General Staff: War Office, *Training Manual*, 7.
101. Adkin, *From the Ground Up*, 53; Christopher M. Burgess, *The Diary and Letters of a Fighter Pilot* (Barnsley: Pen and Sword, 2008), 121.
102. RAFM, *Frederick Louis Bernard Burns*.
103. IWM, *J. W. Larrett*.
104. Adkin, *From the Ground Up*, 54.
105. RAFM, *Frederick Louis Bernard Burns*.

106. Adkin, *From the Ground Up*, 60; IWM, *Private Papers of R. Davidson*, Documents 7996.
107. Adkin, *From the Ground Up*, 60; IWM, *R. Davidson*.
108. FAST, *RAF Circular No. 246, South Farnborough*, July 26, 1916; Dye, *Bridge to Airpower*, 43; Frederick Libby, *Horses Don't Fly: A Memoir of World War I* (New York: Arcade, 2002), 167.
109. Dye, *Bridge to Airpower*, 43.
110. TNA, *Reports and Miscellaneous Correspondence*, AIR1 1157/204/5/2474.
111. FAST, *RAF Circular No. 246*; TNA, *Approved List of Spares for Sopwith "Salamander,"* AIR10 782.
112. Joubert De La Ferté, *Forgotten Ones*, 39.
113. IWM, *R. Davidson*.
114. IWM, *R. Davidson*; TNA, *Reports and Correspondence on FE2b Aeroplanes*, AIR1 941/204/5/970.
115. Adkin, *From the Ground Up*, 58; IWM, *R. Davidson*.
116. IWM, *A. E. Herbert*.
117. Stanley Spooner, "A Warning to Pilots," *Flight: First Aero Weekly in the World* 262 (1914): 2; IWM, *A. E. Herbert*.
118. TNA, *Experimental Air Speed Indicator Mk 5*, AVIA 14/107/30.
119. Joubert De La Ferté, *Forgotten Ones*, 29.
120. William A. Robson, *Aircraft in War and Peace* (London: Macmillan, 1916), 103.
121. IWM, *Private Papers of E. A. Gray*, Documents 12363; Adkin, *From the Ground Up*, 62.
122. IWM, *S. Burdett BEM*.
123. IWM, *E. A. Gray*; IWM, *S. Burdett BEM*; Adkin, *From the Ground Up*, 62.
124. Joubert De La Ferté, *Forgotten Ones*, 40; TNA, *RFC Work Summaries 1916*, AIR1 759/204/4/164–170.
125. TNA, *Walter Sydney Teasdale*, ADM188 569/4700; TNA, *Reports and Testing of Bomb Racks*, AIR1 2151/209/3/258.
126. Dye, *Bridge to Airpower*, 8.

GENDER, RACE, AND HEROIC AVIATION IN INTERWAR ARGENTINA, 1920–40

Marc Alsina

On a sunny fall day in early April 1920, thousands of Argentine men, women, and children lined the principal avenues in downtown Buenos Aires. They waited in eager anticipation to catch a glimpse of the day's heroes: the military aviators Capt. Pedro Zanni, Capt. Antonio Parodi, and Lt. Marcos Zar. In the preceding month, the three pilots had independently completed international "raids" in a burst of aviation activity not seen since before World War I. The magazine *Caras y Caretas* declared the flights "a triumph" that "highlights the degree of advancement and expertise that [our] pilots . . . have achieved."[1] When the aviators were spotted walking down the avenue, "the crowd cheered enthusiastically . . . and from balconies, female hands threw in their wake a veritable shower of flowers." The journalist noted that for the "young soldiers," the acclamation was a "most beautiful and worthy compensation for the wonderful effort made for the glory of national aviation."[2]

Twenty years later, on April 22, 1940, another crowd gathered to celebrate a great aviator at the "Sixth of September" airport outside Buenos Aires. Police and military personnel had to be called in to control the throngs of spectators. The national press had been tracking Carola Lorenzini's month-long raid to all fourteen Argentine provinces. As Lorenzini finally arrived over the airfield in her Argentine-made Focke-Wulf biplane, she conducted a series of dramatic aerobatic maneuvers to thrill her fans. Upon landing, the crowd surged around her airplane. *La Prensa* newspaper reported that a "little girl . . . gave a bouquet of flowers to Miss Lorenzini, who had to . . . sign many autographs for various [female] admirers."[3]

Although none that day knew it, Lorenzini's raid ended the Heroic Age of aviation in Argentina. The twenty-year span from 1920 to 1940 represented the apex of popular enthusiasm for celebrity aviators in Argentina and much of the world. Distance, altitude, and speed records were being surmounted on a routine basis. Aviators were now conquering oceans and continents on their great flights. These feats were steeped in a rhetoric of a scientific conquest of the sky, distance, and time. For the North Atlantic nations, this era culminated with Charles Lindbergh's solo Atlantic crossing in May 1927. Aviators like Lindbergh were held up as ideal, masculine members of their nations, races, and humanity as a whole.[4] Alongside heroic male aviators stood more controversial celebrity women pilots, such as Amelia Earhart and Adrienne Bolland, whose feats challenged gendered social norms and assumptions of female biological inferiority.[5]

In Argentina, the popular acclaim heaped on celebrity aviators was driven by a multitude of popular and official discourses vying to articulate a modern national identity. The arrival of millions of European immigrants after 1880 transformed Argentine political, cultural, and economic life. Originally a rural nation on the extreme fringe of the Atlantic world, Argentina was increasingly an urbanized, industrial, and cosmopolitan society whose citizens conceived of themselves as "modern." Argentines were eager to follow the path of "modern progress"—the tidal wave of ideas, practices, and objects arriving from Europe and North America that seemed to promise power, prosperity, and international prestige. Elites and common people alike competed to define a national ethos, character, and narrative in light of the tremendous demographic, political, and technological changes of the early twentieth century. Social commentators expressed anxiety over the fitness of the Argentine "*raza*" (race) for modernity—believing it essential for national survival—while simultaneously seeking to modify or reject aspects of social and material progress radiating from the North Atlantic nations.

The contested visions of national identity that coalesced during the interwar period were understood in biological and cultural terms. They were embedded in prevailing notions of race in Argentina, North America, and Europe. Elites, officials, and the media harnessed ostensibly scientific notions of race and eugenics to advocate for new forms of state control over men, women, and children. Alongside debates over the biological health of the national *raza*, amorphous discussions of national cultural identity took place as social commentators searched for a narrative to knit together Argentina's cosmopolitan community. Where the liberal elite of the belle époque had looked only to Europe for cultural inspiration, after World War I, a growing nationalist movement saw "authentic" Argentineness, or *Argentinidad*, residing in the local premodern countryside.

Such racial-biological and cultural notions of identity were profoundly gendered. Public health officials, policymakers, and intellectuals intensely debated the biological capabilities of men and women and discussed how these concerns should steer the future of masculinity and femininity in their society. The demands of urban and industrial life convinced many commentators that Argentine men needed unprecedented levels of energy and willpower to contend with the velocity of modern life. Heroic aviators were widely believed to possess these qualities in abundance and were therefore considered representative of the positive, normative qualities men need to succeed in the new technologized world.[6]

Narratives around female pilots proved much more contentious. While Argentine men were essential for securing the material progress of the nation, women were traditionally ascribed to domestic roles. Prevailing attitudes concerning biology claimed women were incapable of meeting the physical demands of flight. Even as growing numbers of international female pilots undermined this argument, most Argentine intellectuals maintained that women had a duty and "natural" predisposition to uphold the moral and spiritual qualities of the nation from the home, not the cockpit. Nevertheless, the pressures of modern progress seeping in from the North Atlantic created a small window of opportunity for *aviadoras* like Carola Lorenzini to take on the heroic endeavor and win the support of the Argentine crowds.

This chapter investigates why the Argentine people were so transfixed by and invested in heroic aviation—in essence, what meaning they ascribed to *aviadores*, *aviadoras*, and their great raids. It first analyzes the interplay among racial-biological and cultural identities and the resulting popular discourses that swirled around heroic male aviators. It then highlights the trials, tribulations, and triumphs of Argentina's two most prominent celebrity aviators of the period, Pedro Zanni and Eduardo Olivero, before concluding with an investigation of the gendered cultural associations around women pilots as an incarnation of *la mujer moderna* (the modern woman) in the Argentine popular imagination. Ultimately, I argue that the national media's coverage of Argentina's two famed *aviadoras*, Myriam Stefford and Carola Lorenzini, demonstrates the limits of social change in interwar Argentina. By the end of the Heroic Age of aviation, the media had enshrined the selective incorporation of feminist ideas and images as a core tenet of a uniquely Argentine form of progress.

In the midst of tremendous change, Argentines were asking themselves deep questions about what it meant to be a proper man or woman in a modern society. They projected these self-interrogations onto their *aviadores* and *aviadoras*: Who could or should be a pilot? What made them great? Do we have what it takes to thrive in the recently dawned technological age? The answers—it seemed to many—were written in the sky.

MALE HEROIC AVIATION AND THE RACIAL-BIOLOGICAL ANXIETIES OF MODERNITY

The technology of flight arrived in Argentina at a time of unprecedented social change, population growth, and economic development. The advent of the railroad, the refrigerated steamship, and the end of the bitter civil wars that characterized the nineteenth century had opened the fertile Argentine countryside to European markets. Soon the economy was growing at an unprecedented rate as elite landowners made millions of pesos feeding Argentine wheat and meat to a rapidly industrializing Europe. Much like the United States, Argentina became a major destination for European immigrants, largely from Spain and Italy. The population of the capital city of Buenos Aires alone grew from around 180,000 in 1869 to over 1.5 million by 1914.[7] The city became a cosmopolitan mixture of different nationalities, ethnicities, and classes, all vying for a piece of the immense wealth passing through its port. In 1912, the republic instituted universal male suffrage, beginning a turbulent democratic period. While their parents remained off the voter rolls, second-generation immigrants increasingly dominated the nation's politics. The period of open democracy lasted until a coup d'état in 1930 initiated a series of fraudulently elected conservative and military governments.

The excitement and promise of early flight captured the national imagination in belle époque Argentina. It was the great scientific "conquest" of its time. Aviation prophets soon began forecasting the transformation of nations and the world as man expanded his dominion over the sky. Enthusiasts proclaimed that the next step in the march of progress would be the dawn of the "Air Age," in which time, distance, and topography would no longer be obstacles in the development of civilization.

The events of aviation's Heroic Age proved a simultaneous source of inspiration and anxiety in Argentina. Popular media for adults and children featured exciting stories of adventure and danger in which the airplane was depicted as a tool of exploration, escape, and dominance. Readers learned that with flight came power, especially over those who lacked wings. Such narratives seemed to be confirmed in the real world. Heroic flights of daring aviators became a benchmark with which to measure national capability and biological fitness.[8]

The great drama of aviation technology needed its protagonists, and these were the hero pilots. Citizens in the United States, Europe, and many other countries embraced their own national aviation heroes, such as the Wright brothers, Louis Blériot, and Hubert Latham, who risked everything to take to the sky. At a time when rudimentary airplanes seemed just as likely to kill their operators as lift them off the ground, the pilots who braved the unknown to further the "conquest of the sky" were lauded as heroic, larger-than-life personalities emblematic of their nations' technological and social progress. Early aviation in Argentina was no different. Early aviators in Argentina, both local and foreign, emerged as popular heroes, the earliest nonpolitical national celebrities in a new age of tabloid journalism and mass spectator events.[9]

No Argentine aviator reached greater heights—both in the skies and in national fame—than Jorge Newbery (1875–1914). Newbery became an international celebrity in 1912 when he achieved a world-record altitude of 6,250 meters in a Morane-Saulnier monoplane. He was an ardent supporter and organizer of early aviation who seemed to encapsulate the national ethos of belle époque Argentina as a nation dedicated to a liberal, cosmopolitan culture defined by European immigration. Newbery was a second-generation immigrant from the United States who returned to his father's home country to train as an engineer at Cornell University. A gifted athlete, he was depicted in popular media as embodying the masculine qualities of energy, willpower, and courage that the new era of progress demanded. His comfort and fluency with the latest modern inventions and cultural fads from Europe and North America, combined with his dedication to Argentine national aggrandizement, made Newbery a darling of high society and the media. With men like Newbery at the helm, national commentators and journalists saw a bright future for an energetic and modern Argentina at home with the great North Atlantic nations.

On March 1, 1914, tragedy struck when Newbery was killed in a flight accident while preparing to cross the Andes by plane. His death was a major blow to Argentine aviation, which experienced a crisis of confidence and a decline in activity until after World War I. Newbery was forever enshrined as the greatest "martyr" of national aviation. Annual remembrances on the anniversary of his death continued for decades; his name would eventually be emblazoned on airports, schools, and flight clubs around the country. Newbery became a towering benchmark of fame, personality, and legacy whom all subsequent Argentine aviators sought to equal.[10]

The end of World War I brought a new wave of war surplus airplanes, aviators, and public enthusiasm for flight in Argentina. Rapid advancements in airframe and engine technology—spurred by unprecedented investments from the combatants—had transformed the fragile wood-and-wire airplane into aircraft capable of previously unimaginable feats. Aviators were now crossing mountain ranges, oceans, and continents. The flurry of aviation activity caused a new boom in popular interest in flight, featuring dozens of air shows, festivals, short-lived businesses, and articles in major newspapers and magazines. The Argentine public looked to their aviators to take up the mantle of heroic aviation that had been left vacant since Newbery's death.

The *aviador* who came closest to matching Newbery's public image was Capt. Pedro Zanni (1891–1942), the premier local hero pilot of the 1920s. He epitomized the masculine traits of energy and tenacity expected of great fliers. A second-generation Italian immigrant with a working- to middle-class background, Zanni represented an increasingly common pattern among Argentina's celebrity pilots of the interwar period. He learned to fly in the military, earning his pilot's license at the army's aviation school in 1913. He first came to national prominence in 1919 after completing several successful flights over the Andes Mountains.

In 1922, he set his sights on a far bigger prize: an aerial circumnavigation of the world. Around-the-world flights were just becoming a technical possibility. Dozens of aviators from the United States and Europe were already preparing attempts. Beyond the obvious challenges facing Zanni as a pilot, a circumnavigation flight was primarily a struggle of resources. The estimated cost of 250,000 pesos was the equivalent of the government's entire civil aviation budget for 1923.[11] The circumnavigation also required landing permission and access to supplies in over twenty countries.

In a testament to Argentina's relative wealth and international prominence, Zanni succeeded in putting together the pieces by early 1924. The Argentine people proved more than willing to open their pocketbooks for Zanni's cause; by the end of his attempt, he would raise over half a million pesos. The prospect of one of their own surmounting a great international challenge inspired many Argentines. As one journalist expressed, the great challenge revealed Zanni's "faith, energy, tenacity, spirit of sacrifice and sacred love for all that represents the glories of the homeland."[12] For

Figure 3.1. A tired Capt. Pedro Zanni poses for a photograph after crossing the Andes in 1920. *El Hogar*, March 26, 1920. Courtesy of the Hemeroteca de la Biblioteca Nacional Mariano Moreno.

the aviation community itself, the circumnavigation flight was a moral imperative: "Argentine condors . . . must proclaim what a race can [do] when its individuals nest in their breasts healthy and strong hearts, dominating with their skill and will."[13]

Zanni and his mechanic Felipe Beltramé left for Europe on February 23, 1924, where they acquired three Fokker C.IV single-engine airplanes. The main airplane was christened *Ciudad de Buenos Aires* (*City of Buenos Aires*). His timing could not have been more perfect. By June, there were four teams—one each from the United States, France, Portugal, and Britain—working their way around the world.[14] On July 26, Zanni and Beltramé took off from Amsterdam, heading first to Paris before turning southeast to cross the northern Mediterranean and Middle East. They followed a path similar to that of the European teams. All flew east over the southern edge of Asia, cutting across the Indian subcontinent before using Indochina to reach the Chinese mainland coast.[15] Japan was the last port of call in advance of the dangerous crossing of the Pacific Ocean. Zanni—like the others—planned to chart a course across the northern Pacific, using Soviet, Japanese, and American islands to refuel and navigate.

Zanni's task was extraordinarily difficult. Before he had even left Europe, three of the four competing flights had ended in failure. In the end, only the US team reached their goal, albeit losing half of their airplanes along the way. Despite battling bad weather, Zanni and Beltramé managed to cross the Middle East and South Asia without incident, arriving in Hanoi on August 18. But the following day, one of their aircraft's wheels suddenly sank into the mud on takeoff, preventing the airplane from reaching an adequate velocity. The Fokker languished in its takeoff roll before hitting the edge of the airfield and cartwheeling into a nearby rice paddy. Fortunately, no one was badly injured, but the flight was delayed until one of the replacement airplanes they had prepositioned in Japan could be delivered to Hanoi.[16] On October 11, 1924, Zanni and Beltramé touched down in Kasumigara, Japan, the last stop before the Pacific crossing.

There the two fliers' luck finally ended. The aerial expedition halted when Zanni could not get steamships to deposit supplies along the Aleutian Islands and Alaskan coast before winter set in. The original shipping contractor had delayed sending ships to Japan after news broke of the accident in Hanoi.[17] The national media began calling on Zanni to give up the dangerous effort. On November 3, he officially suspended the raid. The tabloid *Crítica*, an ardent supporter, reported that the devastated Zanni would have "preferred to have died in the attempt to cross the Pacific, before abandoning the flight, against his will."[18]

The Argentine people were dispirited by the premature end to the flight, but media outlets maintained their praise for Zanni himself. He had flown thousands of kilometers—and matched the efforts of all the European teams. According to the magazine *Caras y Caretas*, Pedro Zanni's flight across Europe and Asia revealed him to be "an essentially strong and healthy organism to face fatigue for long weeks, at the same time as variation in climate, heights, air currents, etc."[19] In late 1924, in the wake of Zanni's raid, another *Caras y Caretas* writer was left hopeful for the future of the Argentine *raza*: "The interesting thing is to verify that men of the fortitude of Zanni abound in this land. Let us see in the effort of this brave new man the impetus of a new race that wants to emerge imposing itself against all the obstacles that big enterprises demand."[20]

Such language, loaded with racial-biological conceptions of identity and capability, reflected deep-seated anxieties about the "fitness" of the Argentine people for the changes brought by modernity. Heroic aviation drew the attention of social commentators, journalists, and writers because it was the newest measure of national aptitude. In their minds, great feats were not simply the result of an individual's expertise and training. As one writer in *El Hogar* magazine argued, the triumphs of aviators were "collective feats," the "fruit of a work in which all the forces of the nation have collaborated, and to which industry, technology, and science are most directly linked."[21] But this assessment of the technical demands of flight was not the prevailing sentiment of the public. A prominent military official complained in 1921 that "the public, who with so much passion usually judges the meritorious efforts of our pilots . . . ignores . . . that modern, fully furnished airplanes have already been built in our workshops."[22]

The public's gaze was fixed firmly on the attributes of the pilots themselves. As the historian Willie Hiatt found in Peruvian heroic aviation, the *aviador* was lauded for his manly energy, willpower, and courage while "the airplane was almost incidental to [his] feat."[23] By the early 1920s, this discourse of masculine capabilities was increasingly medicalized and quantified as the field of aviation medicine arrived in Argentina. Aviators and military officials returning from Europe after World War I brought back new ideas concerning flight training and aviation medicine that had arisen as a result of the unprecedented demand for combat pilots. Argentine military officials in the newly created Servicio Aeronáutico del Ejército (Aeronautical

Service of the Army) were well aware of these developments and quickly sought to implement similar medical screenings locally.

In 1922, the Gabinete Psico-Fisiológico de la Aeronáutica Militar (Psycho-Physiological Cabinet of Military Aeronautics) was opened under the direction of Dr. Agesilao Milano (1877–1937). Using the latest electro-mechanical devices from Europe, doctors attempted to quantify physical and mental traits such as the sense of balance, reaction times, and attention span.[24] In the process, practitioners in Europe and Argentina endeavored to formally and medically define the ideal man for flight. As Dr. Milano emphasized in a 1925 article for *Aviación* magazine, military pilots "constitute a group of chosen men who enjoy a special prestige before their comrades and the general public . . . because they must have a select psychic and physical constitution."[25] Since humans are terrestrial creatures, aviators had to muster "not only all their physical energy, but also and in great proportion all of the moral energy, all of their intelligence." They needed "inalterable *sangre fría* [cold blood]," the ability to stay calm under duress.[26]

According to Dr. Milano, the ideal candidates for pilots were young, energetic men with quick reaction times, preferably under thirty years old. By the end of the 1920s, such medical exams were extended to civilian pilots as well, since "a weak person, a crazy person, a childish person [*un chiquilín*], cannot pilot an airplane."[27] Articles in the popular media asked "Could you serve as an aviator?" while encouraging their readers to try at-home equilibrium tests to see if they were up to snuff.[28]

The popular and official emphasis on the biological qualities of pilots and heroes reflected the prevalence of eugenics and social Darwinism, which understood humanity to be divided into a racial hierarchy.[29] The Argentine identity coalescing by the interwar period was a tangled web of highly politicized sentiments that blended ostensibly scientific ideas of race with more nebulous cultural notions of heritage and kinship. Racial-biological notions of identity were plastic in much the same way as their cultural elements, with medical officials, intellectuals, and others alternatively emphasizing a collective "white" identity while also claiming minute stratifications between ethnicities or even the regional origins of Argentina's many inhabitants.[30]

Argentine elites had opened the door to European immigration during the late nineteenth century in an effort to replace the "inferior" preexisting Hispanic, Afro-Argentine, Indigenous, and mixed-race populations whom they saw as antithetical to modernity. But the arrival of millions of immigrants in the ensuing decades created profound tensions in Argentine society. Officials complained that they were receiving "lesser" Latin peoples from Italy and Spain, as opposed to the supposedly more industrious Anglo-Saxon and Germanic peoples.[31] They saw the waves of new arrivals as unhygienic, possibly diseased, and politically radicalized. Argentine government officials increasingly turned to medicine to "cure" these perceived "social pathologies." In the eyes of reformers and officials, only the power of modern, scientific public health could combat the "illnesses" of "poverty, vagrancy, crime, hysteria, and street violence" and thus save the "national race."[32]

The scientific legitimization of the "*higienista*" (hygiene) movement—as it became known—was derived in part from new ideas of social Darwinism emphasizing racial competition. The historian Adriana Novoa has shown how the concept of Darwinian extinction deeply permeated the worldviews of Argentine scientists and intellectuals. After the arrival of Darwin's theory of natural selection, "races" were in competition, and the process of progress demanded sacrifices. The evolution of mankind and civilization required the extinction of inferior races.[33] Argentines soon wondered if they, too, would pass into history, casualties of the unending march of progress. Popular media, in periodic summations of Darwin's theory of natural selection, emphasized that "*darwinismo*" was still at work on the human species. One such popular science article stressed that natural selection "has been applied to the struggle between nations."[34] Another in 1929 concluded, "The process of racial evolution began with rigid selection. The weak, succumbed; the strong, conquered."[35]

This racial anxiety, a fear of degeneration or lack of fitness for modernity, underpinned the veneration of the hero aviator. Two qualities—consistently at the fore in popular and industry media—were central to these positive evaluations of pilots: energy and willpower. Medical exams at the Gabinete Psico-Fisiológico tested a candidate's resistance to fatigue. Doctors demanded that pilots avoid an "excess of food, alcohol, tobacco, women, etc.," all of which were believed to weaken the body's resistance to the forces of flight.[36] Repeated exposure to such stresses risked "the aviators' neurosis" caused by the "excessive expenditure of nervous energy."[37] Willpower, required for moral and hygienic discipline, enabled the pilot to overcome his environment.[38] Women, rarely referenced in aviation medicine publications from the 1920s, represented the antithesis of these qualities. They were supposedly burdened by a biologically determined lack of willpower, discipline, and emotional and physical resilience. Thus the qualities necessary for modernity were fundamentally masculine in the eyes of the aviation community and most of Argentine society.

The importance of an individual's energy and willpower extended from the nation's heroes into wider society. In the popular media, energy was the currency of modernity. It was what enabled individuals to weather the storm of social and material change experienced since the late nineteenth century, particularly in Buenos Aires. Typically embedded in discussions of energy and modernity were critiques of the perceived violence and chaos of velocity. Not only was velocity in the new machines zipping over Argentine roads and across her skies, but it was also in the demographic and cultural changes rocking the nation. One prominent social critic for *El Hogar* magazine wrote in his 1920 column entitled "The Problem of Life" that "now velocity is everything. We live in a continuous race, hurrying to get to a place where we have nothing to do. It is a violent, horrible rush, full of urges, of frights, of violence. A telegraph put here, gasoline over there, cars, electric trains, airplanes, submarines, gliders . . . the chaos!"[39]

The intensity of the experience of urban modernity was linked to the prevailing public health discourse on mental illness. This was most noticeable in the diagnosis of "hysteria" in women, often deemed a "side effect of modern urban stresses" affecting the supposedly more fragile female constitution.[40] But the risks of modernity extended to society as a whole. One author, of a 1925 short story titled "The Man of the Future," feared the effects of "scientific and industrial development" on the human race: "Many indications make us fear that man is decaying pitifully, that [he] has paid very dearly for his acquisitions, and that maybe the time will soon come of the bankruptcy of body and brain. . . . There is no doubt that, overall, those who live in big cities are increasingly losing their physical energy."[41] Regardless of the morality attributed to material progress, the energy pilots supposedly possessed in abundance was considered essential to surviving the present and future.

Even as men like Pedro Zanni were celebrated, the Argentine aviation community was troubled by a persistent problem inherent to aviation at the time: most heroic flights failed or were marred by difficulties. Of course, for something to be heroic, there had to be a realistic possibility of failure. The sheer volume of flights attempted in the North Atlantic nations ensured there were enough successes to keep people largely optimistic about their aerial capabilities. In Argentina, the situation was quite different. Out of about half a dozen major raids undertaken by the country's celebrity pilots, only one succeeded in its original goal and timeline. Popular media frequently debated why the nation lacked successful heroic aviators.[42]

In the midst of this debate, journalists and writers began to articulate not just a modern racial-biological identity but a modern Argentine *cultural* identity. They weaved the disappointments of Argentina's Heroic Age of aviation into a new national narrative of struggle and tenacity in the face of bad luck and adversity. This hard-luck incarnation of *Argentinidad* found its most complete expression in the trials and tribulations of the last heroic Argentine aviator to complete a great international raid: Eduardo Olivero.

EDUARDO OLIVERO AND THE "HARD-LUCK" OF THE ARGENTINE NATIONAL NARRATIVE

Eduardo Olivero, born in the provincial city of Tandil in 1896, learned to fly at sixteen. A second-generation Italian immigrant, Olivero left for Italy to join that nation's armed forces in 1915; he subsequently gained distinction as a fighter pilot on the Austrian front. He survived the war relatively unscathed and returned to Argentina. While on a routine flight in 1920, Olivero's cockpit was suddenly engulfed in flames. Although he managed to land the airplane, he was permanently disfigured by the burns. The following year, he was in a severe car accident, injuring his head and eyes. For the rest of his life, Olivero wore sunglasses in an effort to cover his facial scarring. His reputation as a hard-luck pilot was firmly solidified by 1921, as a *Caras y Caretas* journalist called him "[an] admirable pilot so ironically punished by luck."[43]

In 1924, Olivero decided to attempt a great raid from New York City to Buenos Aires. He brought into the project his friend Bernardo Duggan, who agreed to finance the flight. After almost two years of planning, in early 1926, Olivero and Duggan traveled to Italy, where they purchased a Savoia-Marchetti S.59 single-engine flying boat, which they named the *Buenos Aires*. They also hired the well-known Italian mechanic Ernesto Campanelli to accompany them.

The risks presented by a flight from New York City to Buenos Aires were clear to the aviators at the outset. They had selected a flying boat to compensate for the lack of infrastructure along their route. Olivero made this decision despite having never flown a water-based airplane and not knowing how to swim.[44] The aviators were particularly worried about the tropical weather at the equator. They added an enlarged radiator and water-cooling system to help the airplane's single engine keep them aloft in the hot and

Figure 3.2. From left to right, Duggan, Olivero, and Campanelli are depicted as quintessential modern heroes in their tailored suits. *La Prensa*, August 11, 1926. Courtesy of the Hemeroteca de la Biblioteca Nacional Mariano Moreno.

humid air over the tropical jungle. Finally, Duggan and Olivero elected to leave their radio behind to save space and weight, a decision they would come to regret.[45]

On May 24, 1926, Olivero, Duggan, and Campanelli took off in the *Buenos Aires* from Miller Field outside New York City to much fanfare in the international press. According to *The New York Times*, the aviators anticipated reaching Buenos Aires in seventeen to twenty days.[46] In the end, their aerial "Odyssey"—as it was later dubbed—took almost three months. They first headed down the US East Coast before flying out over the Caribbean Sea. There they encountered incessant tropical storms. Numerous times, as they continued south and east along the northern coast of South America, their airplane was lightly damaged on landings or takeoffs, causing delays for repairs. As Olivero recalled in his 1927 memoir, *Mis impresiones*, the journey was a jarring combination of elegant dinner parties with local dignitaries and near-death experiences in remote jungles, rivers, and ocean inlets.[47]

The most dramatic period came in late June when the three men disappeared for over a week in the Amazon jungle. While flying from Paramaribo, Guyana, to Para, Brazil, the aviators encountered a sudden storm that exhausted the seaplane's fuel reserves. They were forced to land by the remote island of Maraca on the Amazonian coast of Brazil just as night was coming upon them. While the fliers were unharmed, they found themselves in a region of Brazil without "wired communications," and they had left their radio behind. For the next week, the international press speculated wildly about their fate. Brazil dispatched naval vessels to search for them to no avail. The aviators eventually reached a town onboard a fishing boat where they managed to make contact with a steamship chartered by the Argentine newspaper *La Nación*.[48]

The flight resumed shortly after their reappearance, but the bad luck continued. As they made their torturous journey along the Brazilian east coast, the *Buenos Aires* again disappeared for four days. This time they had run out of fuel during a storm between Araranguá and Rio Grande do Sul in southern Brazil.[49] Having definitively proven to the world the utility of radios in such endeavors, the three beleaguered aviators finally landed in Buenos Aires after traveling nearly fifteen thousand kilometers in eighty-one days. In an end befitting the journey, they arrived on Friday, August 13.[50]

The reaction to Olivero's and Duggan's journey seems to have been mixed in Argentina. Certainly, their great adventure over the wilds of Latin America captured the public imagination. But the men had become the butt of jokes among *porteños*—the people of Buenos Aires. When their arrival seemed assured, one *Crítica* columnist castigated his countrymen: "What are the airmen going to say when they learn that they are awaited with a tremendous stock of jokes and ridicule?"[51]

These fears proved overblown. Once the aviators arrived in Buenos Aires, the national press hailed them as heroes. The setbacks of their journey were now harnessed to emphasize their greatness. Thousands of Argentines crowded at the river's edge to greet the aviators who were subsequently honored at dozens of banquets, sporting events, and parades.[52]

The popular tabloid *Crítica* provided the most sensationalized coverage, publishing dozens of articles, drawings, photographs, and maps about the flight and its meaning. Despite the hyperbolic rhetoric, its pages contain the clearest illustration of how the flight was understood in terms of the national identity. *Crítica*'s journalists matched the qualified praise found in other publications, deeming the trio "the Heroes of Bad Luck."[53]

But some *Crítica* articles went so far as to argue that the struggles of the crew mirrored those of the Argentine people, and their tenacity in the face of such trials was representative of the true Argentine spirit, even if this was not always recognized. Whereas European heroic aviators were "nothing more than . . . lucky . . . , our boys have shown that they are phenomenal, patient, suffering, persevering, impenetrable to fear and impervious to despondency."[54] These authors claimed that the public's mockery of the flight revealed a failure to grasp its meaning. The pilots were exhibiting the very essence of what it meant to be Argentine, which in this context was encapsulated by the word "creole," or the traditional, rural culture of the Argentine countryside: "It is necessary to exalt the tenacity, ingenuity and patience, quintessential creole virtues . . . of our brave pilots. . . . How many obstacles they have had to overcome in the long months that their Odyssey has lasted. But like the little creole horse, slowly no more, and without fainting, they have reached the goal."[55]

Crítica's contributors harnessed the imagery and rhetoric of the countryside, and in particular the myth of the gaucho, the landless horsemen of the premodern Argentine countryside, in a fashion similar to that of cowboys in the US imagination. The rural horsemen, often of mixed race and associated with Spanish colonial heritage, were deemed incompatible with modernity by liberal elites and were largely eliminated in a series of military campaigns in the late nineteenth century. Soon after, nationalist writers began to cultivate a romanticized image of the horsemen as archetypes of a noncosmopolitan and rural *Argentinidad*—resurrecting them as a symbol of Argentine identity.[56] These mythical gauchos were portrayed as fundamentally white, Spanish, and aggressively masculine in their independence, violence, and restlessness.[57] Nationalists painted them as tragic figures who helped realize Argentine independence from Spain only to be marginalized and eventually eradicated by Europeanized elites.

This narrative was laid out in the most famous text of *gauchesque* literature from the nineteenth century, José Hernandez's epic poem *El Gaucho Martín Fierro*, which *Crítica*'s editors chose to reprint alongside coverage of Olivero and Duggan. Drawings of gauchos appeared alongside renderings of the aviators. A banner over the coverage of their arrival read "It is the Gaucho they carried inside that made them arrive." Another image featured "Juan Pueblo," represented by an individual wearing traditional rural clothing, looking on admiringly as Olivero embraced his mother, and Duggan his wife (see fig. 3.3). Battling long odds and facing tragic defeat but persevering were thus cast as Argentine narratives borne out by the struggles of their great aviators. Just as the gauchos eventually succumbed to the forces arrayed against them, sacrificed in the construction of Argentine civilization, so too had many of Argentina's heroic pilots died in the conquest of the sky. The history of Argentine aviation was cast as a tragic yet inspiring narrative of masculine sacrifice and tenacity in the service of progress.

When *Crítica* hailed Olivero and Duggan as embodying the gaucho spirit, it might have seemed a victory for the growing nationalist movement. Two heroic Argentines were being draped in the laurels not of European civilization and progress but of a mystical spirit emanating from the countryside. But the construction of such a narrative was in reality far less

Figure 3.3. On the left, "Juan Pueblo" looks on in tears as Olivero and Duggan embrace their mothers. On the right, a stoic gaucho rides his horse. *Crítica*, August 13–14, 1926. Courtesy of the Hemeroteca de la Biblioteca Nacional Mariano Moreno.

exclusionary than nationalist intellectuals had hoped. This hard-luck version of *Argentinidad* could be applied to any ethnic group or nationality in the country. Even if the rural archetype of the gaucho was becoming a national symbol, most of the nation's famous pilots were the children of recent immigrants who nevertheless were said to embody authentic gaucho qualities. Zanni and Olivero were both second-generation Italo-Argentines. Mainstream culture emphasized assimilation and the negotiation of differences among Argentina's enormous immigrant class.[58]

The culture of aviation reflected this shift as the Heroic Age of aviation waned in the early 1930s. The discourses swirling around flight were increasingly focused not on negotiating ethnic or national differences but on reinforcing or transcending class hierarchy. Aviation, despite its undoubtedly elitist origins, was rapidly becoming a technology of common people—and in the process, losing some of its prestige. Both the narratives pushed by the aviation industry and the prevailing image of the male pilot were changing. Whereas the industry in Argentina (as well as Europe and North America) was initially happy to trumpet the new technological capabilities of airplanes on great raids, by the 1930s, they were emphasizing the safety and regularity of commercial aviation.[59] Refraining from narratives of "extraordinary" aviation, they now asserted that the future of their industry was so ordinary that everyday people would soon be flying as passengers and pilots. The *aviador* was transforming from an exceptional individual whom the common man should emulate to an identity *of* the common man. In Argentina, this change melded with a developing masculine culture in the working and middle classes that promoted technical skill, knowledge, and inventiveness as a means to socioeconomic upward mobility and dignity.[60]

THE *AVIADORA*, MODERN FEMININITY, AND THE ARTICULATION OF ARGENTINE PROGRESS

Yet as the locus of aviation culture moved down the class ladder, creating new opportunities for common people to participate in the industry, half of the Argentine population remained conspicuously out of the equation. Whereas modern masculinity was essential for the nation, intellectuals and government officials were ambivalent at best about the possibilities offered by *la mujer moderna*—the modern woman. Narratives of heroic aviation and biological fitness created a space for a handful of prominent female fliers in the 1930s. But in the end, Argentine intellectuals and media outlets largely rejected *la mujer moderna*. They constructed a narrative of national progress that venerated material improvement while pushing back on the interwar period's most divisive social question in Argentina: the role of women in the modern age.

Argentine women had always shown an interest in aviation, whether as spectators, enthusiasts, or pilots. Women of all social classes were markers of the emotional weight of great flights and served as a necessary feminine opposite to the masculinity of aviators. Pilots became sex symbols. When *Mundo Argentino* magazine asked its readers who their ideal man would be, dozens of girls and young women responded they would marry a handsome aviator. Celebrity pilots were mobbed by groups of women, inflating their social cachet.[61] Women's role in the pageantry of aviation reached its zenith when heroic aviators died in the line of duty. During the funeral processions, the media often described women weeping for their fallen heroes. Fund-raising efforts for monuments and public remembrances were frequently undertaken by women.[62]

Yet when it came to women hopping into the cockpit themselves, the situation was quite different. Aviation remained an almost exclusively male space—*aero clubes* (air clubs) generally discouraged women aspirants. Prospective *aviadoras* had to find individual instructors willing to train them, something a handful succeeded in doing. The nation had its first licensed female pilot, Amalia Celia Figueredo de Pietra (1895–1985), in 1914; about a dozen more women would follow her by 1930.

However, women rarely flew after receiving their licenses, and none became a prominent national figure. Women pilots did not fit the prevailing narrative of aviation, which was steeped in the rhetoric of a masculine conquest of nature. When men flew, the media described their exploits as demonstrations of bold and courageous dedication to this scientific conquest. When a woman took to the skies, her flight was invariably a poetic and emotional journey that had little to do with the furtherance of progress.[63]

Women were largely seen as biologically unfit for the cockpit. Their bodies and minds were supposedly too fragile to handle the velocity, violence, and risk. From the outset of powered flight, there were a few local journalists who advocated *for* women pilots. Their arguments ranged from the logical—women are generally smaller and lighter than men—to the ludicrous, such as women's eyes having a wider field of view. But for every positive argument for women pilots, there were far more detractors who believed their supposed natural weakness made them less able aviators.[64]

Early narratives of Argentine aviation typically depicted women as sentimental and naturalistic—and thus counterproductive to the male aviators' progressive mission, which demanded total dedication and sacrifice.[65] When a woman insisted on flying anyway, she was embedded in a tragic narrative of liberation gone wrong. By the interwar period, flight was a frequent metaphor for liberation from social obligations.[66] Girls and young women wrote to *Mundo Argentino* that their greatest happiness would be to fly away from their lives in an airplane.[67] In popular fiction, the narrative around the *aviadora* was remarkably consistent. A young woman, on the verge of adulthood and marriage, dreams of a different life. Her soul craves grand things. Flight offered a metaphorical and literal escape from her natural destiny as a mother and wife.[68]

This narrative was reinforced by the frequent usage of the *aviadora* in popular culture to represent *la mujer moderna*, or the "Modern Girl" archetype of the North Atlantic. Argentine media during the interwar period was flooded by images and stories primarily from the United States that depicted a modern womanhood of greater freedom and empowerment. *La mujer moderna* was wealthy, active, athletic, and independent. She wore lighter and more revealing clothing. She smoked cigarettes in public, drove motorcars, and flew airplanes. The young and beautiful woman pilot, dressed in a flight suit with pants, posing alongside her aerial stead, was one of the most radical depictions of North American modernity (see fig. 3.4). They were stand-ins for both the material progress represented by the sleek new aircraft and the radical social progress represented by the female presence in the cockpit.

The visibility of *aviadoras* in popular culture ensured they were a frequent topic of conversation even though they were exceptionally rare in Argentine society. The airplane, and the speed it represented, was drawn into seemingly unrelated social debates on gender relations. In one example, a columnist for *Mundo Argentino* created an imaginary conversation between two women, one a traditional "sentimentalist," the other a modern "materialist." The traditional woman condemned modern love, saying, "There is no time for flirting, there is no time to lose." The modern woman replied, "I am a girl of my time. It's true, flirting has entered materialistic terrain. And it is logical. For we live in the century of the airplane, the submarine, and the Charleston."[69] As another columnist wrote, "Anything that keeps the modern woman motionless horrifies her."[70] Modern love was one of dancing, sports, and perpetual motion.

The discourse around the demands of modernity for women centered on energy and willpower too. But whereas such qualities were essential for the

Figure 3.4. *La mujer moderna* on the airfield was a staple of interwar advertising as companies sought to associate their products with chic, North American modernity. *El Hogar*, September 27, 1930. Courtesy of the Hemeroteca de la Biblioteca Nacional Mariano Moreno.

Figure 3.5. Stefford in 1931 on the eve of her great raid. Images of Stefford generally emphasized her feminine beauty despite the addition of flight gear. *Caras y Caretas*, August 15, 1931. Courtesy of the collections of the Biblioteca Nacional de España.

modern man, in popular narratives, they were dangerous for women. When it came to *la mujer moderna*, and especially the *aviadora*, one word consistently came to the fore: *inquietud*, or restlessness. She was dissatisfied with her traditional social roles and had an unstoppable desire for greater things. This supposedly created a fatal tension between her natural femininity and unnatural masculine drive. For the *aviadora* in popular fiction, her restlessness invariably resulted in her death, or the death of a loved one. The woman pilot was portrayed as a fundamentally tragic figure.

This narrative seemed to be borne out in reality, or at least that was how it was depicted in the media. The first prominent woman aviator in Argentina, Myriam Stefford, was the perfect incarnation of *la mujer moderna*, an image she purposely cultivated. Born Rosa Martha Rossi in Switzerland in 1905, she became a famous actress in European cinema at a young age, changing her name to Myriam Stefford. In 1930, she married the well-known Argentine writer and millionaire Raúl Barón Biza and moved to Buenos Aires. Stefford soon decided to take up aviation, training with the World War I German fighter pilot Luís (Ludwig) G. Fuchs. As would later be remembered, "her desire was as strong as her will. And her will was so unyielding that she was sure to triumph: she would be a great aviator."[71] In a mere two months, she earned her license.

But Stefford was not content to end her aviation career there, reportedly declaring, "I cannot limit myself to the tranquil life of the lady who has obtained a *brevet*."[72] She decided to attempt the heroic: a raid to all fourteen Argentine provincial capitals in a light airplane. The "Circuit of the Fourteen Provinces," as it was known, was a challenge created by a prominent *aero club* in 1926 to promote the creation of flight infrastructure in the interior of the country.[73] For much of the interwar period, many of the provinces still lacked paved runways, navigational aids, and weather reporting services. By 1931, two teams of male aviators had completed the circuit in 1926 and 1927, while a third team—Alberto Riggi O'Dwyer and the mechanic Octavio Occo—had died preparing an attempt.[74]

Stefford elected to use her B.F.W.m 23 two-seater monoplane *Chingolo*,[75] which was woefully underpowered for a long-distance flight. But Stefford evidently loved her "*avioneta*" (little airplane), as the press called it. During interviews, she frequently called it her "*pajarito gaucho*" (little gaucho bird) and would repeat her slogan: "Little bird with wings of paper and a heart of steel."[76] Stefford also decided to bring along her instructor Fuchs for assistance, although he emphasized in the press that she could have done the raid by herself.[77]

On August 18, 1931, Stefford and Fuchs took off from Morón Airport outside Buenos Aires. Over the next six days, they flew to Corrientes, Santiago del Estero, and Jujuy. But on the morning of August 26, on their way to San Juan, a crucial bolt in the flight control system snapped. The airplane crashed in a "sad and desolate plain" of scrub brush near the town of Marayes, killing both pilots instantly.

The public was shocked by the news of Stefford's death. When her casket arrived in Buenos Aires, thousands showed up at the train station to pay their respects. As *Caras y Caretas* remembered one year later, seemingly "all of the people of Buenos Aires" visited her memorial.[78] In a romantic gesture that likely would have pleased Stefford's sense of drama, her widower Raúl Barón Biza eventually commissioned a massive marble mausoleum in her honor outside of Córdoba.[79]

For the press, Stefford's life and death were a confirmation of the narrative around women and flight. She was wealthy, foreign, and feminine, yet with an "unstoppable" will. Journalists fell over themselves emphasizing her femininity in light of her heroic death: "The desire to perform a magnificent feat did not kill in her the delicacy of her feelings as a woman and as an artist."[80] According to the newspaper *La Razón*, "She presented that interesting duality: a very eighteenth-century woman, worthy of shining in the halls of the Sun King, and a woman of her time, eager for glory and triumph in the middle of this twentieth century. . . . For being feminine she fell in love with glory and with masculine recklessness she wanted to conquer it."[81] Even as social commentators remarked on her masculine drive, they painted it in feminine terms, such as in the previous quotation where she "falls in love with glory." Stefford's life was now firmly embedded in the tragic narrative of the *aviadora*, a woman who "lacked nothing, but dreamt of glory."[82]

The cautionary overtones of these memorials reflected the growing rejection of *la mujer moderna* in popular culture and politics.[83] As the 1930s wore on, mainstream social thought increasingly separated material and social progress. Previously, most intellectuals believed that social progress, in this case represented by feminism, followed material modernization for better and for worse.[84] But the crises of the Great Depression, the rise of Communism and Fascism, and the possibility of another global war eroded this narrative. Social conservatives, who were ascendant in this period, argued that feminism—particularly in the form of women in the workplace—was a failed experiment. One correspondent for *La Prensa* wrote in 1931 that *la mujer moderna* was a rarity even in the supposed heartland of modernity, the United States. She concluded that there should be different "models" of women for different societies—in other words, that social progress should be tailored to local culture.[85]

As the decade progressed, commentators went a step further, arguing that the lack of social progress for women was one of the reasons their society was relatively peaceful. An editorial for *El Hogar* magazine in June 1936 claimed that Buenos Aires was "one of the cities with the greatest moral cleanliness in the world." It continued, "Our time is characterized neither by faith, nor by tolerance, nor by tranquility. The airs from outside, which still nourish us, arrive loaded with terrible omens." The abandonment of the household by women in other countries had led to unemployment, diminishing public religiosity, and an emptiness in the "soul of the family."[86] But in Argentina, as another columnist wrote, "the Argentine woman has not returned to her home because she never abandoned it."[87] In essence, the role of women as the guardians of ostensibly premodern values like the primacy of family and religion made Argentina a beacon of calm, tolerance, and morality for the world.

Yet the modern aspirations of Argentine identity made it difficult to disentangle material and social progress completely. There was too much uncertainty over the direction of these forces. In a future air age, women might have to fly. The commercial aviation industry was already targeting market campaigns toward women to convince them to fly as passengers.[88]

More consequentially, most industrialized nations had at least one famous woman aviator. Women like Amelia Earhart were clearly demonstrating their capabilities in the cockpit.[89] What did it say about the fitness of the Argentine race for modernity that they lacked great *aviadoras*?

This problem was clearly evident in the coverage of Myriam Stefford's death. Remembrances of Stefford in a booklet honoring her life emphasized her fundamental foreignness—using English words like "sportswoman" or "recordwoman"—and described her drive to perform masculine activities as unlike her Argentine counterparts, "who only think of 'pleasing' and conquering a [social] position, either through their beauty or the solution of marriage."[90] Yet at her funeral, a civil aviation department official declared Stefford "the prototype of her sex in the modern age" and a "precursor of the woman of the future, [who], alongside of men will tomorrow be a very powerful factor in the perfecting of mankind."[91] This discrepancy between the supposed future of humanity and the desired role of women in Argentine society remained a source of tension for the aviation community and the public.

The answer for most Argentines was to celebrate the local woman pilot, but only within the heroic mold of the 1920s. Argentine women could fly if they were extraordinary, proof of the biological capabilities of the *raza*. But the *aviadora*, unlike the *aviador*, did not become an identity of the common Argentine—at least according to the national media. Instead, the narrative of women and flight shifted from claiming that women *could* not fly to that they *should* not fly. The presence of a heroic *aviadora* was taken as evidence that Argentine women were fit for modernity but had made the choice to largely abstain from North Atlantic feminism.

Just as these ideas were solidifying, the first authentically local woman hero pilot emerged on the national scene, Carola Lorenzini (1899–1941). Lorenzini was Argentina's Earhart. She was an international celebrity and the first woman to receive a commercial pilot's license in Latin America. Lorenzini was undoubtedly a hero in Argentine society, a source of inspiration for women and men alike. But as we shall see, hero status could be just as constraining as it was empowering.

Lorenzini was born in 1899 in a rural town in the province of Buenos Aires. Her friends and family remembered her as physically gifted, disciplined, and hardworking.[92] After leaving home, she worked as a typist for a telephone company in Buenos Aires. In 1930, Lorenzini took her first ride in an airplane and never looked back. She saved money from her job and finally began flying regularly in 1933. The following year, Lorenzini approached

Figure 3.6. Lorenzini just prior to breaking the South American women's altitude record in 1935. Much like Earhart, Lorenzini was frequently seen wearing pants, which was transgressive at the time. Archivo General de la Nación Argentina, Departamento Documentos Fotográficos, box 788. Courtesy of the Archivo General de la Nación Argentina.

military aviation authorities, offering to fly one of the models recently produced by the state aircraft factory. Aircraft manufacturers during the period frequently harnessed the image of the woman flier to sell their wares. Argentine military authorities agreed to Lorenzini's proposal and gave her access to state aircraft for most of her career. In 1935, she used an Argentine-designed and built airplane to capture the South American women's altitude record.[93]

Lorenzini soon became known for her skill as an aerobatic pilot. Her stick-and-rudder skills impressed her fellow aviators and the many crowds that gathered to watch her exhibitions. After witnessing one of her aerobatics displays one journalist noted, "It seems that space itself responds to the demands of the *aviadora*; and the stability of the machine, easily achieved after a series of spectacular [maneuvers], gave the exact impression that the airplane was . . . moved by the harmony of nature and not by the feminine hand that guided it."[94]

In 1940, Lorenzini took up the mantle of heroic female aviation left vacant since the death of Myriam Stefford nine years earlier. She convinced military authorities to sponsor her own fourteen provinces raid in one of their Focke-Wulf biplanes. Lorenzini's whirlwind tour caused a national sensation. Departing Buenos Aires on March 24, 1940, she completed the raid in less than a month, stopping at dozens of provincial cities and towns. People were particularly impressed with her aerobatic shows over city centers—a practice normally prohibited by this time. Nearly every stop featured parties, banquets, and honorifics. In a gesture that touched many Argentines, Lorenzini flew over the site where Stefford and Fuchs had been killed and dropped a wreath of flowers. When she finally arrived back in Buenos Aires on April 21, a huge crowd gathered to celebrate, reminiscent of the greetings extended to male aviators ten years earlier. The media noted the hundreds of girls and young women who showered Lorenzini with flowers and begged for her autograph.[95]

Lorenzini's life inspired a powerful cognitive dissonance in the Argentine media. She was difficult to fit into a gendered mold. She had the physical presence of a man and was characterized as disciplined, diligent, and hardworking, traits usually associated with laboring men. Yet all commentators noted her lovely smile, warm demeanor, and feminine qualities.[96] Lorenzini—who was forty-one in 1940—was older than most famous pilots, male or female. Her credentials as an authentic Argentine were unquestioned due to her rural upbringing and self-financing of her flight training, which distinguished her from the wealth and foreignness of the archetypical *aviadora*.[97]

By the early 1940s, Lorenzini was an omnipresent feature of national aviation. Officials knew that she would guarantee crowds, and they all but required her to appear at nearly every major aviation event. But as Lorenzini came to realize all too well, her heroic status had strict limitations. Aviation authorities refused to admit her into the fold of professional aviation. She was fired from her job at the telephone company in the late 1930s because of her dedication to aviation. For years afterward, she petitioned state authorities to give her a salaried job in the industry. Although vague promises were made, officials stonewalled her. Despite her clear skill, she was denied a professional license twice in the late 1930s. In her letter of protest, she complained that her examiners were adding irrelevant and unfair questions to ensure her failure. Only after her fourteen provinces raid in 1940 did authorities grant her a commercial license—a fact they then trumpeted as a South American first. Then in a betrayal that shocked even the national press, there were rumors that military authorities were revoking Lorenzini's access to the Focke-Wulf airplane she made famous. Although they reversed course, for Lorenzini, this was the last straw. She arranged for a salaried job in the private sector, turning her back on state authorities.[98]

Tragically, a week before she was finally to begin her career as a salaried pilot, she was killed in a flight accident. On November 22, 1941, military officials invited Lorenzini to perform aerobatics to honor a contingent of women fliers from Uruguay. Her Focke-Wulf airplane had just come back from maintenance when she hopped in the cockpit. In the midst of an aerobatic maneuver, there was a sudden problem with one of the control surfaces. Lorenzini, already in a steep dive, could not recover. She was killed instantly on impact.

Over the next two days, more than seventeen thousand Argentines filed past her casket to pay their respects. Continuing its tradition of extensive and emotional coverage of martyred aviators, one *Crítica* article declared Lorenzini "an authentic *gaucha*. The Argentine woman had in her, her best example. Her highest representation."[99] Another emphasized her remarkable drive to surmount the many obstacles to her aviation career: "In the first place, she was a woman; in addition she was poor and had to work. But the will of Carola overcame everything."[100]

Even in death she could not escape the tensions of her life, as journalists emphasized the foundational femininity behind her obviously masculine qualities. As one writer concluded, "Her creole soul never denied the condition of her sex, although [her] vocation was something at odds with love and home."[101] Lorenzini's mother lamented in an interview, "She had too much courage to be a woman." Nevertheless, the most moving piece published in *Crítica* sought to reassure readers that the message of Lorenzini's life would endure: "The reality is tremendous and harsh; Carola Lorenzini has died, but as the best tribute to her glory, ten determined and generous Argentine girls like her must come immediately to take up her post to pick up her lesson in boldness and courage."[102]

This was not to be. Lorenzini died flying for free to promote women in flight, invited by the very authorities that had spurned her. In perhaps the ultimate tragedy, she was the last of her kind. No woman pilot in Argentina ever again matched her public persona; it would be nearly forty years before women would be accepted into the fold of professional aviation in Argentina. Lorenzini's life was a reminder of what Argentine women could do but chose not to, at least according to the mainstream press.

By the 1940s, the direction of Argentine modernity and progress was no longer defined by the unbridled acceptance of material and social change. While the men of the nation forged material modernity with their energy and willpower, women were left to safeguard the supposedly premodern national soul. Concerns of biological fitness created space for heroic Argentine women to fulfill the role of *la mujer moderna* in their society—and even be celebrated for it. But their presence was only tolerated because they were extraordinary. In the popular imagination, when women took flight, liberation became tragedy. And according to many social commentators, this mirrored the overall trajectory of North Atlantic feminism. For the betterment of their society, a woman like Carola Lorenzini had to remain the exception to the rule; the future of the average Argentine woman had to remain largely the same as her forebearers. As a result, modern progress was effectively rendered Argentine through a gendered articulation of social change—the promotion of the modern man and the rejection of *la mujer moderna* and its most visible representative, *la aviadora*.

NOTES

1. "Los Andes son cruzados por el capitán Pedro A. Zanni," *Caras y Caretas*, March 27, 1920, 35–36. For the coverage of Zar, see "El Teniente Marcos Zar en Asunción," *Caras y Caretas*, April 3, 1920, 4. Unless otherwise noted, all translations are my own.
2. "El homenaje popular tributado a los aviadores Zanni, Parodi y Zar," *Caras y Caretas*, April 3, 1920.

3. "Una crecida cantidad de público recibió ayer en Seis de Septiembre a la aviadora Carola Lorenzini," *La Prensa*, April 22, 1940.
4. For the reception and popular discourses of male celebrity aviators in interwar Europe and North America, see Bernard Rieger, *Technology and the Culture of Modernity in Britain and Germany, 1890–1945* (New York: Cambridge University Press, 2005), 116–57; Robert Wohl, *The Spectacle of Flight: Aviation and the Western Imagination, 1920–1950* (New Haven: Yale University Press, 2005), 9–48; and Charles L. Ponce de Leon, "The Man Nobody Knows: Charles A. Lindbergh and the Culture of Celebrity," in *The Airplane in American Culture*, ed. Dominick A. Pisano (Ann Arbor: University of Michigan Press, 2003), 75–104.
5. For the history of women pilots in North America and Europe, see Liz Millward, *Women in British Imperial Airspace, 1922–1937* (Ithaca: McGill-Queen's University Press, 2008); Rieger, *Technology and Culture of Modernity*, 138–53; Joseph C. Corn, *The Winged Gospel: America's Romance with Aviation, 1900–1950* (Baltimore: Johns Hopkins University Press, 1983), 71–90; and Susan Ware, *Still Missing: Amelia Earhart and the Search for Modern Feminism* (New York: W. W. Norton, 1993).
6. The historiography of modern Argentina has generally focused on the perceived *negative* physical and psychological qualities elites and the state sought to mitigate through public health, criminal justice, and other forms of social control. A major exception has been research on "matrimonial eugenics" in the region, especially in Nancy Leys Stepan, *"The House of Eugenics": Race, Gender, and Nation in Latin America* (Ithaca: Cornell University Press, 1991), chap. 4. For the history of social control, public health, and Argentina, see Donna J. Guy, *Sex and Danger in Buenos Aires: Prostitution, Family, and Nation in Argentina* (Lincoln: University of Nebraska Press, 1991); Natalia Milanesio, "Redefining Men's Sexuality, Resignifying Male Bodies: The Argentine Law of Anti-Venereal Prophylaxis, 1936," *Gender and History* 17 (August 2005): 463–91; Julia Rodríguez, *Civilizing Argentina: Science, Medicine, and the Modern State* (Chapel Hill: University of North Carolina Press, 2006); Yolanda Eraso, "Biotypology, Endocrinology, and Sterilization: The Practice of Eugenics in the Treatment of Argentinian Women During the 1930s," *Bulletin of the History of Medicine* 81 (2007): 793–822; Adriana Novoa, "The Act or Process of Dying Out: The Importance of Darwinian Extinction in Argentine Culture," *Science in Context* 22 (2009): 217–44; and Diego Armus, *The Ailing City: Health, Tuberculosis, and Culture in Buenos Aires, 1870–1950* (Durham: Duke University Press, 2011).
7. Leandro Losada, *La alta sociedad en la Buenos Ares de la "Belle Époque": Sociabilidad, estilos de vida e identidades* (Buenos Aires: Siglo Veintiuno, 2008), 46.
8. This exemplified broader trends in science, technology, and the ideology of civilizational dominance promulgated by the North Atlantic powers. Michael Adas, *Machines as the Measure of Man: Science, Technology and Ideologies of Western Dominance* (Ithaca: Cornell University Press, 1989), introduction and chapter 3.
9. Raúl Larra, *Jorge Newbery, el conquistador del espacio* (Buenos Aires: Aerolíneas Argentinas, 1975), 112.
10. For examples of the coverage around Newbery in life and death, see the funerary booklet *Jorge Newbery: Homenaje* (Belgrano: Talleres Gráficos "Roma" de Magrini

y Assenti, 1914), and his most recent biography, Alejandro Guerrero, *Jorge Newbery* (Buenos Aires: Emecé, 1999).

11. Pedro Leandro Zanni, *Raid aéreo Amsterdam-Tokio. Su desarrollo* (Buenos Aires: Imp. Ferrari Hnos., 1926), 5.
12. "La vuelta al mundo en aeroplano: Partida de la misión argentina," *Aviación*, February 29, 1924, 6–7.
13. "La vuelta al mundo en aeroplano: Partida de la misión argentina," *Aviación*, November 30, 1923, 2.
14. For an accounting of the various attempts in mid-1924, see "La vuelta al mundo y los grandes raids," *Aviación*, August 10, 1924, 17–18.
15. The US Army team chose to travel west from Seattle, Washington, surmounting the treacherous Pacific crossing first.
16. Zanni, *Raid aéreo Amsterdam-Tokio*, 27–28.
17. Zanni, *Raid aéreo Amsterdam-Tokio*, 35–36.
18. "Zanni lamenta abandonar el raid," *Crítica*, November 3, 1924, 3.
19. "Zanni," *Caras y Caretas*, August 30, 1924, 54.
20. "El esfuerzo del aviador Hillcoat," *Caras y Caretas*, December 6, 1924, 46.
21. "Nosotros y la aviación," *El Hogar*, April 8, 1921, 3.
22. Francisco Torres, "Aviación y aviadores nacionales," *Aviación*, June 1921, 30.
23. Willie Hiatt, *The Rarified Air of the Modern: Airplanes and Technological Modernity in the Andes* (New York: Oxford University Press, 2016), 25–26.
24. Agesilao Milano, *Cómo debe seleccionarse el personal militar de la aviación. Métodos modernos usados con ese objeto* (Córdoba: "La Semana Médica," Imp. de Obras de E. Spinelli, 1921), 5.
25. Agesilao Milano, "Instrucciones para el régimen higiénico navegante," *Aviación*, August 10, 1925, 11.
26. Agesilao Milano, "Fisiologia-inaptitud e higiene del aviador," *Aviación*, February 28, 1922, 29.
27. Older men were less desirable, as they reportedly were more sensitive to the cold and suffered from poorer kidney function at high altitude. "El sentido del equilibrio. ¿Sirve usted para aviador?," *El Hogar*, May 18, 1923, 5.
28. "Pruebas para la aviación. Cómo puede hacerse un aviador," *El Hogar*, August 22, 1919; "Pruebas a que debe someterse todo aspirante a aviador militar," *Aviación*, April 1921, 26; "El sentido del equilibrio," 5; "El mal de los aviadores," *El Hogar*, May 16, 1924, 34; "El mal de los aviadores," *El Hogar*, December 19, 1924, 53.
29. Rodríguez, *Civilizing Argentina*, 5.
30. For the history of race in Argentina, see Paulina L. Alberto and Eduardo Elena, *Rethinking Race in Modern Argentina* (New York: Cambridge University Press, 2016). For the region, see Stepan, *House of Eugenics*; and Julia Rodríguez, "A Complex Fabric: Intersecting Histories of Race, Gender, and Science in Latin America," *Hispanic American Historical Review* 91 (2011): 409–29.
31. Rodríguez, *Civilizing Argentina*, 4–5.
32. Rodríguez, *Civilizing Argentina*, 6.
33. Novoa, "Act or Process," 237.

34. Pedro Gamboa, "La ciencia al alcance de todos. La selección natural," *El Hogar*, February 21, 1919.
35. "La teoría general de la evolución animal," *Crítica*, November 2, 1929.
36. Milano, "Fisiologia-inaptitud e higiene," 31. This call for discipline and moderation was a common feature of Latin American "eugenic hygiene" practices. As Nancy Leys Stepan has shown, public health officials and scientists across the region adopted Neo-Lamarckian notions that "linked a sanitary environment to racial health." Thus things like alcohol, tobacco, drugs, and sex, if unchecked, could be "racial poisons" that undermined the long-term health of the user's race. See Stepan, *House of Eugenics*, chap. 3.
37. "La enfermedad de los aviadores," *Caras y Caretas*, June 12, 1920, 18.
38. "Las dos primeras conferencias del curso actual," *Aviación*, August 10, 1925, 16. The frequent reference to "willpower" was spurred by popular understandings of Friedrich Nietzsche's amorphous notion of "will to power." Nietzschean characterizations of willpower—as a means to master oneself and nature in order to overcome the banality of everyday existence—appealed to pilots and supporters of aviation. Wohl, *Spectacle of Flight*, chapters 4 and 6. The European Fascist aviation community was particularly enamored of Nietzschean philosophy and saw themselves as cases par excellence of the "new nobility" or "Nietzschean supermen" demanded by their vision of modernity. Fernando Esposito, *Fascism, Aviation, and the Mythical Modernity*, trans. Patrick Camiller (Hampshire: Palgrave Macmillan, 2015), 80–114, 210–67, 348–76.
39. "El problema de la vida," *El Hogar*, April 9, 1920, 15.
40. Rodríguez, *Civilizing Argentina*, 74.
41. "El hombre del futuro," *El Hogar*, January 2, 1925, 55.
42. See "Nosotros y la aviación"; "Y nosotros . . . ," *Crítica*, February 22, 1927, 3; and "¿Por qué los aviadores argentinos no salen a conquistar gloria?," *Mundo Argentino*, February 16, 1927, 7.
43. "El aviador Eduardo Olivero," *Caras y Caretas*, June 18, 1921, 62.
44. He learned how to fly a flying boat at the Savoia factory in Italy, but it is unclear if he learned how to swim too. Eduardo Olivero, *Mis impresiones* (Buenos Aires: Talleres Gráficos Tuduri, 1927), 16.
45. Olivero, *Mis impresiones*, 30.
46. "Arrive Here to Try Argentine Flight; Dugan, Olivero and Campanelli Plan Trip from Here to Buenos Aires," *New York Times*, May 13, 1926.
47. Olivero, *Mis impresiones*, 131–59.
48. "Duggan Party Safe at Vigia in Brazil," *New York Times*, June 21, 1926.
49. "Duggan Found near Mastardas Bay," *New York Times*, August 5, 1926.
50. A fact that one *Crítica* correspondent found very amusing. "Hoy: ¡Viernes 13 de agosto! ¿Llegarán los aviadores?," *Crítica*, August 13, 1926.
51. "La verdad sobre el raid del Buenos Aires," *Crítica*, August 11, 1926, 14.
52. Evidently, they received particular attention from Argentine women, especially the more attractive Duggan. "Duggan, Olivero y Campanelli. El entusiasmo femenino," *Caras y Caretas*, August 21, 1926, 65.
53. See, for example, "Critica saludó desde el cielo ayer, la llegada de los héroes," *Crítica*, August 14, 1926, 6.

54. "La verdad sobre el raid del Buenos Aires," 14.
55. "Heroísmo y buena suerte," *Crítica*, August 12, 1926.
56. Rodríguez, *Civilizing Argentina*, 17–18.
57. As the work of the historian Oscar Chamosa has shown, the appropriation of the gaucho as the symbol of Argentine identity did not challenge the "myth of the white Argentina," since the "non-European rural populations" associated with the horsemen were still subordinated to white, urban culture. The celebration of a "mythical" gaucho did not translate into increased opportunities for the rural mixed-raced population either. Since the rural "folk type" was perceived through the lens of Spanish heritage, they were characterized as essentially white, but of a lower class than people of pure European ancestry or with whiter skin. Nevertheless, Argentine identity continued to be burdened by a fundamental contradiction: "The exotic other was at the same time the authentic national Self." The way mainstream Argentine culture accommodated this tension was to mythologize the rural, mixed-race gaucho or peasant as a *historical* aspect of the nation. See Oscar Chamosa, "People as Landscape: The Representation of the Criollo in Early Tourist Literature in Argentina, 1920–30," in *Rethinking Race in Modern Argentina*, eds. Paulina L. Alberto and Eduardo Elena, 53–72 (New York: Cambridge University Press, 2016).
58. For the successful integration of Italians into Argentine society, see Samuel Baily, *Immigrants in the Lands of Promise: Italians in Buenos Aires and New York City, 1870–1914* (Ithaca: Cornell University Press, 1999), 82, 217. The continued prevalence, if not dominance, of nationalist sentiments was due to the unavoidable reality of the "nation's visibly subordinate position in global economic, political, and cultural circuits." Matthew Karush, *Culture of Class: Radio and Cinema in the Making of a Divided Argentina, 1920–1946* (Durham: Duke University Press, 2012), 6, 10. For the "culture of mixture" in Argentine popular culture, see Beatriz Sarlo, *Una Modernidad Periférica: Buenos Aires 1920 y 1930* (Buenos Aires: Ediciones Nueva Visión, 1988), 28.
59. For the decline of the Heroic Age of aviation in the North Atlantic nations, see Wohl, *Spectacle of Flight*, chapter 6; and Corn, *Winged Gospel*, epilogue.
60. As the Argentine historian Beatriz Sarlo found in her studies of interwar popular culture, technical know-how was "poor people's knowledge." Such knowledge was frequently the purview of the many European immigrants who worked in the nation's factories and workshops. The aura of science, technology, and progress conferred respectability onto those who possessed technical skills but lacked formal education. Beatriz Sarlo, *La imaginación técnica: Sueños modernos de la cultura argentina* (Buenos Aires: Ediciones Nueva Visión, 1992), 3–6.
61. *Mundo Argentino* magazine was especially emblematic of this culture, with its write-in sections for readers frequently referencing aviation. For the pilot as a sex symbol, see the cover of *Mundo Argentino*, August 21, 1929. *Mundo Argentino* was not unique though, as other newspapers and magazines, like *El Hogar*, often featured photographs of dashing pilots and their fans. For examples, see the coverage of Antonio Parodi and Pedro Zanni in March and April 1920 or of Ramón Franco in February 1926 in *Caras y Caretas*, *La Prensa*, *Crítica*, *Mundo Argentino*, and *El Hogar*.
62. This supporting role for women began with the first heroes of Argentine aviation, such as Teodoro Fels, Jorge Newbery, and Benjamin Matienzo. Fels later recalled the feeling

of "vanity" due to the attention of women. Newbery and Matienzo—both killed in accidents—were honored by monuments and remembrances sponsored by women's organizations. Letter by Teodoro Fels, reprinted in "Héroes olvidados que fueron ídolos de las muchedumbres," *Caras y Caretas*, September 12, 1931, 129–33; María Esther Rega Molina, "Tribute," in *Jorge Newbery: Homenaje*, 7; Comisión de Señoritas Pro Monumento a Matienzo, *Memoria de la Comisión de Srtas. Pro Homenaje a Matienzo en el primer aniversario de su trágico vuelo: 1919–28 de mayo-1920* ([San Miguel de Tucumán]: Comisión de Señoritas Pro Monumento a Matienzo, 1920), 33–38, 55.

63. The historian Robert Wohl noted this gendered narrative in European and US aviation culture as well. Robert Wohl, *A Passion for Wings: Aviation and the Western Imagination, 1908–1918* (New Haven: Yale University Press, 1994), 280. For a characterization of the journey of a woman "aeronaut" in contrast to the "conquests" of her male colleagues, see "Una aeronauta argentina: La señorita Raquel Cabrera Bernet," *Boletín del Aero Club Argentino*, August 10, 1911, 18.
64. See, for example, "La mujer y la aviación," *El Hogar*, October 22, 1915, 44; "La emotividad femenina," *El Hogar*, April 18, 1919, 10; and "Charlas femininas: Mujeres modernas," *Mundo Argentino*, November 9, 1932, 52.
65. See the short stories of E. Ramirez Angel, "Un vuelo largo," *El Hogar*, February 11, 1916, 35; and Carlos E. D'Alkaine, "Longchamps . . . Longchamps," *Mundo Argentino*, June 21, 1933, 20–21, 23. Such gendered aviation culture was commonplace among the North Atlantic nations as well, perhaps best encapsulated by the culture of France's airline pioneers who created "*La Ligne*" from Toulouse to Buenos Aires in the late 1920s. See Wohl, *Spectacle of Flight*, chapter 4.
66. Liberation was a frequent theme of aviation culture around the world and with men as well. As Robert Wohl reveals about the depiction of flight in interwar Hollywood movies, "Flying was essentially a form of masculine escape from the bonds of earth, humdrum existence, and the constraining responsibilities of everyday life, especially the demands of nagging women." When men were liberated, they were fulfilling their masculine desires, whereas when women flew, it undermined their femininity. Wohl, *Spectacle of Flight*, 152.
67. There are numerous examples of this in the biweekly "Readers' Page," which *Mundo Argentino* maintained from at least 1919 to 1922.
68. See, for example, Amadeo Tovia, "Lia Wood," *Caras y Caretas*, October 1, 1921, 45–46; Valetín de Pedro, "La colegiala y el aviador," *La Prensa*, October 18, 1931; and Beatriz Eguia Muñoz, "El aeroplano," *El Hogar*, March 11, 1927, 4.
69. "El amor y los deportes," *Mundo Argentino*, July 29, 1931.
70. "Charlas femininas: La juventud," *Mundo Argentino*, July 4, 1934, 40.
71. *Myriam Stefford* (Buenos Aires: pub. anon., 1931), 7. Many of the details of Myriam Stefford's life for this section come from this posthumous "homage" book. The booklet was published anonymously, but inside are firsthand recollections of private conversations and letters, which suggests the author was Stefford's close associate.
72. *Myriam Stefford*, 10.
73. At the time, there were only fourteen provinces, with the rest of the country still being organized into territories.

74. Antonio Biedma Recalde, *Crónica histórica de la aeronáutica argentina*, vol. 1 (Buenos Aires: Círculo de Aeronáutica, Dirección de Publicaciones, 1968), 195–98. The men were killed when their modified SVA biplane crashed during a test flight, probably due to a mechanical failure.
75. The chingolo is a type of Andean sparrow, known as the rufous-collared sparrow. Although Argentine society considered her decidedly foreign, Stefford embraced the nascent Argentine identity, at least superficially.
76. "Corrientes-Santiago del Estero," *Jornada*, August 24, 1931, reprinted in *Myriam Stefford*, 25–26.
77. *Myriam Stefford*, 11.
78. "Recordando a Miryam Stefford. La influencia maléfica de un brillante," *Caras y Caretas*, August 27, 1932, 11.
79. The monument was completed in 1935 and still stands today. "Una historia de amor y tragedia," *La Voz*, January 30, 2018, https://www.lavoz.com.ar/ciudadanos/una-historia-de-amor-y-tragedia (page no longer extant).
80. "Myriam Stefford," *La Unión de Buenos Aires*, reprinted in *Myriam Stefford*, 73.
81. "Mujer antes que todo," *La Razón*, reprinted in *Myriam Stefford*, 84.
82. "Recordando a Miryam Stefford," 11.
83. Eraso, "Biotypology, Endocrinology, and Sterilization," 796; Gregory Hammond, *The Women's Suffrage Movement and Feminism in Argentina from Roca to Perón* (Albuquerque: University of New Mexico Press, 2011), 140.
84. See, for example, "Los Estados Unidos," *El Hogar*, December 21, 1928, 3.
85. "La mujer norte americana," *La Prensa*, December 20, 1931.
86. "Moral de Buenos Aires, moral Argentina," *El Hogar*, June 19, 1936, 3.
87. "La mujer argentina no abusó de su libertad," *El Hogar*, January 24, 1936, 3.
88. See, for example, Luis Pozzo Ardizzi, "El aeroplano y la mujer," *El Hogar*, November 1, 1929, 11; "Guía de la mujer práctica. Para viajar en avión," *El Hogar*, December 27, 1929, 68–69.
89. A fact noted in the Argentine media. See, for example, "Amelia Earhart, la aviadora que asombró al mundo," *Mundo Argentino*, August 11, 1937, 62; and "La mujer pájaro," *Ciencia Popular*, June 1937, 367.
90. *Myriam Stefford*, 10.
91. Speech by Sr. Mundin Schaffter, quoted in *Myriam Stefford*, 58.
92. In my account of Lorenzini's life, I utilize Bonvissuto's very sympathetic biography. In the tradition of Argentine histories at the time, Bonvissuto reproduced many of his primary sources—letters, newspaper articles, speeches—in full in the text. Vicente Bonvissuto, *¡Adiós Carola!* (Buenos Aires: El Cazador Libros, 1978), 13–16.
93. "Una aviadora argentina bate el récord sudamericano femenino de altura," *Caras y Caretas*, April 13, 1935, 48.
94. Article from *La Capital* of Santa Rosa on January 28, 1940, reprinted in Bonvissuto, *¡Adiós Carola!*, 124.
95. "Carola Lorenzini dió fin a una hazaña de singular significación," *Crítica*, April 21, 1940.
96. Bonvissuto, *¡Adiós Carola!*, 54, 76, 129; see also coverage of Lorenzini's death in *Crítica* on November 24, 1941.

97. Reprint of *Mundo Argentino* article from November 30, 1938, in Bonvissuto, *¡Adiós Carola!*, 77; "A costa de muchos sacrificios Carola llegó a ser aviadora," *Crítica*, April 21, 1940.
98. Bonvissuto, *¡Adiós Carola!*, 220–21.
99. "Homenaje silencioso y conmovido," *Crítica*, November 24, 1941.
100. Untitled, *Crítica*, November 24, 1941.
101. "La gloria nos ha robado una hija," *Crítica*, November 24, 1941.
102. "Estaba en el corazón del pueblo," *Crítica*, November 24, 1941.

4

CIVIL AIR TRANSPORT AND THE COLONIAL CONTEXT IN THE INTERWAR PERIOD

Marc Dierikx

On February 27, 1936, the Dutch professor of cartography and future prime minister Willem Schermerhorn flew aboard KLM's scheduled flight from Amsterdam to the Dutch East Indies. His journey had started in the early hours of the 22nd and was already a day behind schedule because of adverse weather. Now they were flying over the Indus River Delta, on their way to land at Karachi airport. Things were *not* going well, as Schermerhorn noted in his diary:

> I will not easily forget these last few hours in my life. . . . I need to write down this first impression. At the edge of the rainstorm we continued to circle for about an hour and every time we got close the entire machine was blown up and down, so that the suitcases hit the floor. There was no question of making it [to the airport]. We made one plunge from a height of two hundred and fifty meters to fifty meters above the sea, as could be read on the barograph later on. . . . We were only ten kilometers from the airport but there it was dogs' weather. . . . We diverted to Navanagar, but the field was not to be found. What was on our map was not clearly marked and in small print. Moreover, the field was broken up in the middle and cattle were walking on it. For half an hour the pilot . . . tried to land [to no avail]. . . . After what seemed another hour or so, a well-marked airstrip [Bhuj] came in sight and the whole airplane cabin was as happy as a child, because we had only twenty minutes of fuel left!

> After flying for six and a half hours we were safely on the ground. I will not soon forget this moment of joy and relief![1]

SOCIETAL IMPORTANCE

Flying the colonial air routes required a certain panache, not just of the flight crews, but also of the passengers who risked the unknown. Schermerhorn's diary of his ten-day journey to the Dutch East Indies bears evidence of this. Boarding an airplane was about trusting one's life to modern technology and the skills of the crew in a hazardous environment. As travelers, airline passengers formed a category unto themselves.

Scheduled long-distance air services across continents were still recent phenomena in 1936. They dated from the beginning of the decade. Ten years before that, commercial air transport had started out in Europe as an experiment to discover whether there would be a market for rapid travel by airplane. Enthusiasm ran high. When the first international airline flights took off in the spring of 1919, they were commonly announced as signs of a new age in which air travel would "shorten" distances across the globe. The new mode of transport held a magic aura that captivated popular imagination. In the first years of peace, newspaper publications the world over heralded the coming of the air age. In 1919, Dutch papers alone contained more than a thousand articles about the possibilities of air traffic. They had roaring headlines like "The Flying Future," "World Air Traffic," "Our Country and Air Traffic," and "Over the Atlantic."[2]

Air links were seen as instruments contributing to a new form of worldwide connectedness, since all peoples and countries share the same air medium. To some, the belief in the good of aviation was almost like a religion.[3] Nonetheless, air transport took time to catch on. Aviation technology was not yet ready to foster scheduled flying and maintain the timetables needed to make the new mode of travel attractive. Airplanes, often with a single engine, were still accident-prone machines. Some early airlines only hired pilots who had previously proven themselves capable of surviving an emergency landing. The custom of handing out life vests to passengers before flights over water entailed more than a discrete warning. The situation only began to change with the spread of multiengine aircraft in the mid-1920s.

Given these circumstances, passengers were few. Attracting clientele was no easy matter. Flights were sparse, and only the "busiest" routes boasted daily departures. There was also the question of price; airline tickets were expensive. In Europe, a flight from Amsterdam to London cost the equivalent of a worker's monthly wages. Early airlines advertised to a select class of businessmen, politicians, and government officials on missions that involved some urgency. Of these passengers, only a small minority were women, more often than not spouses accompanying their husbands. Therefore, load factors were low. On average, airplanes carried no more than two passengers on each flight.[4] Nonetheless, early air travelers were decades ahead of general society in developing a new sense of distance (or the relativity of it).[5] For the first time in history, it became possible to have breakfast in Paris and lunch in London.

Because airplane load factors were low, financial losses were endemic and considerable. In the first twenty years of commercial aviation, not a penny was earned in profits. Airlines could only survive if they received government subsidies. Income largely depended on the carriage of freight, in particular mail. In the early days, air transport meant mail transport. Indeed, in the United States all scheduled flying involved airmail operations until the mid-1920s.[6]

There were other factors that influenced the development of air travel. At the beginning and at the end of air journeys, airports were poorly connected to surface infrastructure, generally difficult to get to, and lacked the comforts now associated with air travel. In many cases, the aircraft hangar was the only permanent building on the landing ground; it combined its technical functions with a corner set apart for passenger handling. The air base itself was little more than a large grass area with a wide thirty-odd-yard circle chalked in the middle, a simple arrow indicating the most common landing direction, and a windsock. In the absence of weather forecasting and radio communications, air transport developed on the basis of services over relatively short distances. The natural characteristics of the landscape and climate—seas, mountains, valleys, plains, and dominant weather patterns rather than borders or the presence of traditional physical infrastructures such as (rail)roads and waterways—were decisive for the development of the air routes.[7]

In defiance of these realities, countries that had colonies in Africa and Asia—including France, Britain, the Netherlands, and Belgium—devised plans to use air transportation to reduce travel time between the motherland and overseas territories. An air service, it was thought, would strengthen existing bonds. Even for early planners, the dream was to use colonial services as an initial phase toward the construction of a worldwide air network, although it was not before the mid-1920s that technology began to catch

Figure 4.1. Imperial Airways poster advertisement. National Air and Space Museum, ca. 1930. Courtesy of the Smithsonian Institution.

up with aspirations and the first real steps were taken. Proposals were put forward to develop national airmail services. It was well understood that improved mail connections were valuable in business affairs and for personal correspondence. They could also be an important factor in enhancing colonial rule itself.

In the initial postwar years, technology proved a serious impediment to realizing such visions. Although record flights appeared to demonstrate the opposite, aviation just was not ready. In June 1919, British airmen John Alcock and Arthur Whitten Brown flew a modified bomber across the Atlantic. They crash-landed in a bog on the west coast of Ireland. When local people who came out to help them asked where they had come from, their reply, "We are Alcock and Brown. Yesterday we were in America," brought on roaring laughter. Nonetheless, both were knighted for their achievement and received a prize from the secretary of state for war and air, Winston Churchill.[8] Other record-breaking flights brought similar stories. From November 12 to December 10, 1919, the Australian brothers Ross and Keith Smith amazingly managed to fly from Britain all the way to Australia, securing serious prize money and knighthoods. Although such flights served as technological trailblazers for other endeavors, their societal impact was not significant. Plans to develop regular air services to the colonial outposts were potentially more important.

In the early 1920s, France and Spain established a chain of airstrips at military forts they held in North Africa. These subsequently doubled as staging posts for makeshift civilian air services. Regular flights from Toulouse along the Spanish coast to Casablanca in Morocco, operated under the direction of Pierre-Georges Latécoère, started in September 1919.[9] French national ambitions dictated the expansion of such services, with the consent of the government in Paris. More money poured in when various efforts were reshuffled and combined in 1921 to form the Compagnie Générale d'Enterprises Aéronautique. In 1923, the government formally stepped in to oversee developments. The pressure to achieve success was high; this also applied to the pilots, whose pay depended on the completion of each flight.[10] In May 1923, the first Latécoère proving flight reached Dakar in French-held Senegal on Africa's west coast. Two years later, a regular airmail service was set up along the 1,900-mile-long route from Toulouse. The route was supported by the French government, which sought to use the service to strengthen the bonds between France and its protectorate Morocco.[11] From April 1927, the French mail service was extended across the Atlantic to Natal in Brazil. It operated under the name Aéropostale, following a merger with a French-Brazilian aviation enterprise.[12] Passengers were not carried on the Dakar route (operated by Air France from 1933) until 1936. Despite various grand schemes, the African air transport situation did not change much until the mid-1930s, when a new French company, Aéromaritime, appeared on the scene to operate flights from Dakar to Pointe-Noire in French Equatorial

Africa (Congo-Brazzaville). Aéromaritime also offered a service to Niamey (Niger), where it connected with a third French company, Régie Air Afrique, that offered service all the way to Tananarive on the island of Madagascar, off the East African coast.[13] France specifically pursued speeding up air communications with the aim of bringing overseas governors under the control of Paris and to "help displaced French adventurer-diplomats."[14]

Plans to operate a service to the French colonies in Asia took longer to reach fruition. The French used their League of Nations mandate territories Lebanon and Syria as staging posts. Civilian flying in Indochina began in 1926 under the guise of Air Asie. A second company, Air Union-Lignes d'Orient, was set up in France in 1927 to start survey flights with seaplanes between Marseilles and Beirut the following year. Then in 1929, Air Asie and Air Union-Lignes d'Orient merged to form Air Orient, which began regular flights to Beirut on June 6, 1929. In January 1930, Air Orient expanded its operations from Marseilles through Damascus to Baghdad. It also initiated a twice-monthly service from Saigon to Bangkok in October. For the overland route segments, the company used Dutch-built Fokker aircraft. The two services were connected in April 1931. Ten and a half days and several plane changes were needed to cover the 7,500-mile distance from Marseilles, including a stretch by car from Beirut to Damascus.[15] In May 1932, operations were reorganized as a weekly service from Damascus to Saigon. The first roundtrip Paris-Saigon-Paris flight took off on December 21, 1933, but the plane crashed in a snowstorm in France during the return journey.

Plans for imperial aviation were also fermenting in London. By 1920, a string of provisional airfields had been established along a projected East African route from Cairo, Egypt, to Cape Town, South Africa. Two South African military pilots, Pierre van Ryneveld and Christopher Quintin-Brand, took off from London in February 1920 and headed for Cape Town. They were knighted upon completion of their flight on March 20. In the years that followed, Britain focused on aviation in Europe. But at the end of November 1924, Director of Civil Aviation William Sefton Brancker set off with pilot Alan Cobham for a proving flight to India in preparation for a possible air service. In Brancker's vision, Britain had to develop air communications "or cease to be an empire." Convinced that aviation advertised England and enhanced British prestige throughout the world, Cobham also made a survey flight to South Africa late in 1925 and another one to Australia in 1926. Tens of thousands of people crowded the embankment of the Thames and cheered upon his return to London on October 1, 1926. He was welcomed back as a national hero.[16] The next year, Cobham set off again for Africa—this time in a flying boat with his wife, Gladys; a cameraman; and a crew of three. His mission was to reconnoiter a possible water-based route for air services and shore up the necessary support from colonial authorities.[17] In the British perception, water-based flying offered cost savings versus airport construction.

After the proving flights to South Africa and Australia, a British scheduled air service to India received priority. The importance of India as the jewel in the British crown was, after all, that much bigger. In April 1924, a single flag carrier, Imperial Airways, was formed through the merger of the four private airlines then operating in Britain. As its name suggested, Imperial Airways aimed to offer air services between England and the British Empire, India in particular. Initially, money, distance, and airplane technology stood in the way. It was not before the Imperial Conference of 1926 that something of a coherent strategy on air services was put forward. A plan was presented to establish a network of "All Red Air Routes" that would knit the empire closer together.[18] A liberal subsidy contract was drawn up with the government that enabled Imperial Airways to prepare a service to Cairo and Karachi in British India (today, Pakistan).[19] As a first step, Imperial Airways took over the Royal Air Force service across British-mandated territories in the Middle East in 1927. Two years were needed before the service was extended to Karachi. Thereafter, Imperial Airways concentrated on the route to India, neglecting its European services to the effect that it had, by 1933, withdrawn from all but the London to Paris and London to Cologne routes.[20]

Scheduled operations across Africa took longer to initiate. Not before February 1931 was a regular air mail and passenger service started from Cairo to Mwanza on the Southern shore of Lake Victoria in Tanganyika (Tanzania), going on to Cape Town in 1932.[21] *The Times* proudly called the first scheduled flight from London "an Imperial event of outstanding importance."[22] But on a continent where intercolonial trade was scant and only the upper classes had money for travel, there was limited demand for scheduled air services. As far as demand existed, it was primarily geared toward mail and freight.[23] Air services catered to the elite. One commentator summarized the Imperial Airways passenger list as "a microcosm of colonial and overseas society."[24]

Taking pride in the state's possession of vast colonies in East Asia, Dutch plans for an air service were quick off the mark. Early in 1923, an initiative was launched to investigate whether a trial flight to Batavia (contemporary Jakarta), the capital of the Dutch East Indies, would be possible. The idea originated with a young pilot Bram Thomassen à Thuessinck van der Hoop. The plan was underwritten by private funding, with the Dutch aircraft tycoon Anthony Fokker supplying the airplane. The machine departed from Amsterdam on October 1, 1924. On the third day of the flight, things went wrong: Engine failure necessitated an emergency landing in Bulgaria. A new engine had to be brought up from the Netherlands by train. The aircraft and its cargo of 281 letters reached Batavia fifty-four days after departure on November 24, the day Cobham and Brancker took off from London destined for British India. Meanwhile, in Batavia, the Dutch crew was welcomed by an outrageous crowd of enthused colonials (fig. 4.2).[25] But although the importance of a national airmail service to the Dutch East Indies was evident, preparations for such a service moved forward by chance rather than by plan. In 1927, two privately funded flights proved that an air connection might now be technically feasible. After this, developments caught momentum. Recognizing that an air service would be beneficial for colonial rule, both the government in The Hague and the colonial authorities in Batavia sponsored its development. An advertisement appearing early in 1928, a time in which mail flights were still only contemplated, already lauded

Figure 4.2. Colonials welcoming the arrival of the first Dutch plane in the East Indies. November 23, 1924. Courtesy of Leiden University Library, the Netherlands, KITLV Collection, CC BY License.

the speed of a possible Dutch service that would combine transportation by train to Marseilles, then by ship to Medan on the island of Sumatra, and thereafter by air to its final destinations in the Dutch East Indies.[26] After a series of test flights in 1928 and 1929, scheduled flying of a trial mail service began in September 1929.

Plans were also developed in Belgium. On February 12, 1925, pilot Edmond Thieffry took off from Brussels headed for the Belgian Congolese capital Léopoldville (Kinshasa). Like the Dutch flight a few months earlier, the journey took more time than planned: fifty-one days, longer than the sea voyage the airplane flight was supposed to eradicate.[27] In March 1926, three army officers—George Medaets, Jean Verhaegen, and Willy Coppens—did much better, completing their journey flying south along the river Nile in just twelve days.

The Belgian case was radically different from those in neighboring countries as Congo already had an air service. Plans had been nascent since 1911. In April 1920, the Ligne Aérienne Roi Albert took off as the first more or less scheduled air service operating in Africa. As it reduced travel time between Léopoldville and Stanleyville (Kisangani) from eighteen days by river boat to a mere fifteen hours of flying—a huge improvement in communications for the colonial administrators—it was heavily subsidized.[28] In subsequent years, promoting air transport in the Congo took center stage over the development of air services from Brussels, where the national airline Sabena primarily served as a learning organization. If, in 1929, the air network in the Congo encompassed nearly 2,500 miles, Sabena's network in Europe was no more than one-eighth of its length, although passenger numbers from Brussels were substantially higher.[29]

Once air mail started arriving on a regular basis, initiating passenger air transport to the colonies became the next step. Government and business communities were again the first to benefit. Transporting officials further strengthened ties between the home government and its overseas representatives and reinforced business bonds through executive travel. It also underscored the sense of national prestige and pride of the colonial achievement felt at the time and aided an administration generally by tightening the grip of the home country. In Holland, it was thought that airplanes might even be used for the rapid deployment of colonial police or troops in areas of unrest.[30] Air services, many believed, would ultimately alter the "social structure of empire" and ease colonial settlement, then an important prospect.[31] By the middle of the 1930s, it had become possible to take an airplane flight from Europe to faraway destinations in Asia and Africa. In the minds of visionaries, the colonial world was drawing nearer. Before 1940, some ninety thousand people used air transport to fly between Europe and the colonies in Asia and Africa.[32]

In a wider sense, the air services to the colonies played a role in altering the perception of geography. Increased exchanges of news and press messages brought the colonial territories mentally closer. Cities in India and Southeast Asia—such as Karachi, Rangoon, Singapore—that were not previously part of the average European's topographical knowledge now became well-identified places on the map, only a few flying days away. Maps showing colonial air routes were distributed widely through newspapers and billboard advertisements and in schools, creating a more immediate sense of topography. The geography of the air routes became a topic in education. British travelers marveled at the vastness of the empire as it stretched out below them.[33] Cultural exchanges benefited too, enabling performing artists to do shows at home and overseas.[34]

For a colony, the airplane might reduce the relative isolation of outposts of empires by permitting visits and meetings to take place on relatively short notice between individuals otherwise geographically far apart.[35] In the Dutch East Indies, it became possible to wake up on Sumatra in the morning and be present for a lunch meeting in Bandung, Java. This opened up new business opportunities and intensified cooperation between regional colonial administrators. A journey from the oilfields near Balikpapan on Borneo (Kalimantan) to Batavia was reduced from a seven-day trip by ship to a seven-hour flight.[36] On the other side of the spectrum, speedy communications also opened up completely new perspectives for colonial settlers. The 1939 monthly airline magazine *KNILM Nieuws*, published in Batavia, held out the novel option that affluent air travelers from the Dutch East Indies could book a flight to Europe for a winter sports vacation in the Swiss Alps.[37]

Nonetheless, contrasting views also existed and held that the annihilation of distance between the center and periphery of an empire "will only help the work of exploitation . . . of resources . . . and economic impoverishment."[38]

OBSTACLES TO OVERCOME

The right to operate services on the air routes to the colonies was by no means undebated. At the core of many diplomatic skirmishes lay prestige. The issue resided in the legal structures that underlay international civil aviation as such. In the context of the Versailles Treaty, twenty-six countries, including Britain and France as the major colonial powers, decided that absolute national sovereignty should rule the air medium. The principle was laid down in the Paris Convention of 1919, relating to the regulation of aerial navigation. Hence, flights crossing borders needed prior permission from each state that was to be overflown; this included colonial possessions.

The two largest colonial nations subsequently proved very reluctant to allow foreign services to cross their territories in Africa and Asia. Nonetheless, the vast British Empire made London the central actor in establishing nascent world air services. Against this background, London regarded intercontinental air services not as a topic in international transportation but as a legal and political issue. As Britain's overall policies were geared toward establishing the "All Red Air Route," allowing foreign air services to cross imperial territory was hardly a foregone conclusion.

Imperial Airways initiated the first segment of its planned route with scheduled flights between Cairo, Egypt, and Basra, Iraq, in 1927. Both London and the British government in India regarded it as unthinkable that foreign air services would be allowed to operate over imperial territory before Britain would have its own.[39] Initial thinking was that services catering to foreign interests could only be permitted in a framework of international cooperation, with the sections that traversed British territory reserved for British operators. This would leave Britain's sovereign rights in the air untouched.[40] French policy was drawn up along similar lines, although a formal directive to foster a *Ligne Blue* did not exist. Nonetheless, Paris, which paid between 60 and 85 percent of the total cost of French air transport, was as reluctant as London to allow foreign services across its overseas territories.[41]

Other governments followed these restrictive practices. The idea that colonial rule necessitated a *national* air service to the overseas possessions was held in common by all colonial powers. Operating such an air service was considered so important to national prestige that *not* having one was almost unthinkable. National chauvinism dictated perceptions. Colonial air services were not only considered flag carriers, but they were measured against those of other colonial powers in terms of speed and standards of service. These elements added weight to controversies over operating rights. Foreign air services infringed on an imperial prestige that was there to be protected.

In Europe, Italy only allowed airplanes flying to the colonies to make technical refueling stops on its territory. Greece, crucially situated on the route across the Mediterranean, demanded firm commitments from Britain, France, and the Netherlands to include Athens as a scheduled stop on all colonial flights so that Greece would feature prominently in the world air network. Further afield, problems were of a more fundamental nature, and international politics played a bigger role. Turkey, for example, had been a German ally in the war and was therefore not a signatory to the Paris Convention. Angora (Ankara) limited foreign use of its airspace to a single carrier, Germany's Junkers Luftverkehr, which it had allowed to fly in 1925.[42] The policy for Syria, under French mandate at the time, was made in Paris, which meant that "foreign" air services were allowed only if they provided for a prominent French role.[43] Egypt, where Britain had a considerable power base, approached the air services issue from a more practical point of view and demanded rebates for Egyptian officials in exchange for cooperation and permission to land.[44]

Bigger problems existed in Persia (Iran). From the beginning of the 1920s, the country tacitly steered away from Britain as the dominant foreign power and developed sympathies for Germany. In aviation terms, this led to a deal with Junkers Luftverkehr in 1925 to operate a service to Tehran through Germany's new de facto ally, the Soviet Union. When Imperial Airways wished to establish a route from Cairo to Karachi in 1929, the Persians demanded British planes make a stop in Tehran, not just in Bushire or Jask on the Persian Gulf as Imperial Airways had planned. This involved an unwelcome detour for Imperial, and London refused—at the cost of not receiving the desired rights and having to reroute operations through the emirate of Sharjah on the other side of the Persian Gulf. The Dutch proved more pliable to Persian demands for a quid pro quo, even if it meant transporting some of the Persian mail for free.[45]

Settling the Persian issue brought The Hague face-to-face with London. A British permit would be needed before a Dutch air service could cross the vast expanse of British India. London, however, was in no hurry to agree to this. For starters, it was felt that Imperial Airways had to be well established in India before any foreign air activity could even be contemplated. The extension of the Imperial Airways service from Karachi to Rangoon was only planned for 1933. Allowing KLM to operate along the route years ahead of Imperial Airways would mean that important centers of the British Empire like Calcutta, Rangoon, and Singapore would be linked exclusively by a foreign airline. Here colonial prestige and aviation diplomacy intersected.

After a year of negotiations, Britain and the Netherlands drew up an agreement in June 1930 that would allow KLM to operate across British India in exchange for Dutch consent to grant reciprocal facilities, when applied for later, for a British service across the Netherlands' territory to Australia.[46] It would prove a recipe for prolonged discussion and conflict.

Developments on the African continent were not radically different. Here, too, the larger colonial powers blocked foreign initiatives. For the Belgians, the organization of a scheduled service to follow the trial flights to Congo presented unexpected problems. Negotiating agreements on passage and traffic rights with Britain and France was one of the key factors that held up the opening of a Belgian scheduled service. Initial diplomatic talks for a route following the river Nile from Cairo over British territory were launched. But in 1928, Brussels suddenly settled on negotiations with France, hoping they could build on the pioneering work of the French carrier Latécoère that was already flying through Dakar. The Belgians hoped to open their service by 1930, but talks did not progress. Strangely, the French were not the only ones slow to move. In Brussels, the Belgian Foreign Ministry dragged its feet to keep a possible alternative deal with the British afloat while airline planners pleaded in Paris. Thinking about organizing a future air service across Africa to Madagascar, the French-held island off the East African coast, Paris was in no hurry to allow a foreign airline to fly before French services were firmly established. A tentative agreement was reached in January 1929 but remained a dead letter. Paris revoked its consent and decided that the "integrity of the French colonial airspace" was more important than the maintenance of good aeronautical relations with its smaller neighbor in Europe.[47]

Nonetheless, an agreement was signed in May 1930, under which the Belgians received rights for a route to the Congo, with the condition that it be operated jointly with the French. Nothing came of it. In Belgium, the economic crisis of the 1930s meant that government money for nonremunerative airline adventures—however prestigious—was scarce. In France, lingering doubts about the joint Franco-Belgian service were heightened in March 1931 by the sudden collapse of Aéropostale as the result of a political scandal over subsidies. This spelled drama for the Belgians: There could be no question of allowing a Belgian service to operate before French aeronautical interests in Africa had been restructured. Brussels felt humiliated. The eight Fokker aircraft purchased in 1930 to operate the route remained in their hangar at Brussels's airport, collecting dust. It was February 23, 1935, before Belgium could finally initiate its air service to the Congo.[48]

For London, the ultimate goal of the colonial air route to Asia was to see Imperial Airways operating all the way to its naval stronghold Singapore, and from there to Australia. This led to protracted discord with the Dutch controlling sovereignty over the Dutch East Indies. For the linkup to Australia, London needed consent from The Hague. In 1930, the Dutch had readily signed a bilateral agreement to this effect without giving the matter too much thought. After all, their short-term objective had been to ascertain operating rights for a KLM service to Batavia. But in 1932, Britain and Australia began colluding to expand the empire's air route from Singapore to Sydney as a joint Anglo-Australian service under the aegis of the 1930 Anglo-Dutch agreement. It was even explicitly stated "that consideration will not be given to any suggestion for inclusion of foreign interests until the possibility of a co-operative British-Australian service shall be fully exhausted."[49] The service began operating in January 1934 as a British-Australian joint venture, Qantas Empire Airways, of which Imperial held 51 percent of the shares.[50]

This effectively meant that the Dutch were sidelined, since the air service was legally British and thus covered by the bilateral agreement of 1930. Although Dutch pleas for an air service of their own to Australia went unheeded, an opportunity to put a foot in the door emerged later in 1934. With government consent, KLM entered its brand-new Douglas DC-2 airplane in the Melbourne Air Race, a flying contest around half the world, starting in England. What if a Dutch plane beat the competition, thus demonstrating the possibilities of rapid airmail delivery to Australia? Surely the British and the Australians would then grant the Dutch traffic rights. The strategy proved counterproductive. Although the KLM plane finished second in Melbourne, its very success strengthened Anglo-Australian resistance to allowing the Dutch to enter the market for air transport to Australia. In the years that followed, demands to initiate a service from Batavia were blocked time and again with references to sovereignty and the bilateral air agreement. It was only after eight years of exasperating negotiations that The Hague managed to get permission for its desired Dutch air service to Sydney. What brought the long-coveted "trophy" within reach in 1938 was the unexpected decision in London to reequip the landplane-operated Singapore-to-Sydney service with British-built Short flying boats. This technological changeover necessitated the construction in the Dutch East Indies of a whole new infrastructure for the refueling and servicing of flying boats. The Dutch successfully made a major issue out of this to finally secure rights for their long-demanded Sydney route.[51]

Facing the prospect of a Dutch ban on British and Australian flying boat operations over the Netherlands' Indies territory, the Australian government grudgingly accepted that the Netherlands' Indies airline KNILM would start operating flights to Sydney in July 1938. This was, however, not to the liking of KLM, which claimed its own place on the prestigious Australia route. In Batavia, KNILM resisted this for fear that KLM would thus gain a foothold in air transport within the Dutch East Indies, KNILM's exclusive domain. As a compromise, The Hague proposed that KLM would participate in a KNILM-operated service to Sydney under a charter contract. Under pressure from the cabinet in The Hague, the two "sister companies" agreed that KNILM would *temporarily* operate the Australia link under a joint brand name: *Intercontinental Airways. Combined Netherlands Indies and Dutch lines KNILM-KLM.*[52]

The first KNILM machine left for Sydney on July 3, 1938, but there was no cause for celebration. It soon became apparent that the service would not attract enough passengers to break even. Worse yet, to protect Qantas Empire Airways, the Australian government in Canberra continued to hinder the Dutch wherever possible. The new Australian foreign minister, Henry Gullett, told the Dutch flatly that he did not consider himself bound by an aviation agreement that had been signed by his predecessor. Gullett absolutely refused to allow KLM to operate in Australia. Constantly opposed by the Australians, KNILM was forced to operate the heavily loss-making route to Sydney on its own. To alleviate the financial strain, the colonial government promised the company a separate subsidy arrangement.[53]

Despite this government support, KNILM was forced to reduce the frequency of its Australia service by half to once a week in August 1939. With international tensions in the Pacific region rising, its aircraft were needed elsewhere. The expansion of the war in Europe in May 1940 did not resolve the controversy. Due to the ongoing conflict, Imperial Airways withdrew from the Singapore-Sydney connection in June 1940. Still, Britain and Australia maintained that there was no room for a Dutch service if this involved KLM. Even the unexpected death of Henry Gullett, who perished with two other cabinet members in a plane crash near Canberra in August of that year, did not change the situation. Allies or not, Australia—and by extension, Britain—persisted in an obstructive aviation policy toward their colonial neighbor.

NATIONALITY AND SERVICE ON BOARD

Although early airlines liked to claim the comfort they offered on board was comparable to that of first-class rail or sea travel, actual conditions for air passengers were spartan. While some poster ads, particularly for the shorter European routes, showed comfortable cabins with leather upholstered seats, most aircraft were equipped with lightweight wicker chairs or metal-frame seats covered with cloth.[54] The railway-style amenities of serving onboard luncheons by uniformed cabin attendants existed only on French Air Union aircraft operating the Paris-to-London route in 1927.[55] Most other services offered nothing to eat or drink. Engine noise was so deafening that passengers had to be supplied with earplugs. Conversation was impossible while the engines were running—and for a time afterward, as normal hearing only returned gradually after landing. Amenities did include a tin or a paper bag at every seat for depositing the effects of air sickness caused by the combination of low flying, turbulence, and poor ventilation. It was no surprise, then, that early passengers could opt to receive a special certificate, signed by the pilot, that they had actually flown—and now lived to tell the tale. Only the most modern airplanes boasted onboard toilet facilities, although droppings usually disappeared in free fall. Passengers reported unpleasant drafts below. Instructions on the door warned that the facilities were *not to be used above towns*.[56]

Being sufficiently prosperous to afford an expensive ticket was merely one prerequisite to becoming a passenger on an intercontinental flight to Asia. In 1929, Imperial Airways, which started empire passenger services in May of that year, charged £130 (the equivalent of $631 in 1929), including meals and lodging for a one-way trip from Paris to Karachi. This was more than half a year's wages for middle-class people.[57] What did passengers get for all that money? The diary of a Dutch Imperial Airways passenger from August 1929 is, perhaps, telling:

> It is not a journey for women and children. Because it is tiring to spend eight days on board an airplane, flying eight to thirteen hours. The never-ending deafening roar of the three enormous engines is exhausting. The ever-changing landscape takes all your attention every hour of the flight, which is mentally exhausting. The constant movement of the plane is devastating for people who are prone to air sickness and I have seen passengers travelling only short distances in the most agonizing circumstances and heard them swear, with deadly pale distorted faces, that this was a once and only for them.[58]

Prospective travelers had to prepare well in advance and procure the necessary travel documents. Apart from a passport, passengers needed a special visa for Greece, where airplanes made an intermediate stop in Athens. But Greece also required official documental "proof of good moral behavior" from each traveler. A visit to the Greek embassy was only a first step. Across the Mediterranean, Imperial Airways landed in Tobruk, Libya, then an Italian colony. This required an Italian visa. In case the traveler was not British, a visit to the British embassy was also necessary to obtain a visa for Egypt, Palestine, Iraq, and the territories belonging to the British Empire in Asia. For intermediate stops in the Persian cities of Bushire and Jask, passengers needed a Persian visa. However, this could only be obtained after receiving official approval by the Persian envoy in Berlin; the visa would then be issued at the Persian legation in Paris. On top of this, health certificates were necessary for each country along the route where stops were planned.[59]

The earliest air travelers on the empire routes also needed time. Traveling "the modern way" on Imperial Airways (fig. 4.1) took eight days to cover the distance between London and Karachi. From there, onward traveling passengers could either take a ship directly to Singapore or go by train to Calcutta and board a steamer there, which meant another eight days' travel. Thus, the complete journey to Singapore took at least sixteen days—and more if there was no awaiting connection by ship. Since the first part of the journey was by air, one's luggage was limited. Air travel dictated quantity and weight: the airline provided one large and one small suitcase, which, in combination with the passenger, was not to exceed 100 kilos (220 pounds) in total weight. Passengers went on the scales together with their luggage. Anything over the limit led to additional charges.[60]

French services performed slightly better with regard to speed. In 1930, Air Orient claimed it needed only one week to cover the distance from Paris to Hanoi in French Indochina. The Dutch kept a similar pace on their service, although individual flights could take several days longer than scheduled if weather conditions en route were unfavorable or in case of mechanical trouble. Flights lasted ten days on average. Because of these uncertainties, newspapers included daily updates on the progress of each individual airplane along the route.

Passengers traveling to Africa experienced similar conditions. Imperial's service was not fast, even by the standards of its time. When scheduled services started in January 1932, traversing the African continent took eleven days on five separate aircraft, plus two train segments and overnight stays in hot and uncomfortable places.[61] Imperial Airways attracted passengers by appealing to its uniquely British character, promising a home-away-from-home environment on board and immaculately dressed staff in attendance everywhere. Aircraft crews hoisted the national flag from the cockpit on every landing, as was customary in aviation everywhere. Advertisements built on the contrast between Britishness and foreignness. To illustrate this, Imperial Airways' advertisements liked to depict the company's aircraft overflying the Egyptian pyramids at Giza, ships on the Nile on the way from Cairo to Baghdad and Karachi, or unnamed but clearly Indian cities.[62]

Early French passengers were also lured by advertising that used colorful posters portraying the geography traversed. Latécoère billboards showed airplanes overflying a map of Spain and Morocco. The route's ultimate destination was symbolized by a welcoming North African tribesman.[63] When airmail service to Dakar started in 1925, France took a lead in long-distance air transportation. It was not before the end of the 1920s that such transport emerged in other countries, like the German air services to Turkey, Persia, and even China.

In Holland, KLM combined speed and destination in its advertising and used the image of the airplane to stress the swiftness of the services offered. It was an approach that stemmed from earlier campaigns: "See twice as much of Europe in half the time."[64] The juxtaposition of a modern airliner flying over a small globe quickly became a common theme in airline promotion. Other features also found their way into advertising. Imperial Airways stressed "that your journey will be as luxurious, as swift and as interesting as modern science can make it."[65] The French also built on the image of luxury. In 1934, a famous Air Afrique ad depicted a white-clad colonial relaxing in an airplane seat while enjoying the view of an African village below (fig. 4.3). Other ads stressed the contrast between the world of air travel and African life, such as an Algerian village with inhabitants in traditional attire looking up at an airplane passing overhead. More inventive draftsmen came up with alternate approaches, like the subtle difference between Caucasian and colonial people in a 1932 Air Orient poster and touristic aspects of the various cities where night stops were made.[66] In some of its ads, the Dutch KNILM referred to the modernity of flight as compared to ship travel, depicting a sleek, streamlined airplane passing overhead of the traditional ocean liner as the logical next step in transport.[67]

Notwithstanding these national approaches—advertisements were not geared to attract foreign customers—the communality in the imagery stood out. Initially, the airplane itself commanded attention, but from the beginning of the 1930s, new elements were added: a typical landscape or a landmark building on the ground (fig. 4.1 and 4.3). Artists developed ways to portray the links between the airplane and the colonies it serviced. As if

Figure 4.3. Air Afrique poster, 1934. Musée Air France.

to underline the difference between the highly developed European world of the colonial administrators and Indigenous populations, locals were generally represented looking up in awe at the airplane overhead—always approaching, never just passing, as it heralded the progress that a benign colonialism intended to bring (fig. 4.4).

Initially, air transport in the colonies themselves was almost nonexistent. In the early 1920s, only Belgium operated a service in the Congo. France and Britain focused on establishing services connecting Europe to overseas holdings. The foundations of Dutch colonial air transport were laid in earnest in April 1927, when a committee of preparation was established in Amsterdam by leading colonial entrepreneurs.[68] The first scheduled flights in the Dutch East Indies took place in November 1928, even before a regular airmail service from the mother country had been established. With memories of recent political unrest on Java in November 1926 still fresh in the minds of authorities in Batavia, dedicated air transport capacity and control of the widespread Indonesian archipelago were considered of utmost importance to the administration. This translated into a promise of generous government subsidies. As a consequence, a dedicated East Indies airline was founded in July 1928, KNILM. Customers were mainly European colonials. Early advertisements specifically aimed at this group, showing white colonial settlers waving at an approaching airplane while their native servants sat by and watched.[69] The image contrasted with everyday life in the Dutch East Indies. Advertising built on this disparity. KNILM repeatedly used the symbolic image of an airliner passing high over tiny Indonesian natives (fig. 4.4).[70] This remained a popular theme well into the 1930s.[71] It took years before non-Europeans ventured aboard. In an effort to encourage Indonesians to fly, KNILM organized special low-priced demonstration flights, but even by the late 1930s, Native inhabitants accounted for a mere 5 percent of KNILM's passengers, making Dutch colonial aviation a white man's business.[72] Efforts to entice Indonesians to fly, including ads in the indigenous Malay language, were not very successful because of the widespread fear of the new transportation technology. Popular folklore translated the Dutch acronym KNILM into "enter one of these and you will soon die."[73]

The 1930s were a difficult time for colonial aviation everywhere, and the Dutch East Indies were no exception. The worldwide economic crisis did not leave the archipelago untouched. KNILM made do with gradually shrinking subsidies only as the demand for air services began to rise from the middle of the decade.

Figure 4.4. KNILM timetable, written in Malay, 1932. Courtesy of Leiden University Library, the Netherlands, Special Collections, Collection Or. 27.622.

Following the French and British services, Dutch scheduled passenger flights to Asia began in the early 1930s. Although sources are sketchy, it would appear that KLM's clientele was more internationally diverse than that of Imperial Airways or Air Orient.[74] Its main attraction was speed. The service was a commercial hit from the start and developed into the cork on which the Dutch national airline floated. To ensure happy customers, KLM recognized the need to upgrade amenities on board. By the standards of the day, passengers were pampered. The flight engineer served coffee, tea, chocolate milk, raisin bread, and cold marinated or smoked fish. Nonetheless, comfort was not great, due in no small part to atmospheric conditions. Turbulence was a common occurrence, especially in the tropics. When the airplane flew high—a cruising altitude of about ten to thirteen thousand feet was customary—the cabin quickly became cold, even in a hot climate. Passengers needed a jacket to keep warm, or the cabin heating had to be turned on. Flying days were long. Air travel consisted of flights that lasted from twelve to fifteen hours. It was often almost dark when the plane landed. As facilities for night flying did not exist, passengers stayed over in luxury hotels equipped with modern conveniences such as hot showers. In most cases, hotels served European menus. All hotels for the night stops along the route were listed on the tickets issued.[75] Stayovers, however, were short. Passengers typically enjoyed no more than three to four hours of sleep as they had to rise between two and three in the morning in preparation for the airplane's departure at the crack of dawn.[76]

Night stops were, nevertheless, important reference points for the privileged clientele. The airlines operating intercontinental air routes did their best to make trips into lasting travel experiences. Passengers were met by a uniformed driver at each airport who would take them on guided sightseeing tours in whatever light remained. Such excursions were included in the airfare but were too short for the truly interested: "Rome in two hours," Willem Schermerhorn sneered.[77] For those traveling on KLM, these encounters likely contributed to a sense of bonding among passengers who traveled together on a relatively small single airplane for the entire week-long trip.[78] This Dutch approach was exceptional: Airlines generally changed planes at intermediate points. Both the French and the British used multiple aircraft on the services to the colonies in Asia until 1939.[79]

Imperial Airways, for one, cut up its route from London. The first leg of the long journey, from London via Paris to Basel, Switzerland, was covered by plane. But since the three-engine Armstrong Siddeley Argosy biplanes that Imperial used were unable to fly over the Alps, passengers traveled from Basel to Genoa by overnight train. There they were pampered with an extensive breakfast aboard an Imperial Airways vessel moored in the harbor before a motor launch would take them to their flying boat for the Mediterranean crossing. Imperial needed the next four days to take its passengers to Alexandria in Egypt. There they went from the harbor to the airport by bus to board a De Havilland Hercules landplane for the remainder of the journey to India.[80]

For the happy few who could afford it, air travel made colonial life more interesting. Dutch East Indies advertisements promised passengers the ability to "travel above your worries—cool, fast and comfortable."[81] The airplane's speed and its cool environment, free from the eternal dust and grime of the tropics, meant that flying quickly became popular with the colonial elite. The clientele was exclusive; tickets were anything but cheap. KNILM catered to the Dutch ruling class, who may have been pleased to learn in 1928 that life insurance policies now also covered the risk of airplane crashes.[82] To entice the general public to fly, KNILM organized more than one thousand short air tours over the various cities it served during its first two years of operation.[83]

The service from Batavia to Bandung, both on the isle of Java, was an immediate success. In February 1929, after just three months, the frequency of flights was doubled.[84] KNILM expanded its network in March 1930 with service to Singapore and in September of that year to Medan on Sumatra. As they covered a distance of almost eleven hundred miles, flights took ten to eleven hours, but this still represented a significant saving of time; the same journey by ship took almost three days. To keep passengers happy on such long flights, KNILM provided lunch baskets to be taken on board.[85] The opening of new services, such as night flights out of Surabaya, typically drew crowds of several hundred colonials. Passengers who lined up to be taken on a short flight over the city were enthused. One participant noted, "The spectacle was overwhelming! The first impression we got was that of the greatness of *La Ville Lumière* in the Indies."[86] Flights from Surabaya to the island of Bali (already a holiday destination because of its distinctive Hindu culture) were also popular with the colonial elite. Nonetheless, the highest load factors were achieved on the routes to and from the oil industry centers Balikpapan and Tarakan on the island of Borneo. But KNILM's principal contribution to colonial society remained the transportation of mail. Within two years, airmail service became the backbone of operations, although the journey from the airfield to the addressee could still be quite long and part of the time gained in flight was lost on the ground afterward.

Figure 4.5. KNILM advertisement, 1938. Courtesy of Leiden University Library, the Netherlands, Special Collections, Collection Or. 27.622.

Throughout the 1930s, the top Dutch priority was expanding the air network to Australia. When KNILM finally opened its service to Sydney in 1938, the airplane's prowess at "conquering distance and time itself" was advertised as an "amazingly fast and delightfully serene" way to travel between London and Australia. In the words of the airline's advertising department, "Romance and glamour [were] inseparably bound." The Dutch planes covered the distance in eight days, compared to the month-long journey by ship.

As before, advertising emphasized modernity and speed with the head-on profile of an approaching Lockheed Electra commanding visual attention.[87]

The Dutch emphasis on speed and dynamism stood in sharp contrast with competing British-Australian operations, which utilized slower—but bigger and more luxurious—Short C-class flying boats. Imperial Airways and Qantas Empire Airways advertised their aerial operations by consciously linking contemporary aviation to the older traditions of luxury ocean liners. Flying boat service from London to Australia, which began on June 26, 1938, required ten to fourteen days to complete. The Commonwealth's larger airplanes held up to seventeen passengers, who could move around from their seats to a smoking and dining room and an observation deck; this contrasted with the static seating arrangements on board the smaller land-based Dutch aircraft in which passengers were generally expected to remain in their seats.[88]

The Dutch service, following the overland route over Europe, Egypt, Iraq, India, Siam (Thailand), Singapore, and the Dutch East Indies, advertised itself as one big tourist trip with luxury hotels and sightseeing options all along the way. For the nine-day journey from Amsterdam to Sydney, the KLM/KNILM travel brochures listed them all. The most noticeable stop was on the island of Bali. "Fly to Bali and be Charmed," a typical KNILM pamphlet suggested. In contrast to other landing places, Bali, the natural beauty of which was described in terms of the "Last Paradise on Earth," was promoted by reference to its exotic culture, especially that embodied in the dress of its female population. To entice the predominantly male flying public, the spirit of the island was persistently captured in photographs depicting bare-breasted, mysterious-looking young women "whose rhythmic gait heightens the beauty of their goddess-like forms."[89]

In a period in which public reference to sexuality was scant, brochures in 1938 and 1939 advertising air services to Bali were sprinkled with images of topless dancing girls. One booklet promised, "In the evenings, when the blessing of the gloaming descends over the landscape, when the cool sea wind rustles through the palm tops and sings its lullaby of the leaves . . . when out of the far distance the gentle sing-song of the gamelan is carried along by the breeze, then Bali is most beautiful. . . . Then the young, slender dancing girls dance, their graceful movements accompanied by music that is one intense enchantment and rapture. Then . . ."[90] With these three suggestive dots, the brochure ended. Even with war approaching, colonial air travel retained an element of magic.

Figure 4.6. KNILM folder, promoting Australian tourism to Bali, 1938. Courtesy of Leiden University Library, the Netherlands, Special Collections, Collection Or. 27.622.

CONCLUSION

The development of interwar colonial air services was of considerable significance to European countries that had overseas possessions. Initially, developments focused on the transportation of mail, which was important to speed up business, governmental, and personal communications between the home country and the colonies. For this reason, governments and postal authorities financially supported long-distance air services. Once they began to carry passengers in the 1930s, these services also played an important role in extending globalization, promoting more effective governance, and enabling business officers to obtain a tighter grip on corporate affairs around the world.

The legal structure underlying international aviation acted as a complicating factor in this. The combination of national prestige and absolute sovereignty in the air meant that air services depended on agreements between governments. Aviation became one of the bargaining chips in bilateral affairs. The controversies over air services to East Asia and Australia provide examples of this from the colonial era. They are indicative of the many skirmishes over commercial landing rights that would follow after the Second World War, shaping global air transport to a degree few airline passengers realize.

Looking at practical aspects of the kind of long-distance air transport discussed here, airlines pampered their customers, treating them as tourists on an air cruise. In this context, national styles developed, either focusing on luxury, as in the British example, or on the speed of service, as in the Dutch example. In more ways than one, colonial air services were the precursors of the worldwide air tourism that we know today. Despite the enormous growth in air transportation and its opening up to the masses since the 1960s, national styles in the air have remained distinguishing features of airline operations. National symbols on the tails of airliners bear evidence of these traditions and are used to attract passengers through promises of experiencing the alluring and exotic places that are within the airline's reach.

NOTES

1. Willem Schermerhorn, diary entry, February 27, 1936, Netherlands National Archive (NNA), The Hague, "W. Schermerhorn, 1918–1976," 2.21.183.74, Collection 312, inv. no. 56 (author's translation from Dutch).
2. All Dutch newspaper clippings from https://www.delpher.nl/nl/kranten, the big newspaper digitization project of the Netherlands National Library. Sample articles mentioned are "De vliegende toekomst," *Sumatra Post*, January 4, 1919; "Het wereldluchtverkeer," *De Telegraaf*, January 8, 1919; "Ons land en het luchtverkeer," *Haagse Courant*, January 27, 1919; and "Over den Atlantischen Oceaan," *Algemeen Handelsblad*, June 14, 1919.
3. Jacques Arnould, *Et la Ligne Vivra! Latécoère 11 Avril 1927* (Toulouse: Éditions Privat, 2016), 31.
4. International Civil Aviation Organization (ICAO) Circulars, *The Economic Situation of Air Transport: Review and Outlook* (Montreal: ICAO, various years).
5. Emmanuel Chadeau, *Le Rêve et la Puissance: l'Avion et son Siècle* (Paris: Fayard, 1996), 132.
6. F. Robert van der Linden, *Air Lines and Air Mail: The Post Office and the Birth of the Commercial Aviation Industry* (Lexington: University Press of Kentucky, 2002), chap. 1.
7. Chadeau, *Rêve*, 131.
8. Mark Quinn, ed., *A Century of Irish Aviation: Pioneers and Aviators* (Dublin: Avolon, 2015), 27.
9. François Pernot, "Le role des aviateurs militaires français dans le défrichement des lignes aériennes dans les années vingt et le début des années trente," in *Actes du Colloque International l'Aviation Civile et Commerciale des Années 1920 à Nos Jours* (Paris: Service Historique de l'Armée de l'Air, 1994), 47–51.
10. Antoine de Saint-Exupéry, *Vol de Nuit* (Paris: Gallimard, 1931), chap. 4; Jean-Pierre Gaubert, *L'Aéropostale: La Religion dur Courrier* (Portet-sur-Garonne: Éditions Loubatières, 2002), 29–30.

11. Guillemette de Bure, *Les Secrets de l'Aéropostale: Les Années Bouilloux-Lafont 1926–1944* (Toulouse: Éditions Privat, 2006), 57–62.
12. Laurent Bonnaud, "Brésil, l'autre rive (1925–1935)," in *Actes du Colloque International*, 73–110; R. E. G. Davies, *Rebels and Reformers of the Airways* (Shrewsbury: Airlife, 1987), 283–98.
13. Robert Espérou and Gérard Maoui, *Air France: Des Origines à Nos Jours* (Paris: Le Cherche Midi, 1997), 31–33; Henri Mézière and Jean-Marie Sauvage, *Les Ailes françaises: L'Aviation marchande de 1919 à nos jours* (Paris: Éditions Rive Droite, 1999), 25–28.
14. Gordon Pirie, *Air Empire: British Imperial Civil Aviation 1919–1939* (Manchester: Manchester University Press, 2009), 79.
15. Camille Allaz, *History of Air Cargo and Airmail from the 18th Century* (London: Christopher Foyle, 2004), 91–92; Espérou and Maoui, *Air France*, 18; Mézière and Sauvage, *Les Ailes françaises*, 24.
16. Pirie, *Air Empire*, 84–88.
17. Alan Cobham, *Twenty Thousand Miles in a Flying Boat: My Flight Round Africa* (London: George Harrap, 1930).
18. "Report of the Imperial Air Communications Special Sub-Committee," November 17, 1926, British National Archives, Kew (London), Air Ministry, AIR 5, no. 907.
19. Robin Higham, *Britain's Imperial Air Routes 1918–1939* (London: G. T. Foulis, 1960; repr., Fonthill Media, 2016), 93–97.
20. Higham, *Britain's Imperial Air Routes*, 66–74.
21. R. E. G. Davies, *A History of the World's Airlines* (London: Oxford University Press, 1964), 180–82; Peter Lyth, "The Empire's Airway: British Civil Aviation from 1919 to 1939," *Revue Belge de Philologie et d'Histoire* 78, nos. 3–4 (2000): 865–87.
22. *The Times*, January 20, 1932.
23. Gordon Pirie, "Passenger Traffic in the 1930s on British Imperial Air Routes: Refinement and Revision," *Journal of Transport History* 25, no. 1 (2004): 75.
24. Gordon Pirie, *Cultures and Caricatures of British Imperial Aviation: Passengers, Pilots, Publicity* (Manchester: Manchester University Press, 2012), 83, 85–111.
25. Marc Dierikx, *Vliegende Hollanders: Het ware verhaal van Anthony Fokker & Albert Plesman* (Amsterdam: Boom, 2020), 75–91.
26. KNILM advertisement 1928, Leiden University Library, Special Collections, Or. 27.622. inv. no. 7. With gratitude to Ms. Doris Jedamski and Ms. Geke Burger for cooperation to use materials from this collection.
27. Edmond Thieffry, *En avion de Bruxelles au Congo Belge: Histoire de la première liaison aérienne entre la Belgique et sa colonie: Bruxelles-Léopoldville, 1925* (Brussels: Schaumans, 1926).
28. Guy Vanthemsche, *La Sabena, 1923–2001: Des origines au crash* (Brussels: De Boeck, 2002), 23–25, 60–81.
29. Vanthemsche, *Sabena*, 63–65.
30. Marc Dierikx, *Blauw in de lucht: Koninklijke Luchtvaart Maatschappij 1919–1999* (The Hague: Sdu, 1999), 41–42.
31. Pirie, *Air Empire*, 99–100.

32. Figure calculated from Pirie, *Cultures and Caricatures*, 86; Dierikx, *Blauw in de lucht*, 371.
33. Pirie, *Air Empire*, 101; Pirie, *Cultures and Caricatures*, 136.
34. "De eerste vrouwelijke passagier," *Sumatra Post*, June 8, 1931.
35. Pirie, *Air Empire*, 101; Pirie, *Cultures and Caricatures*, 173.
36. Jan Meijer, *Indië en de Vliegende Hollander* (Deventer: Van Hoeve, 1941), 8–9.
37. *KNILM Nieuws* 5, no. 4 (1939), advertisement 1928, Leiden University Library, Special Collections, Or. 27.622. inv. no. 4.
38. Pirie, *Air Empire*, 108.
39. Foreign Office note on KLM's proposed scheduled flights to Batavia, December 14, 1929, British National Archive, Kew (London), Foreign Office Papers, FO 371, inv. no. 14095.
40. Marc Dierikx, *Begrensde Horizonten: De internationale burgerluchtvaartpolitiek van Nederland in het interbellum* (Zwolle: Tjeenk Willink, 1988), 71–72.
41. Sacha Markovic, "Le Rôle de l'État dans la Naissance de l'Aviation Commerciale Française (1918–1933)," *Revue Belge de Philologie et d'Histoire* 78, no. 3–4 (2000): 980–86.
42. "Bilateral Agreement between Greece and the Netherlands on Air Services," June 1933, NNA, 2.05.37, Buitenlandse Zaken, DEZ, inv. no. 4346. See also Dierikx, *Begrensde Horizonten*, 73–76, 111–13.
43. Dierikx, *Begrensde Horizonten*, 76.
44. Dierikx, *Begrensde Horizonten*, 106–10.
45. Letter from the Dutch envoy in Teheran to the Foreign Ministry in The Hague, February 28, 1930, NNA, 2.05.37, Buitenlandse Zaken, DEZ, inv. no. 4312.
46. Letter from the Foreign Office to the Dutch envoy in London, April 7, 1930, NNA, 2.05.44, Netherlands Legation in London, inv. no. 1161.
47. Vanthemsche, *Sabena*, 75–77.
48. Vanthemsche, *Sabena*, 70–79; Mézière and Sauvage, *Les Ailes françaises*, 10–17.
49. Letter from Australian Prime Minister Joseph Lyons to the Dominions Office in London, June 8, 1932, British National Archive, Kew (London), Foreign Office Papers, FO 371, inv. no. 16413.
50. Dierikx, *Begrensde Horizonten*, 130, 136.
51. Marc Dierikx, *Clipping the Clouds. How Air Travel Changed the World* (Westport: Praeger, 2008), 14–15.
52. Concept agreement between KLM and KNILM on Australia air service, January 9, 1939, KLM Archive, Amstelveen, series RvB.
53. Letter from Tom Elink Schuurman to Patijn (Netherlands Minister for Foreign Affairs,), May 12, 1939, NNA, 2.05.48.14, Consulate-General Sydney, inv. no. 76; Letter from Hendrik Nieuwenhuis (KNILM) to the Board of KLM, July 31, 1939, KLM Archive, series R-5; Dierikx, *Begrensde Horizonten*, 146–55; Marc Dierikx, *Bevlogen Jaren: Nederlandse Burgerluchtvaart tussen de Wereldoorlogen* (Houten: Unieboek, 1986), 113–14.
54. Chadeau, *Rêve*, 140.
55. Espérou and Maoui, *Air France*, 20.

56. *Bataviaasch Nieuwsblad*, June 17, 1930.
57. Pirie, *Cultures and Caricatures*, 83–84.
58. C. W. Wormser, "Over drie werelddeelen: Ervaringen van een luchtpassagier," *Sumatra Post*, September 9, 1929 (author's translation from Dutch).
59. Description by C. W. Wormser of a flight on Imperial Airways from Paris to Karachi, July 14–22, 1929, "Over drie werelddeelen."
60. Wormser, "Over drie werelddeelen."
61. Robert L. McCormack, "Imperial Mission: the Air Route to Cape Town 1918–1932," *Journal of Contemporary History*, 9, no. 4 (October 1974), 77–97; Pirie, *Cultures and Caricatures*, 125–32.
62. Charles G. Dickson, "Poster: Cairo-Baghdad-Karachi Service, Imperial Airways," 1982–814/1, Science Museum Group Collection Online, ca. 1930, accessed May 1, 2025, https://collection.sciencemuseumgroup.org.uk/objects/co8016842/poster-cairo-baghdad-karachi-service-imperial-airways; William Constable, "India by Imperial Airways poster—Vintage Airline Travel Poster—Constable 1935," Heritage Posters, ca. 1931, accessed May 1, 2025, https://www.heritage-posters.co.uk/product/india-by-imperial-airways-poster-vintage-airline-poster-constable-1935/.
63. Poster, Lignes Aériennes G. Latécoère, "France—Espagne—Maroc" (1919), in Espérou and Maoui, *Air France*, 15.
64. G. I. Smit, R. C. J. Wunderink, and I. Hoogland, *KLM in beeld: 75 jaar vormgeving en promotie* (Naarden: V+K Publishing, 1995), 26–29, 36.
65. Imperial Airways advertisement (1931), in Pirie, *Air Empire*, 139; Pirie, *Cultures and Caricatures*, 118.
66. Poster, Air Orient, "Europe—Far East" (1932), in Espérou and Maoui, *Air France*, 19, 25.
67. KNILM timetable 1938, Leiden University Library, Special Collections, Or. 27.622. inv. no. 8.
68. Letter from Koningsberger to De Graeff, May 24, 1927, NNA, 2.21.211, Collection A. C. D. de Graeff, inv. no. 12.
69. KNILM advertisement 1930, Leiden University Library, Special Collections, Or. 27.622. inv. no. 7.
70. KNILM timetable 1928, Leiden University Library, Special Collections, Or. 27.622. inv. no. 21.
71. KNILM, Peratoeran Perdjalanan, 1932, Leiden University Library, Special Collections, Or. 27.622. inv. no. 21.
72. KNILM, *Annual Report 1937*, 6, private collection.
73. "Kalo Naik Ini Lekas Matti," *Algemeen Handelsblad voor Nederlandsch-Indië*, June 1, 1931.
74. Pirie, *Cultures and Caricatures*, 123–44; Chadeau, *Rêve*, 144–47.
75. Espérou and Maoui, *Air France*, 29.
76. Information based on diary entries by a Dutch passenger, Joop Hardeman, written during his air trip from Amsterdam to Batavia, May 3–10, 1934, accessed June 2006, https://www.stamboomhardeman.nl. See also Pirie, *Cultures and Caricatures*, 125–27, 131.
77. Schermerhorn, diary entry, February 22, 1936, NNA.

78. Description by C. W. Wormser of a flight on Imperial Airways from Paris to Karachi, July 14–22, 1929, *Sumatra Post*, September 9, 1929. Hardeman, diary entry; Schermerhorn, diary entry, February 22–March 3, 1936, NNA.
79. Espérou and Maoui, *Air France*, 21, 29.
80. Wormser, "Over drie werelddeelen," *Sumatra Post*.
81. *Soerabaijasch Handelsblad*, March 20, 1933.
82. *Bataviaasch Nieuwsblad*, October 31, 1928.
83. *Bataviaasch Nieuwsblad*, September 27, 1930.
84. *Bataviaasch Nieuwsblad*, July 16, 1929.
85. Letter from Enthoven to Koningsberger, January 25, 1927, NNA, 2.10.54, Ministry of the Colonies, inv. no. 427. See also *Bataviaasch Nieuwsblad*, September 27, 1930.
86. *Het Nieuws van den Dag voor Nederlandsch-Indië*, August 15, 1930.
87. KNILM advertisements 1938, Leiden University Library, Special Collections, Or. 27.622. inv. nos. 4, 6.
88. Pirie, *Cultures and Caricatures*, 154–56, 179–82.
89. KNILM leaflets, January 1939, Leiden University Library, Special Collections, Or. 27.622. inv. no. 11.
90. Brochure, *To Bali with KNILM* (1939), Leiden University Library, Special Collections, Or. 27.622. inv. no. 11.

"DETROYATTABOY"

Michel Détroyat and the 1936 National Air Races

Rénald Fortier

The interwar years, those two troubled decades between the world wars, were among the most fascinating periods in the history of flight. Engineers working in the United States and across Europe made remarkable strides in aerodynamics and construction. Military and civilian aircraft flew higher, faster, and farther than ever before—and did so with ever greater reliability. Even the terrible turmoil of the Great Depression could not stifle the progress of aviation.[1]

At the same time, the spectacle of flight became entrenched as a worldwide phenomenon. Indeed, the most famous fliers became firmly established as truly global celebrities. Charles Lindbergh and Amelia Earhart, or "Lady Lindy" as she was often called, were as well known and beloved as contemporary stars of the silver screen, including Charlie Chaplin and Mary Pickford.

That passion for wings did not go unnoticed in dictatorships like the Soviet Union, Japan, Italy, and Germany. Their pilots were promoted as the harbingers of a new age and of a new breed of men who possessed superhuman qualities unconstrained by the bonds of time and space. Record-breaking flights and international competitions were used to demonstrate the superiority of the political systems that had made possible their successes. Increasingly, advanced aircraft industries capable of producing high-performance machines were seen as prerequisites for laying claim to major power status. One textbook example of this use of aviation's power to fascinate was Fascist Italy's air minister, Italo Balbo, a ruthless thug with the looks of a movie star.[2] Even declining democratic powers like France and the United Kingdom could not and did not ignore the propagandistic potential of flight, though the governments of these countries seemed unable to muster the flair and bravado of their dictatorial counterparts.

Even though the United States was enmeshed in the global spectacle of flight, it somehow stood apart. The tensions and conflicts breaking out in Asia, Africa, and Europe during the 1930s seemed so far away to the country's citizens and statesmen. While times were hard, enjoying oneself seemed like a good idea. A day at the races might do the trick.

Among the many great spectacles of the American aeronautical past, the National Air Races (NAR), held annually during the 1920s and 1930s, attracted tens of thousands of people to live events, which were followed by far greater numbers through coverage in daily newspapers and radio broadcasts. As events of Americans, by Americans, and for Americans, the NAR were an ideal representation of the country's fascination for all things aeronautical. Despite being an American event, the NAR nonetheless welcomed many visitors, as well as the odd participant, from foreign lands on both sides of the Atlantic Ocean. Among these, none made a larger splash in the NAR than the winner of the 1936 contest, Frenchman Michel Détroyat.

Figure 5.1. A beaming Michel Détroyat after his victory in the 1936 edition of the Charles E. Thompson Trophy unlimited class race. Anonymous, "Results of the Air Races," *Aero Digest*, October 1936, 34.

BROADENING THE FIELD AT THE NATIONAL AIR RACES

American aviation enthusiasts were not, of course, the only people enthralled with aerial races; their European counterparts had been attending international competitions since before World War I. One of these was the Coupe Deutsch de la Meurthe. First established in 1906, but only awarding a winner for the first time in 1912, the event offered a cash prize and gaudy trophy to the pilot who achieved the fastest time over a set distance. Interrupted by the onset of World War I, a second iteration of the competition was held only twice during the 1920s before being recreated in 1932 by the Aéro-Club de France. The annual competition was created to commemorate one of the club's most famous presidents and the eponymous founder of the first Coupe, the late oil magnate, arts patron, and musical composer Henry Deutsch de la Meurthe (1846–1919). During the thirties, the event was held in two 1,000-kilometer (620-mile) stages separated by a ninety-minute refueling stop. As the competition was restricted to airplanes with an engine capacity of less than 8,000 cubic centimeters (490 cubic inches), the race severely tested the machines and their pilots.

Owing to a lack of interest on the part of foreign airplane manufacturing firms, the impact of the Coupe Deutsch de la Meurthe was muted throughout the 1930s. Worse still, the limited power of the engines mounted on the racing airplanes also meant that these thoroughbreds would not bolster in any way the strength of the beleaguered French Air Force.

In 1934, eager as always to boost interest in the NAR, the leadership of National Air Races of Cleveland, Inc. in Ohio cast an eye toward France, as well as toward Italy and the United Kingdom. NAR organizers were deeply impressed by the performance of France's Caudron C.450 and C.460 racing airplanes, superbly streamlined and successful machines designed by the *Société anonyme des Avions Caudron*, a subsidiary of the French automobile giant *Société anonyme des Usines Renault*. These two airplanes were very similar, but the C.460 had a retractable undercarriage.

The capabilities of the Caudron racers were highlighted on August 8, 1934. While flying the C.450, the famous French aviatrix Hélène Boucher broke two world speed records recognized by the *Fédération aéronautique internationale*, the Paris-based world governing body for all manner of aeronautical records: a general record over a distance of 1,000 kilometers (620 miles), with a speed of more than 254 mph, and a female record over a distance of 100 kilometers (62 miles), with a speed of more than 256 mph.

Figure 5.2. English language version of the ad published by the *Société anonyme des Avions Caudron* to celebrate the accomplishments of its airplanes since 1933. *Flight*, November 12, 1936, 51.

Three days later, Boucher reached a speed of more than 276 mph over a 3-kilometer (1.86 mile) course to set another new female world speed record.

The famous French aviator Raymond Delmotte ended the year with a bang by flying at more than 314 mph on December 25 at the controls of a C.460, thus setting a new landplane world speed record. The individual whose record he overcame was the late James Robert "Jimmy" Wedell, a famous American racing pilot and airplane designer who had exceeded 305 mph in early September 1933 at the NAR in a Wedell Williams Model 44.

A C.460 flown by Delmotte won the 1935 edition of the Coupe Deutsch de la Meurthe, achieving a speed of almost 276 mph. Flying another airplane of that type, Maurice Arnoux was able to reach almost 292 mph during his final laps around the circuit. Although this represented a record for the competition, an engine problem forced the renowned pilot to perform an emergency landing in a nearby field. Fortunately, he was not injured.[3]

Before the end of 1934, representatives from the National Air Races of Cleveland had contacted organizations in France to see if a Caudron racer might take part in upcoming closed-circuit competitions such as the Louis W. Greve Trophy race (limited to airplanes with an engine capacity of less than 550 cubic inches) or the Charles E. Thompson Trophy race (an unlimited class race); these were two of the main events of the NAR.

For whatever reason, National Air Races of Cleveland was unable to secure the appearance of a French racer in 1934 or 1935. All the same, in 1935, Louis William Greve, president of National Air Races of Cleveland, invited the well-known French aerobatic pilot Michel Détroyat (1905–56), who was in Cleveland to entertain the crowds attending the NAR, to take part in the 1936 trophy race aboard a Caudron racer; Détroyat readily accepted the invitation. He was already on record for having pointed out, during the formal dinner that followed the 1935 edition of the NAR, that there were racing airplanes in France that could defeat the fastest American machines.

Détroyat soon realized, however, that obtaining the permission of his employers, the well-known airplane manufacturers *Société anonyme des ateliers d'aviation Louis Bréguet* and *Société anonyme des Avions Morane-Saulnier*, would not be as easy. Taking part in an overseas competition in an airplane designed by a competing manufacturer was not the sort of thing that company executives smiled upon.

In mid-1936, however, Air Minister Pierre Cot (1895–1977), a leading figure in the *Front populaire*, a group of left-of-center political parties that had won the French general election held in May, gave his blessing to the idea of shipping a Caudron racer to the NAR. The airplane's high speed would undoubtedly impress the American public—and remind potential enemies of France that the country's aircraft industry could produce formidable machines.

Aware that Détroyat would be attending the NAR with his aerobatic airplane, Cot contacted his employers. Both Bréguet and Morane-Saulnier agreed to let their chief test pilot go to the United States. In turn, Caudron agreed to let Détroyat pilot one of its machines in the NAR. The airplane he would fly was the very C.460 that had won the 1935 edition of the Coupe Deutsch de la Meurthe.

By the end of July, American newspapers were reporting that the French Air Ministry had pledged to support Détroyat's participation in the NAR. Indeed, a number of French pilots were confident he would also break the transcontinental speed record set in January 1936 by the famous businessman aviator Howard Robard Hughes Jr., who had piloted a modified Northrop Gamma (fitted with a special 1,000-horsepower Wright SR-1820-G2 radial engine) from Burbank, California, to Newark, New Jersey, at an average speed of 259 mph.

Détroyat tested his C.460 in early August and was most impressed by its handling characteristics and capabilities. He later claimed he had spent only fifteen minutes or so in the air.[4]

"YOU WILL BE A PILOT"

Maurice Marie Michel Détroyat was born in Paris on October 28, 1905.[5] Like countless children of his generation, he was fascinated by aviation. Détroyat's family had deep links with the French armed forces. His father was a veteran cavalry officer who ended his illustrious career as a major general. An uncle of Détroyat's was a brigadier general in that same arm of the *Armée de terre*, while another was an admiral in the *Marine nationale*.

In 1923, Détroyat informed his father he wanted to be a pilot. The latter told him he would be a cavalryman. Two weeks later, Détroyat enlisted in a dragoon regiment. Even though he loved horses, the life of a mounted soldier did not suit him. Still, he behaved flawlessly in the hope of pleasing his father. Learning that his unit was to provide three men who were willing to join the *Aéronautique militaire* of the *Armée de terre*, Détroyat informed his father, who graciously gave his blessing.

Détroyat first took to the sky in April 1925. His instructors soon realized he was a singularly gifted pilot. Upon graduation in 1926, Détroyat went to a fighter regiment based at Le Bourget, a suburb of Paris. The pilots of his elite unit spent much of their time doing aerobatics.

In May 1927, for example, his commanding officer ordered him to perform over a huge and restless crowd at Le Bourget that was awaiting the arrival of the young American pilot Charles Augustus Lindbergh. Minutes after Lindbergh landed, Détroyat and a friend rescued him from the delirious crowds that threatened to overwhelm him. Asked by the American ambassador, Myron Timothy Herrick, to drive the hero of the hour to the safety of his embassy, Détroyat, his friend, and an accompanying officer got lost as their car negotiated the narrow streets in darkness. Lindbergh seemed mildly amused, or so Détroyat thought.

Toward the end of May, during a visit to Le Bourget, Lindbergh asked Détroyat if he could pilot one of the Nieuport Delage NiD 29 C1 fighters of his unit. The unrelenting pace of the past few days had worn him down. He wanted to relax, if only briefly. Détroyat's commanding officer, Maj. Armand Pinsard, a well-known World War I fighter ace, grudgingly gave his blessing. He offered his own airplane to Lindbergh and ordered Détroyat to fly with him. The flight, prepared in secret, was to be kept short and simple. Détroyat led Lindbergh over Paris early in the morning and lower than permitted. As Détroyat indicated his wish to land, Lindbergh indicated he wanted to do some aerobatics. Détroyat complied, until a flare went up from the military airfield. Détroyat immediately landed. Lindbergh landed a few minutes later.

Détroyat left the military later that year. He soon got a job at Morane-Saulnier as a second pilot and instructor before being promoted to test pilot in 1928. He soon began to accumulate successes of all sorts. His undisputed talent as an aerobatic pilot made him very popular. As months turned into years, Détroyat took part in countless airshows in Europe and in the territories of French North Africa. He also proved to be a top-notch flying instructor.[6]

In January 1934, Détroyat married Fanny Barois, a young pilot and daughter of an industrialist. Within a month, the couple was in New Orleans, Louisiana, where Détroyat dazzled assembled crowds at the Pan American Air Races, a one-off event held as part of the celebrations accompanying the opening of Shushan Airport. This was Détroyat's first visit to the United States; at some point later on, he joined the staff of Bréguet and Morane-Saulnier as chief test pilot.[7]

"WORLD ACES TO THRILL THRONGS"

Given the heavy construction work underway in 1936 at the Cleveland Municipal Airport, National Air Races of Cleveland was forced to find an alternate location for the sixteenth edition of the world's premier air classic, as the NAR were sometimes called.[8] The parties involved agreed in May to hold the various events at the Los Angeles Municipal Airport in Inglewood, California.[9]

Working feverishly to assemble the best program possible, the event's managing director, Clifford W. "Cliff" Henderson, traveled to nearly fifty American cities, delivering speeches in more than thirty of them. He also met many aviation community leaders and examined the airplanes of many potential participants. Henderson secured enough pledges to increase the sums offered to the winners of the planned races from the expected $60,000 to an all-time high of $70,000.[10]

As August 1936 began, workers at the Los Angeles Municipal Airport started to construct the gigantic grandstands where upward of sixty thousand spectators would gather to watch the various events of the NAR during Labor Day weekend. General admission was fifty cents; parking was free.[11]

If one were to believe Henderson, spectators would witness competitions the likes of which had never been seen before. Dozens of new, faster, and more powerful racers—designed, built, and flown by some of the best aeronautical engineers and pilots in the world—were expected to shatter speed records in all major events.

According to the unidentified author of an article published in the popular American monthly *Aviation*, "Reports of super-streamlined flying bullets and mysterious last-minute air race entries are rife throughout the land. Previous pre-race hysteria is far surpassed by the flood of rumors and counter-rumors now circulating from behind closed doors of factories, hangars, private garages and other secret hiding places where the high priests of speed are brewing their strange potions." Unnamed expert observers claimed that speeds of up to 400 mph were a possibility. According to *Aviation*, the NAR had finally reached a footing comparable to that of the International 500-Mile Sweepstakes at Indianapolis, Indiana.[12]

Information concerning Détroyat's participation in the NAR began to appear in French newspapers and periodicals in late July. The Parisian weekly *L'Aéro*, for example, stated that the organizers of that event had invited him to take part in closed-circuit competitions—a first for him and, quite possibly, for a foreign pilot. Still, Détroyat was mainly going to the NAR to perform as an aerobatic pilot, as he had done in 1935.

Détroyat's aerobatic airplane, a Morane-Saulnier MS.234 parasol wing monoplane painted in his favorite colors, red and black, left France on July 25 aboard a cargo ship. His dark blue Caudron C.460 racing airplane sailed aboard that same ship. A trio of mechanics by the name of Barra, Biogon, and Bourrat also made the trip to Los Angeles via the Panama Canal. Détroyat, accompanied by his spouse, left Paris on the morning of August 21 to catch a luxurious ocean liner. His airplanes were already waiting for him in the United States, having arrived at Los Angeles's port at San Pedro the previous day.

Once in the United States, the couple crossed the country on a commercial flight. Two of Détroyat's three mechanics were at the Los Angeles Municipal Airport to welcome them. With his spouse at their hotel, Détroyat and two of his mechanics went to the hangar where the C.460 and MS.234 were being readied for action. Détroyat learned that his mechanics had been bombarded with questions they could barely understand, let alone answer. Moreover, Détroyat learned that his airplanes were never alone. The mechanics took turns, day and night, keeping watch over them. The person on duty slept on a bunk bed beside the airplanes. As accommodating as their American hosts were, the mechanics did not fully trust them. While Détroyat thought they had seen too many gangster movies, he deeply appreciated their devotion.

In the days that followed Détroyat's arrival, American newspapers began to publish information about him. Some of that material was unusual. In California, the daily *Calexico Chronicle*, for example, all but quoted the official guide of the 1936 edition of the NAR: "At the age of 30, Michel Détroyat is an officer in the Legion d'Honneur . . . recently married . . . beau brummel . . . wears silk zipper flying suit and has orderly to help him into it . . . carries cane as his 'mascot' . . . likes American girls and describes them as 'keen' . . . known to friends as 'Mike' . . . one of France's best amateur fishermen . . . sounds like Maurice Chevalier on radio . . . is colorful after dinner speaker." Incidentally, many, if not most, Americans had no idea of how to pronounce Détroyat's last name. He soon became Mister Detroit, or Mike.[13]

American monthly aviation magazines also began covering Détroyat. An unnamed writer working for *Aviation* stated that his C.460 would be a real threat in the Greve Trophy and Thompson Trophy races, the events he was expected to participate in by that time. The article's author thought he might win both races.[14]

As opening day of the NAR grew closer, some American racing pilots found themselves out of the running. On August 30, the already famous Roscoe Turner left California to join other crews waiting for the start of the Vincent Bendix Trophy transcontinental speed race, near New York City. As Turner flew east, he experienced engine problems. Unable to maintain altitude, he crash-landed his Wedell-William Model 44 racer in New Mexico. The airplane settled on its nose and main wheels, but the fuselage behind the cockpit was destroyed. Turner knew he was lucky to be alive. He caught a train to Los Angeles and then went to a hospital to get treatment for his injuries, which included a couple of broken ribs. As spectacular as the various races of the NAR were for gathered audiences, they remained dangerous events during which pilots risked life and limb to win prizes or earn a living.[15]

Détroyat made his first practice runs on the first of September. He was all too aware that many American designers and pilots had no confidence in the capabilities of his C.460. That very day, Détroyat completed at least part of the 150 miles he would have to cover in the Thompson Trophy race at an average speed of 285 mph—more than 30 mph faster than the highest average speed achieved on this circuit in September 1932 by the well-known American aviator James Harold "Jimmy" Doolittle. The American pilots who planned to compete in this race were stunned. Détroyat instantly became the man to beat.[16]

Then, on September 3, an American pilot by the name of Earl Ortman raised the stakes by pushing his recently rebuilt red and gold Marcoux-Blomberg R-3 racer to nearly 300 mph. Having witnessed this performance, Détroyat took off soon after and was able to reach a comparable speed.[17]

As the sun set on September 3, approximately one hundred pilots hailing from various American states were in Los Angeles to take part in one or more races. They would compete for the $70,000 or so in prize money—a 40 percent increase over the $50,000 offered in 1935. According to *National Aeronautics*, the monthly magazine of the National Aeronautic Association (the private national governing body for all US aeronautical records), "The David and Goliath battle of the air between the huge bullet-nose radial powered thunder birds and the shark-like little in-line engine powered racers which has been so spectacular in the past will now reach new climax."[18]

"HOW A FRENCH AIRPLANE TRIUMPHED IN THE UNITED STATES"

Early in the morning of September 4, the first day of the 1936 edition of the NAR, Détroyat easily won the qualifying speed dash, earning $450 in the process.[19] Détroyat spent about fifteen minutes aloft in the late afternoon performing aerobatics for the pleasure of the spectators. The Gilmore Oil Company, an independent petroleum firm from California, sponsored his flights and that of another aerobatic ace, Germany's Gerd Achgelis. Both men also flew in the afternoons of September 6 and 7.

One has to wonder if many people in the audience noticed the symbol that adorned the rudder of the Focke-Wulf Fw 56 Stösser (an advanced training airplane) flown by Achgelis. By this time, the swastika was no longer a benevolent religious symbol of times past; Adolf Hitler's *Nationalsozialistische Deutsche Arbeiterpartei* (Nazi Party) had forever altered its meaning.[20]

The Greve Trophy race, limited to airplanes with an engine capacity of less than 550 cubic inches, was held in the late afternoon of September 6 along a five-mile circuit that participants would circle twenty times. As the six participants took off, Détroyat found himself at the rear of the pack. He soon retracted his landing gear, however, and put his propeller in coarse pitch; the C.460 responded. Détroyat soon caught up with his rivals. He had all but left them behind by the end of the initial laps and concluded there was no need to push his engine too hard. Détroyat's fear that his American rivals had not pushed their racing airplanes during the qualification trials proved unfounded. Toward the end of the race, the French pilot seemingly lost count of the number of times he had gone around the circuit. Ultimately, Détroyat went around a few extra times, just in case.

Détroyat easily won the Greve Trophy race, posting an average speed in excess of 247 mph, more than 30 mph faster than any previous winner of this competition. Harold R. Neumann and his brand-new Folkerts SK-2 *Toots* racing airplane crossed the finish line almost two full laps behind the French pilot. Détroyat's efforts earned him $4,900. The French pilot "flew a marvelous race," said a relative novice in the world of air racing, Robert A. "Rudy" Kling, "and deserves all the credit in the world." Détroyat's C.460 was undoubtedly superior to any airplane competing against it. Still, the very small size of the Greve Trophy race circuit compared to that of the Coupe Deutsch de la Meurthe—in other words, five miles rather than sixty-two—meant that Détroyat was unable to reach or sustain the high speeds his machine was capable of achieving.[21]

Détroyat's victory in the Greve Trophy race boosted his confidence and desire to win the Thompson Trophy. That said, he knew several of his rivals would be flying airplanes that were far more powerful than his C.460. Détroyat did not sleep very well the night before the race. On racing day, September 7, he spent much of the early and mid-afternoon with his mechanics, who had worked throughout the night and morning checking and rechecking the airplane.

As nervous as Détroyat may have been, there were many members of the American aviation community who thought that, barring some sort of mishap, he would win the Thompson Trophy race hands down. Détroyat's airplane was just too fast. With Turner out of the running, only dark horses like Ortman or Harry V. Crosby and his Crosby CR-3 racing airplane were thought to have a chance against the speedy Frenchman. Even so, Ortman later claimed that he "wouldn't even have entered the Thompson race had [he] known that the French plane was being entered."[22]

Only six of the nineteen pilots entered in the Thompson Trophy race were on the starting line in the late afternoon. This time around, Détroyat had some sort of abacus in his cockpit to record the number of times he completed the circuit. Détroyat later indicated that he had readily agreed to let his three mechanics wear blue, white, and red coveralls on that special day to honor the French flag and France itself.

As the pilots soared into the air to begin the first of the fifteen laps they would need to complete around the ten-mile course, Détroyat realized that he could outrun his competitors. During one of the early laps, he reached a speed of 301 mph. As there was no need to push his engine, he slowed down. Unable at times to clearly see the pylons around the circuit, Détroyat made rather broad turns. Even so, his lead was unshakable. Below, the ground crews of the American pilots looked on with increasing consternation.

Seeing how fast Détroyat's machine was, Ortman realized that, barring a mechanical problem, the Frenchman's machine could not be defeated. He therefore throttled back just enough to remain in second place. Toward the end of the race, as visibility grew worse owing to fog, Détroyat almost collided with the Brown B-2 racing airplane piloted by Marion McKeen, who was quite shocked when the C.460 zoomed past him, only inches away.

By the time Détroyat crossed the finish line, he was almost two laps ahead of Ortman. Détroyat was beside himself with joy, as were his mechanics. One of them kissed Détroyat as soon as the latter opened his canopy. Détroyat was close to tears when he saw the French flag being raised at the mast of the airport as the music of France's national anthem filled the air.

The French pilot had won the Thompson Trophy race with an average speed of more than 264 mph—faster than the highest average speed achieved on this circuit, 253 mph, in September 1932 by Doolittle. Détroyat was the first foreign pilot to win the race, as well as the first to take part in it. His victory earned him a sum of $9,500.[23]

Turner, who had left the hospital earlier in the day, saw all this unfold. Beside himself with anger, the famous pilot, who was otherwise known to be "a good fellow and all-around sportsman," rushed to the announcers' booth, grabbed a microphone, and spoke to the crowd, who listened in increasing astonishment.

> It isn't fair for you folks up there in the stands to think that our planes are no good when you see the Frenchman leading the field this afternoon. Not one of the American racing planes in this event cost more than $15,000, and the boys who fly them raised the money to build them. I tell you it isn't fair for any foreign pilot to come over here with a million-dollar subsidy-built airplane and take back the prize money that ought to be divided up among the boys whose efforts and money have made our air races what they are today.[24]

Interviewed by journalists, Détroyat said he felt "no way aggrieved by Colonel Turner's statement. In fact, [he believed] the controversy [would] result in only one way—a general effort toward the development of swifter airplanes, a move forward in aviation."[25]

Even though he smiled at Turner's comments regarding government subsidies, Détroyat defended himself and his airplane. The C.460 racer, he noted, "is two years old and was built and is owned by the Renault company."[26] Developing this type of airplane might have cost a million francs (about $66,000), but all that money was spent by the company. The French government had not spent such a sum, let alone a million dollars, developing the C.460. "The French Air Ministry," said Détroyat, "had nothing to do with building or paying for this plane other than granting the Caudron-Renault company permission to take it out of the country."[27]

Détroyat's comments may have been somewhat disingenuous. He presumably knew that the French Air Ministry had given 9 million francs (about $595,000) in rewards to the competitors who had taken part in the three preceding editions of the Coupe Deutsch de la Meurthe (1933–35). The most successful participant in these races by far, Caudron had received the lion's share, about 5.865 million francs (about $390,000).

Figure 5.3. A few people among the tens of thousands who viewed the 1936 edition of the National Air Races. The platform from which judges and timers could keep an eye on things is in the background. Elizabeth Hyatt Gregory, "Times Flies, but Aviation Keeps Pace with It," *U.S. Air Services*, October 1936, 27.

Be that as it may, no representative of National Air Races of Cleveland officially commented on Turner's outburst. Speaking unofficially, Henderson sharply disagreed with Turner. An unnamed source added that as long as Détroyat and his airplane qualified for a race, in accordance with the regulations, they had every right to participate. Interestingly enough, many, if not most, American pilots seemingly sided with Détroyat, at least privately. One of them agreed to talk to the press. Harry V. Crosby was quoted as saying that "a race is supposed to go to the fastest plane, and Detroyat had the fastest plane. That's all there is to it."[28]

Faced with ongoing controversy, Détroyat graciously withdrew from the Shell Cup race, a competition open to airplanes with an engine of no more than 550 cubic inches in displacement. Having already won $14,850, he preferred to let the American pilots compete for the available prize money. This sportsmanlike gesture was favorably noted in the American press. Détroyat may well have thought that another victory would only increase tension.[29]

An unnamed editorialist in the American monthly *U.S. Air Services* had thoughts to offer on that matter: "Good sportsmanship by a brilliant French pilot. But we have to think what would happen if the situation were reversed. In fact, we can't bear the mental picture of an American flyer abroad being forced by public opinion over there to forego winning another case prize because in three races he had come in first."[30] As it turned out, the fifty-mile Shell Cup race was won by professional racing pilot and parachutist Roger Don Rae. His Rider R-4 completed the event at an average speed of almost 226 mph.

Adding insult to injury, Détroyat's twin victories at the NAR meant that he also won the Clifford W. Henderson Trophy, a nonmonetary award granted to the most successful pilot at the NAR.[31]

"REPERCUSSIONS OF THE AIR RACES"

Within days of the shock caused by Détroyat's victories, many members of the American aviation community took stock of what had happened.[32] The victories, said Henderson, "should awaken the country to the fact that speed planes cannot be built without spending a lot of money."[33] Many wondered where this money would, or should, come from. Henderson was among those who thought that the American government should, somehow, provide some degree of financial assistance. William R. "Bill" Enyart also thought that government money would be most welcome. Given the time it might take for the US Congress to vote on something, the influential head of the Contest Committee of the National Aeronautic Association thought that wealthy Americans could open their wallets to help in the meantime.[34]

Criticizing the frequent poor quality and inaccuracies of the public announcements at the 1936 edition of the NAR, an editorial published in the October issue of the respected monthly *Aero Digest* described Roscoe Turner's heartfelt outburst as the low point: "The unsporting criticism of the winning of the Thompson Trophy by a foreign plane; the show of poor sportsmanship and laxness of the race management in allowing the use of its public address system for criticism of a competing foreign pilot who was doing such a splendid racing job, is inexcusable. This disregard for fair play has left an unpleasant impression of American pilots among unprejudiced Americans, to say nothing of the effect on foreign pilots." The editorialist readily accepted Détroyat's statement that his C.460 had been developed by a private company without using government money. "No further proof that the plane is not a military development (as is contended) is needed than the fact that the plane has been offered for sale to a private pilot in this country."[35]

The stunning results of the 1936 NAR left few people in the American aviation community indifferent. Some commentators in the specialized press, like the one writing for *Aero Digest*, for example, pointed out that the competition had been "especially rich in new engineering design features."[36] Another author writing for this monthly magazine stated that Détroyat's C.460 "created as great an impression by its tremendous speed as by its clean lines, skin-type oil radiator, and fully retractable landing gear. Also impressive was the efficiency of the two-pitch position Ratier propeller which aided in the creation of new speed records in the two events won by Detroyat."[37] Yet another unnamed writer added to these opinions in an in-depth look at the 1936 edition of the NAR published in the monthly *Aviation*: "Of Detroyat's plane the most significant point is that there is no one outstanding feature which overshadows others. The engine, the propeller, and the airplane itself each is a component part carefully balanced to fit into a race plane symposium which has resulted in the finest landplane racer yet developed anywhere in the world."[38]

There can be no doubt that Détroyat's victories at the 1936 NAR sent shockwaves throughout the French aeronautical community. According to the aeronautical columnist of the *Journal des débats politiques et littéraires*, Détroyat's successes were "the result of a magnificent effort that has been sustained with perseverance for several years. It takes on particular importance at a time when the achievements of French airplane manufacturers and the performance of their airplanes are too little known abroad."[39] Better yet, added this conservative daily, one of the most respected in France, "It is the first time, in many years, that an entirely French airplane, both airframe and engine, piloted by a Frenchman, has clearly defeated American competitors in arduous speed competitions on their own ground."[40]

In an interview published by the well-known sports daily *L'Auto*, Marcel Riffard, the gifted aeronautical engineer who had designed the Caudron racer, added his own thoughts: "Détroyat's success was absolutely certain, because we have overwhelming superiority in racing aviation over other countries." Caudron had gained this superiority as a result of its desire to win every edition of the Coupe Deutsch de la Meurthe.

The criticisms expressed by well-known American racing pilot Roscoe Turner were totally unjustified, said Riffard. The French government had not subsidized the construction of the C.460. In any event, the two-year-old airplane's top speed was achieved through careful aerodynamic research rather than the use of pure power. The C.460 was therefore an economical airplane, a counterpart of which could have been developed by an American team with limited funding.[41]

Détroyat had won fair and square, without government assistance. Turner disagreed, wrote Lucien Dubech, a well-known, right-of-center author, literary critic, and sportswriter, in the weekly *L'Auto*: "Too bad for Mr. Roscoe Turner. While he had lacked elegance, all the states of America should not share responsibility. Yet one feels a vague desire to bring said inelegance closer to that with which the Americans welcomed the return of [Olympic gold medalist James Cleveland 'Jessie'] Owens."[42]

However, not everyone in the French press saw blue skies ahead. Even though an opinion piece in the September 1936 issue of *L'Avion*, the monthly of the *Union des pilotes civils de France*, began on a joyful note, Détroyat's victories were also cause for reflection. One of the reasons behind these victories was the fact that the *Société anonyme des Usines Renault* had invested funds in racing airplanes that were not the subject of government orders. Indeed, another reason behind Détroyat's victories was the fact that his Caudron C.460 was designed to take part in the Coupe Deutsch de la Meurthe, a competition whose regulations had been devised without the contribution of the technical services of the French Air Ministry.

The author of the opinion piece published in *L'Avion* had few kind words for these services, which he called the sacrosanct technical services, the monastery of Issy-les-Moulineaux, and grand pedant central. Airplane plans spent weeks and weeks inching through corridors, gathering countless stamps of approval. Once built, the airplanes themselves spent months at the testing establishment near Paris, where they became perfectly safe and so slow as to be all but useless.

In turn, the French aeronautical industry seemed to be as risk-averse as the technical services and testing establishment. How else could one explain the fact that only the *Société anonyme des Avions Caudron* had taken part in the 1936 edition of the Coupe Deutsch de la Meurthe? The great lesson that emerged from the victories of that firm, both in France and in the United States, was that, "faced with a progress to be made, the organizers, builders and pilots knew how to take their responsibilities and the risks."[43]

The unwillingness of the French aeronautical industry to develop tomorrow's airplanes today "promises, for later, a beautiful second-rate aviation, which will pay comfortable fees to foreigners on which it will be dependent, by virtue of multiple licenses." The unnamed author of the opinion piece published in *L'Avion* concluded his text with a heartfelt cry: Did the leaders of the French aircraft industry still possess the enthusiasm, faith, guts, and strength of will necessary to succeed?[44]

"AU REVOIR, GENTLEMEN!"

As columnists and members of the aviation community in the United States and France opined on the results of the 1936 NAR, Détroyat and his spouse were getting ready to go home.[45] Faced with various issues, the French pilot had decided not to pursue the transcontinental speed record. On September 10, the couple boarded an airliner flying to New York City. Interviewed prior to boarding, Détroyat showed no rancor toward Roscoe Turner. Indeed, he wanted to take part in the 1937 NAR with a racing airplane capable of reaching speeds of up to 450 mph. As far as Détroyat was concerned, the C.460 he had flown in Los Angeles was all but obsolete. He claimed, half seriously perhaps, that he might sell it—presumably to an American aviator.

Détroyat and his spouse rested for a couple of days in New York City. On September 12, they answered an invitation sent by the French ambassador, André Lefebvre de Laboulaye, to visit Washington, DC. The aviator was given a hero's welcome by the personnel of the embassy. The couple may have spent some time on Capitol Hill. On September 15, Détroyat and his spouse boarded an ocean liner for home.[46]

An editorial cartoon published in the American weekly magazine *Contact* illustrated the anger felt in certain quarters (fig 5.4). It showed Détroyat sailing away with a bag containing $15,000 in his hands and the Thompson Trophy at his feet, proclaiming "Au revoir, gentlemen!" to four men on a dock. Roscoe Turner was depicted standing and angrily waving his fist at the French pilot. Two seemingly unhappy American pilots sitting at the edge of the dock were identified as Doolittle and Williams, possibly Alford Joseph "Al" Williams.[47]

As Détroyat and his spouse sailed home, the French air minister, Pierre Cot, received a telegram sent by the managing director of the 1936 NAR. In it, Henderson congratulated Détroyat for having won the trophy named after him. He added that the Contest Committee of the National Aeronautic Association invited Détroyat and any other French pilot who was interested to defend these victories at the 1937 edition of the NAR. In a separate telegram, that committee congratulated Cot for the victories won by Détroyat,

Figure 5.4. Editorial cartoon detailing the frustration of many American aviation enthusiasts after Michel Détroyat's victories at the National Air Races. Anon., "Good-Bye, Thompson Trophy, See You Again—We Hope!," *Contact*, September 12–19, 1936, 5.

as well as for the achievements of the French engineers and manufacturers. Cot thanked both Henderson and the committee for their kind words.[48]

"MICHEL DÉTROYAT FEASTED AT CITY HALL RECEIVED YESTERDAY THE GRANDE MÉDAILLE D'OR DE LA VILLE DE PARIS"

Delayed by a thick fog, the ocean liner carrying the Détroyats reached the shores of France during the evening on September 21.[49] Détroyat was in good shape and spirit but might have caught a nasty cold during the crossing. A delegation of the Aéro-Club de France was so eager to congratulate him that it went on board that very day. Journalists from at least two major Paris dailies met Détroyat. "I am very, very happy," said the pilot. "The Americans were very sporting, despite the small nasty remarks of the beginning, remarks which came mainly from Turner." If truth be told, the French pilot regretted the fact that the American pilot had not been able to take part in the Thompson Trophy race; "he would have been soundly beaten!"[50]

Interviewed a day or two later by veteran aviation journalist Jacques Mortane, Détroyat pointed out that he would be very pleased if the devotion and thoroughness of the three mechanics who had made the trip to North America (the "three B's" as he called them) were mentioned in the press.[51]

On October 1, the president of the city council of Paris welcomed Détroyat at city hall. The pilot listened quietly as Raymond Laurent and a regional politician said a few words. Détroyat thanked them both, as well as the people who had helped him achieve his victories, adding that he had merely organized France's contribution to the American racing event. The many people present applauded him profusely. Laurent then handed Détroyat the gold version of the Médaille de la Ville de Paris.[52]

Détroyat was one of the pilots whose 1936 successes were recognized on October 9 at a gala held at the Aéro-Club de France. Hundreds of people were present, including many personalities. The club's president, André Louis Wateau, gave Détroyat the highest award available, the Grande médaille d'or. Modest as usual, Détroyat stated that he owed his victories at the NAR to French technology and the magnificent dedication of his mechanics.[53]

"PLAY *THAT* ONE ON YOUR BAZOOKA!"

There can be no doubt that the victories of Michel Détroyat at the 1936 NAR sent shockwaves throughout the entire American air racing community.[54] Why, with their more powerful engines, were they given the runaround by a foreigner? The consternation reached across the Atlantic Ocean to the United Kingdom, where the founding editor of the well-known British aviation weekly *The Aeroplane*, Charles Grey "C. G." Grey, wrote an editorial entitled "Detroyattaboy." Two paragraphs from this text are worth quoting in full.

> Those concerned with the National Air Races must evidently make their minds whether they want foreign participation or not, or alternatively whether they want to institute a means test. Until these things are made clear the position of the foreign competitor seems to be that he is welcome to add by his presence to the variety, interest and gate-money of the Races provided he is not so tactless as to win back his expenses.

> [. . .]
>
> When we, in the British Empire, are afraid of foreign competition, whether for reasons connected with prize-money or prestige, we state categorically that no others need apply [. . .]. This method is not so sporting that we feel at all proud of it, but at least nobody is thereby led up the garden.[55]

This being said, the victories of Détroyat had their greatest impact within the American air racing community. The shockwaves were felt by a lot of people.

A meeting of the National Air Board, an American group seemingly linked to the National Aeronautic Association, held in the fall of 1936 proved quite animated in that regard. There were some, if not many, who wondered whether foreign pilots and airplanes should be barred from participating in the NAR. Allegations of French government support in the development of Détroyat's Caudron C.460 racing airplane gave weight to this suggestion. After all, American racing teams were "small associations of skilled constructors and experienced pilots working under 'backyard' conditions, risking their own money and relying mainly on prize money to keep going." And yet, according to board member Augustus Thomas Post Jr., a respected aviation pioneer, "Air racing should draw the best from everywhere. [. . .] Should we not attempt to learn something from the world at large rather than to be content to stew in our own juice?"[56] Fellow board member Randolph Fordham Hall concurred. The respected aeronautical engineer reminded all those present that the manufacturers competing for the Pulitzer Trophy, the main event of the NAR between 1920 and 1925, had done so with airplanes sponsored by the US Army and US Navy. That government support had led to great advances in design.

Virtually all members of the National Air Board supported these arguments. They therefore decided that foreign pilots and airplanes should not be barred from taking part in national competitions like the Thompson Trophy unlimited class race and the Vincent Bendix Trophy transcontinental speed race. That said, they did believe that only nongovernmental American participants should be allowed to take part in minor events in the NAR and in all races held at local events.

Regardless of that decision, every member of the American air racing community knew only too well that Détroyat's victories had changed their world forever. To quote Charles F. McReynolds, a prolific aviation journalist, in the December 1936 issue of the American monthly pulp magazine *Flying Aces*, "There is nothing to do now but face the facts and set the stage for 1937." Suggestions and rumors abounded. An editorial in the well-known

Figure 5.5. The superbly streamlined Caudron C.460 flown by Michel Détroyat at the National Air Races. Robert C. Morrison, "On Frontiers of Aviation," *Model Airplane News*, December 1936, 10.

monthly *Aero Digest* suggested that less attention be paid to showmanship and more to advancing aerodynamics. The management team of the NAR might also consider the use of a little more diplomacy in its dealings with pilots.[57]

If one were to believe the respected monthly *U.S. Air Services*, some people suggested that there should be at least two major air racing meets in the United States each year and that the amount of money awarded as prizes at the NAR themselves should be boosted to $100,000 or more. Rumors also circulated to the effect that the chain of newspapers headed by William Randolph Hearst was interested in sponsoring a series of races in various parts of the United States. Some people believed, or hoped, that such a scheme, sponsored by Hearst or some other wealthy patron, could come to fruition.

As Détroyat himself was quoted as saying, he had to a certain point shown the way to American designers and pilots, something for which at least some of them were grateful. Work would immediately begin on new or improved racers. Were Détroyat to participate in the 1937 edition of the NAR, according to some Americans the French pilot had talked to, he would surely meet his match.

Even so, a source of concern for American racing pilots had to do with the strong likelihood that a team comprising at least two French airplanes and, quite possibly, a team with at least one British airplane would cross the Atlantic Ocean in 1937 to do battle with them at the NAR. After all, reminded McReynolds, Détroyat had all but promised to take part in the competitions that year with a brand-new Caudron racer capable of reaching speeds of up to 450 mph. "Play *that* one on your Bazooka!" noted this writer. Two other French pilots would allegedly join Détroyat with equally new Caudron racing airplanes fitted with a powerful new engine.[58]

According to McReynolds, the United Kingdom had also "been hankering to break some air speed records, and the flying Limies figure they might just as well break 'em in America as anywhere else." As an interesting aside, he pointed out that the great Lindbergh, a resident of the United Kingdom at the time, had taken delivery of a specially designed machine, the Miles Mohawk long-range private plane. "It would be rather ironical if Lindbergh were to compete in the American National Air Races flying a British ship."[59]

An additional source of concern for American racing pilots, thought McReynolds, was the possibility that an Italian team might cross the Atlantic Ocean in 1937 if the French and British chose to take part in the premier American air racing event. After all, the Italian dictator, the buffoonish Benito Mussolini, was "always eager for his pilots to show their stuff to the world."[60]

R. C. Wood, the Paris-based member of the National Air Board and a correspondent of *Popular Aviation*, observed that "air races in the next few years should prove to be some of the hottest fought battles for aerial supremacy of recent years." In the meantime, the crowds present at the seventeenth edition of the NAR, to be held in Cleveland in early September 1937, would witness competitions the likes of which had never been seen before. "Monsieur Detroyat certainly started something," concluded McReynolds.[61]

"DÉTROYAT MUST BE PUNISHED!"

Sadly enough, Détroyat did not take part in the 1937, 1938, or 1939 editions of the NAR—and neither did French, British, or Italian pilots.[62] Canceled between 1940 and 1945, inclusively, the NAR only returned in 1946. The most successful racing pilots flew world-famous World War II fighter airplanes of American design that were bought as war surplus. A deadly crash in September 1949 brought the saga of the NAR to a close. Although far less tragic, the fate of the Coupe Deutsch de la Meurthe was equally sad. The 1937 and 1938 editions of the race were canceled, more or less for lack of competitors. In turn, the 1939 edition was canceled as a result of the onset of the Second World War. The Coupe Deutsch de la Meurthe would not be restarted after the end of the conflict.[63]

From 1936 onward, Michel Détroyat became increasingly involved in the rearmament efforts of the French authorities—efforts made necessary by the ever-increasing belligerence of Fascist Italy and, even more so, National Socialist Germany. The situation was indeed dire given the dismal state of the French aircraft industry. The six recently formed *Société nationales de constructions aéronautiques* seemed unable to mass produce airplanes, which left much to be desired anyway. Given that the British aircraft industry was working flat out to supply the machines needed by the Royal Air Force (and that the signing of contracts with German or Italian firms was out of the question), the French government turned to the only aircraft industry able to pull the French Air Force out of the hole it had dug for itself: the United States.

In March 1938, Détroyat secretly test-flew a preproduction example of the brand-new Curtiss P-36 fighter airplane. His glowing report led to the signing of several contracts. Indeed, the French Air Ministry later signed similar contracts with other American aircraft manufacturers, and this until the fall of France, in June 1940.[64] Détroyat, who was in the United States at the time as part of a purchasing mission, was devastated by his nation's surrender. Although aware that Brig. Gen. Charles André Joseph Marie de Gaulle was asking his compatriots to continue the fight, Détroyat chose to return to France to rejoin his spouse and children.

Before long, Détroyat became a supporter of the *État français*. He was also a supporter of Marshall Philippe Pétain, the very elderly head of state of the puppet collaborationist and authoritarian government set up in July 1940 in the southern unoccupied half of France. Whether or not Détroyat gave his support out of conviction, necessity, opportunism, or a combination thereof is unclear. Détroyat's political convictions for a long time before that may have tilted toward the right, but not the far right of the political spectrum.

In 1940, Détroyat wrote at least two letters to German officials in which he proposed that French pilots be used to perform certain services for the German *Luftwaffe* and be offered the possibility of joining an auxiliary transport unit. In 1942, he joined the management of two French airplane manufacturers that produced German observation and transport airplanes. At some point late in that year, Détroyat was chosen to be Pétain's personal pilot. He may have flown him and/or the unsavory head of government of the *État français*, Pierre Jean Marie Laval, on a few occasions.[65] In early July 1944, as Allied forces rushed across France toward Paris, Détroyat, perhaps fearing for his safety, drove to Spain, a neutral if pro-German dictatorship. He now wanted to help free France, anywhere and anyhow. Hoping to advance his cause by offering to participate in the Allied landing in southern

France, which had taken place in August, Détroyat went to Algeria, a French territory under the control of the French provisional government headed by de Gaulle. His offer of assistance was rejected. Virtually under arrest, Détroyat soon returned to France.[66]

Détroyat was formally arrested in October 1944. He stood accused of having cooperated with the German occupation authorities—one of the few well-known French pilots who had done so. Finding the evidence submitted to back the serious charges laid against Détroyat somewhat insufficient, the criminal court dismissed them. He was released in early November 1945, quite possibly after spending a year in jail.

The editorial staff of a new weekly magazine, *Aviation française*, was shocked by the criminal court's decision: "After leading, thanks to the subsidies of betrayal, a high life with the tormentors of the French people, Détroyat must be punished!" This strongly anti-Pétain magazine was not the only Paris-based publication to express anger. A daily newspaper of the French Communist Party, *Ce soir*, for example, stated that the reclassification of Détroyat's case was quite simply scandalous. Another daily of that party, *L'Humanité*, claimed that justice had been trampled. Friends in high places had seemingly protected Détroyat.[67]

Détroyat's release offered no relief from his problems with the new French government, however. In mid-January 1946, he appeared before a *Chambre civique*, a special court for collaborators that dealt with cases of national disgrace. If found guilty, Détroyat would be barred from any function in the civil service or the management of a private firm. He would also lose his right to vote and be expelled from the military and the *Légion d'honneur*, among other things. That said, Détroyat would avoid any more jail time. In the end, he received one of the harshest sentences meted out to date by the special court. Détroyat was condemned to national disgrace for life in January 1946. In addition, he was ordered to give half of his possessions to the state.[68]

Like a few other French aeronautical industry people who, for some reason or other, did not feel comfortable in France, or could not find employment, Détroyat went into exile in Argentina in September 1946. He seemingly went alone. While in Argentina, Détroyat served as the personal pilot of a local millionaire and as an adviser for the Argentinian air force and the country's main airplane manufacturing concern, the government-owned *Fábrica Militar de Aviones*. At the time, the populist dictator Juan Domingo Perón was trying to diversify Argentina's economy, and aircraft production seemed to be a promising area to develop. Given the lack of experience in high-performance airplane design among the country's engineering community, Perón's government invited experienced foreign aeronautical engineers and individuals in search of a home to work in Argentina.

Détroyat returned to France in 1951 as a result of an earlier amnesty that had wiped away his national disgrace. This rehabilitation seemingly included a return of his beloved *Légion d'honneur*. Still, Détroyat was shunned by many. He became one of the civilian transport pilots who flew vital supplies in support of the losing war France fought in the *Fédération indochinoise* between 1946 and 1954, a defeat that led to the independence of Cambodia, Laos, North Vietnam, and South Vietnam. For a brief time, he seemingly worked as an instructor for the head of civilian and commercial aviation in what became South Vietnam.

Once back in France in 1955, Détroyat worked as a ferry pilot on at least a few occasions, delivering private airplanes to their owners all over France. He also took part in several air meets.

Maurice Marie Michel Détroyat died of a cerebral embolism suffered after surgery on the morning of October 5, 1956, in a clinic near Paris. He was almost fifty-one years old.[69] Michel Détroyat came of age during the interwar years, undoubtedly one of the most fascinating and troubled periods in the history of aviation. As a matter of course, he kept abreast of what was taking place in aviation both in France and abroad throughout these years. Indeed, Détroyat was a player, often a key one, in some of the significant aeronautical events that took place during the 1920s and 1930s, from the epoch-making 1927 transatlantic flight of Charles Augustus Lindbergh to the acquisition of American combat aircraft by the French Air Force in 1938–40, not to mention his historic victories in the 1936 edition of the NAR. By that time, however, he knew only too well how dangerous Italy and, even more so, Germany were for a weakened and internally divided France.

While it is true that the huge advances made by aeronautical engineers during the 1920s and 1930s gave birth to commercial aviation and air travel, these advances also paved the way for a new generation of high-performance combat aircraft. In that all-metal and supercharged world, the backyard and shoestring racing airplanes of the NAR were little more than quaint anachronisms. Some of the people involved in the design of these machines had come to accept that fact by the mid-1930s, albeit reluctantly and with regret. Others had not. The stellar performance of Détroyat's Caudron C.460 at the 1936 edition of the NAR shook the American air racing community like never before.

At first glance, the fact that neither Détroyat nor other foreign pilots took part in the NAR after 1936 could be interpreted as a chance to return to the status quo ante for American racing pilots. The onset of the Second World War in September 1939, however, brought to a close the golden age of air racing in the United States. The NAR were canceled between 1940 and 1945. A deadly crash in September 1949 led to their termination.

One could argue that, by the 1930s, both the Coupe Deutsch de la Meurthe and the NAR had evolved into events that, for various reasons, were of no interest to competitors hailing from outside France and the United States. On the one hand, the sleek yet low-powered racing machines allowed to compete were of no interest to countries preparing for war. On the other, these same countries saw no reason to cross an ocean to go against homemade racing airplanes, even though the prize money was nothing to sneeze at.

Romance and adventure, it seemed, were no longer at the heart of aviation by the time the 1930s drew to a close. The aerial atrocities committed in Ethiopia, Spain, and China had seen to that. Indeed, the golden age of air racing in France had ended in 1936. The 1937 and 1938 editions of the Coupe Deutsch de la Meurthe were simply canceled, as were the wartime editions of that competition, of course. It would not be restarted after the end of the conflict.

NOTES

1. I would like to thank the good people at the University of Texas at Arlington who organized the 55th Annual Webb Lectures Series for all their help over the past years. Please note that the translations of quotes found in this text are my own.
2. Robert Wohl, *The Spectacle of Flight: Aviation and the Western Imagination, 1920–1950* (New Haven: Yale University Press, 2005), chap. 2.
3. Anon., "Maurice Arnoux, à la moyenne de 389 km.-h., gagne la Coupe Deutsch de la Meurthe," *Les Ailes*, May 31, 1934, 8–9; Anon., "À Istres, Hélène Boucher bat 4 records du monde," *Les Ailes*, August 14, 1934, 11; Anon., "Raymond Delmotte a volé à plus de 505 km.-h.," *Les Ailes*, January 3, 1935, 14; Georges Houard, "Une nouvelle épreuve de vitesse: La Coupe Deutsch de la Meurthe," *Les Ailes*, May 19, 1932, 1–2.
4. Anon., "French Ace to Enter U.S. Speed Race," *Oakland Tribune*, July 28, 1936, 14; Anon., "Nouvelles de l'aviation," *L'Intransigeant*, August 6, 1926, 4; Michel Détroyat, "Le but initial de mon voyage c'est l'acrobatie," *L'Aéro*, July 31, 1936, 1; Michel Détroyat, "Comment un avion français triompha aux États-Unis," *L'Aéro*, September 11, 1936, 1; Christian de Rollepot, "Le départ de Détroyat pour Los Angeles," *Excelsior*, August 21, 1936, 3; Michel Détroyat, *Tu seras pilote* (Paris: Éditions de France,

1938), 154–55; Roger Peyronnet de Torres, "As de la haute École aériennes et pilote complet, Détroyat bat chez eux les Américains, trois fois de suite, et démontre péremptoirement la valeur de l'aviation française de vitesse," *Le Miroir des sports*, September 15, 1936, n.p.

5. This section's heading is my translation of the title of Détroyat's 1938 book, *Tu seras pilote* (Paris: Éditions de France, 1938).
6. Anon., "Le dernier jour à Paris de Charles Lindbergh," *L'Auto*, May 28, 1927, 1, 2; Anon., "Détroyat," *Match: L'Intran*, September 29, 1936, 3; Anon., "La Coupe Michelin 1929 est en compétition," *Les Ailes*, January 3, 1929, 2; Anon., "La Coupe Michelin—Détroyat et Challe ont matché . . . ," *Les Ailes*, July 6, 1929, 9; Anon., "La Coupe Michelin—le tour de France à la moyenne de 200 km.-h.," *Les Ailes*, July 3, 1930, 3; Roger Peyronnet de Torres, "Michel Détroyat, le champion de la haute école aérienne," *Le Miroir des sports*, June 9, 1931, 366; Anon., *Official Publication—National Air Races, Los Angeles Municipal Airport, Los Angeles—September 4, 5, 6, 7* (Los Angeles: unknown publisher, 1936), 41; Michel Détroyat, *Pilote d'acrobatie* (Paris: Librairie Hachette, 1957), 46–104 and 107–17; Maurice Marie Michel, "Detroyat," Archives nationales, Pierrefitte-sur-Seine, 19800035/137/17375, accessed May 19, 2025, https://www.leonore.archives-nationales.culture.gouv.fr/ui/notice/115654.
7. Anon., "Le mariage de l'aviateur Détroyat a été célébré hier près de Lille," *Le Matin*, January 9, 1934, 2; Anon., "New Orleans Is Air-Minded After Dedicating New Field," *Sunday Star*, February 11, 1934, 38; Anon., "La vie sportive—aéronautique—Détroyat aux États-Unis," *Le Matin*, February 16, 1934, 7; Illinois Central Railroad Company, "Advertising," *Indianapolis Times*, January 17, 1934, 3; Anon., "Sur les terrains d'essais—à Villacoublay," *Les Ailes*, August 5, 1935, 3; Anon., "Détroyat," *Match: L'Intran*, September 29, 1936, 3.
8. This section's heading is taken from Anon., "World Aces to Thrill Throngs," *Calexico Chronicle*, August 6, 1936, 4.
9. Anon., "Air Races May Be Transferred to L.A.," *San Bernardino Daily Sun*, April 22, 1936, 16; Anon., "Air Races Shifted to L.A. from Cleveland," *San Pedro News-Pilot*, May 20, 1936, 1; Anon., "Air Races Awarded Cleveland 5 Years," *Evening Star*, December 10, 1936, C-12.
10. Anon., "$70,000 in Prizes to Be Awarded to National Air Race Pilots This Year," *Calexico Chronicle*, July 16, 1936, 4. In 2025 currency, the sums offered were worth between $1.4 million to $1.6 million.
11. Anon., "Stand Started for Air Races," *San Pedro News-Pilot*, August 3, 1936, 2; Anon., "World Aces"; Anon., "He Gets His Air Race Tickets," *Calexico Chronicle*, August 31, 1936, 2; National Air Races, Inc., "Advertising," *Calexico Chronicle*, September 1, 1936, 4. In 2025 currency, the admission fee was worth about $11.50.
12. Anon., "Speed Marks May Be Broken at 1936 National Air Races," *Calexico Chronicle*, July 28, 1936, 4; Anon., "World Aces"; Secret Agent 1313X, "Preparations for the 1936 Air Races Go on Behind Closed Doors," *Aviation*, September 1936, 15.
13. Anon., "Air Races Lure Foreign Fliers," *Calexico Chronicle*, August 24, 1936, 4; Cy Caldwell, "Cydelites on the News," *Aero Digest*, October 1936, 72; Anon., *Official Publication*, 41.

14. Anon., "1936 National Air Races Program," *Aero Digest*, September 1936, 17; Agent 1313X, "Preparations," 17.
15. Anon., "Turner Escapes Crash Injuries," *Daily Argus*, August 31, 1936, 1; Anon., "Spreckels Leads Chatterton Race," *Evening Star*, August 31, 1936, 1; J. H. Meyer, "The 1936 National Air Races," *Popular Aviation*, November 1936, 20.
16. Anon., "The Record of the Races," *Aviation*, October 1932, 399–401; Anon., "N.B.C. to Carry 2 Plane Races," *Evening Star*, August 28, 1936, B-9; Anon., "French Flier Makes 285 Miles per Hour," *Madera Tribune*, September 1, 1936, 3; Anon., "Brillant vol d'essai de Détroyat en Amérique," *Excelsior*, September 2, 1936, 1; Anon., "Aéronautique—le courrier de l'air," *L'Auto*, September 3, 1936, 2; Jacques Mortane, "Détroyat: L'homme qui a étonné les Américains," *Le Petit Journal*, September 23, 1936, 1; Bernard Musnik, "Détroyat effectue un tour de circuit à la moyenne de 458 km. 654," *L'Auto*, no. 13,043, September 2, 1936, 1; Détroyat, *Tu seras pilote*, 157; Détroyat, *Pilote d'acrobatie*, 206.
17. Anon., "Midget Airplane Repairs Rushed," *San Pedro News-Pilot*, August 27, 1936, 4; Anon., "Three Feminine Fliers Must Be Dropped from Earhart Trophy Context," *San Bernardino Daily Sun*, September 3, 1936, 4; Anon., "1936 Race Planes," *Aviation*, October 1936, 21; Theon Wright, "Air Strength Contest Near on West Coast," *Times-News*, September 3, 1936, 6.
18. Anon., "Famous Fliers, Designers Working on 'Mystery Planes' for National Races," *San Bernardino Daily Sun*, August 18, 1936, 2; Anon., "Two Mexican Officials Will Attend Air Races," *San Pedro News-Pilot*, August 28, 1936, 4; Anon., "Air Races Will Open Tomorrow," *Madera Tribune*, September 3, 1936, 4A; Anon., "Three Feminine Fliers," 4; Anon., "Air Traffic Mark Is Set in July," *Sunday Star*, September 13, 1936, A-9; Leo Baron, "Speeding Planes Take Last Tryouts for Opening of Air Races Today," *San Bernardino Daily Sun*, September 4, 1936, 2; Elizabeth Hyatt Gregory, "Times Flies, but Aviation Keeps Pace with It," *U.S. Air Services*, October 1936, 28; Meyer, "1936 National Air Races," 19. In 2025 currency, the prize money for 1936 and 1935 were worth about $1.6 million and $1.15 million.
19. The title of this section is my translation of Michel Détroyat, "Comment un avion français triompha aux États-Unis," *L'Aéro*, September 11, 1936, 1.
20. Anon., "Chute Jumper Dies in Fall," *San Pedro News-Pilot*, September 4, 1936, 1, 5; Anon., "Woman Wins in Bendix Race," *San Bernardino Daily Sun*, September 5, 1936, 1, 2; Anon., "Aéronautique—les deux premières places de la course New-York-Los Angeles sont remportées par des femmes," *L'Auto*, September 6, 1936, 2; Jean-Gérard Fleury, "Le courrier des ailes—personnel," *Paris-Soir*, August 31, 1936, 10; Anon., "Use Oxygen on Benny Howard," *Times-News*, September 17, 1936, 1; Anon., "Largest Commercial Landplane Placed on Exhibition Here," *Evening Star*, June 6, 1939, 2; Anon., *Official Publication*, 35, 37; Détroyat, *Pilote d'acrobatie*, 203–5; Meyer, "1936 National Air Races," *Popular Aviation*, November 1936, 69. In 2025 currency, the sum won by Détroyat was worth slightly more than $10,400.
21. Anon., "U.S. May Lose Thompson Prize," *Evening Star*, September 7, 1936, 1; Anon., "French Flier Shows Heels to Americans," *San Bernardino Daily Sun*, September 7, 1936, 1, 2; Anon., "Le mois—compétitions," *L'Aérophile*, October 1936, 237; Jacques Desgranges, "Dernière heure—à bord du Normandie—l'Auto, cette nuit, au Havre a souhaité la bienvenue à Michel Détroyat qui revenait d'Amérique," *L'Auto*,

September 22, 1936, 2; Michel Détroyat, "Comment un avion français triompha," 1; Robert A. Kling, "What a Racing Pilot Thinks About," *Sportsman Pilot*, October 15, 1936, 36, 48; Bernard Musnik, "À 398 de moyenne Détroyat enlève le Greve Trophy," *L'Auto*, September 8, 1936, 1; Détroyat, *Tu seras pilote*, 158; Détroyat, *Pilote d'acrobatie*, 207–8. In 2025 currency, the sum won by Détroyat was worth about $115,000.

22. Anon., "U.S. May Lose Thompson Prize," 1; Anon., "French Flier Leaves Air Race," *Madera Tribune*, September 8, 1936, 2; Anon., "Money Makes Planes Go, U.S. Racers Admit," *Marshall Evening Messenger*, September 9, 1936, 1; Anon., "Results of the Air Races," *Aero Digest*, October 1936, 34–35; Loyd B. Dilbeck, "French Ace Wins Air Race," *San Bernardino Daily Sun*, September 8, 1936, 1, 2.
23. Anon., "1936 National Air Races Program"; Anon., "U.S. May Lose Thompson Prize," 1; Anon., "Aviation—Détroyat enlève le Greeve [*sic*] Trophy à 397 à l'heure," *Excelsior*, September 8, 1936, 5; Anon., "French Flier Leaves Air Race," 2; Anon., "Money Makes Planes Go," 1; Anon., "Le mois—compétitions," 237; Anon., "Results of the Air Races," 34–35; Anon., "1936 Race Planes," 20; Anon., "Échos—le drapeau tricolore vivant," *A la page*, October 29, 1936, 2; Desgranges, "Dernière heure," 2; Michel Détroyat, "Comment un avion français triompha," 1; Dilbeck, "French Ace Wins Air Race," 1, 2; Bernard Musnik, "Les trois victoires de Michel Détroyat—triomphe des ailes de France," *L'Auto*, September 9, 1936, 1; Détroyat, *Tu seras pilote*, 160; Détroyat, *Pilote d'acrobatie*, 213–18. In 2025 currency, the sum won by Détroyat was worth about $220,000.
24. Anon., "Poor Sportsmanship at National Air Races and Other Editorials," *U.S. Air Services*, October 1936, 7; Henri Hegener, "De National Air Races," *Het Vliegveld*, November 1936, 317. In 2025 currency, the cost of a racing airplane was equivalent to approximately $350,000.
25. Anon., "Air Prize Winner," *San Francisco Examiner*, September 10, 1936, 1.
26. Robert Myers, "French Ace Wrests Speed Trophy from U.S. with Pace of 264 Miles," *Oakland Tribune*, September 8, 1936, 8.
27. Dilbeck, "French Ace Wins Air Race," 1, 2. In 2025 currency, the sum allegedly spent to build Détroyat's airplane was worth about $1.53 million. In turn, the million dollars mentioned in the press was equivalent to about $23.2 million.
28. Anon., "Coupe Deutsch 1935: 2000 km à 444 kmh," *L'Aéronautique*, May 1935, 126; Anon., "French Flier Leaves Air Race," 2; Anon., "Souvenir Hunters Delay Air Race," *San Pedro News-Pilot*, September 8, 1936, 1; Anon., "Giant Diesel Plane Is Germany's Bid for New Atlantic Service," *Daily Independent*, September 9, 1936, 1, 5; Anon., "Money Makes Planes Go," 1; Anon., "Roger Don Rae Wins Air Race," *San Bernardino Daily Sun*, September 9, 1936, 1, 2; Anon., "Bendix Pledges Southland Not Only Plant, but Home," *Los Angeles Time*, September 10, 1936, 21; Anon., "May 1927–September 1936," *Contact*, September 12–19, 1936, 5; Anon., "Results of the Air Races," 34–35; Anon., "1936 Race Planes," 24; Roger Peyronnet de Torres, "Nouvelles de l'aviation," *L'Intransigeant*, September 11, 1936, 4. In 2025 currency, the sum given by France was worth about $13.8 million, the share of Avions Caudron being about $9.05 million.
29. Anon., "Giant Diesel Plane," 1, 5; Anon., "French Flier Leaves Air Race," 2; Anon., "Souvenir Hunters Delay Air Race," 1; Anon., "Roger Don Rae," 1, 2; Anon., "Results of the Air Races," 34–35; Anon., "Poor Sportsmanship," 7. In 2025 currency, the sum won by Détroyat was worth about $345,000.

30. Anon., "Poor Sportsmanship," 7.
31. Anon., "Giant Diesel Plane," 1, 5; Anon., "French Flier Leaves Air Race," 2; Anon., "Souvenir Hunters Delay Air Race," 1; Anon., "Roger Don Rae," 1, 2; Anon., "Results of the Air Races," 34–35; Anon., "Poor Sportsmanship," 7.
32. This section's title is taken from Anon., "Editorials—Repercussions of the Air Races," *Aero Digest*, October 1936, 70.
33. Anon., "A.S. Air Races Would Redeem Lost Laurels," *Citizen News*, September 9, 1936, 9.
34. Anon., "Money Makes Planes Go," 1.
35. Anon., "Editorials—Repercussions."
36. Anon., "Results of the Air Races," 34–35.
37. Anon., "Results of the Air Races," 34–35; Anon., "Thompson Trophy Race and Other Notes," *U.S. Air Services*, October 1936, 15.
38. Anon., "1936 Race Planes," 18.
39. Anon., "L'Aviation—Michel Détroyat gagne également le 'Thomson [*sic*] Trophy,'" *Journal des débats politiques et littéraires*, September 9, 1936, 4.
40. Anon., "L'Aviation—les victoires de Détroyat," *Journal des débats politiques et littéraires*, September 10, 1936, 4.
41. Jacques Desgranges, "Aéronautique—triple victoire française aux U.S.A.—les raisons de la supériorité technique de l'avion de Détroyat, exposées par M. M. Riffard, créateur de l'appareil," *L'Auto*, September 10, 1936, 2.
42. Lucien Dubech, "Les faits et les gens, revus et corrigés," *L'Auto*, September 9, 1936, 5.
43. Le Colimateur [pseud.], "Courses," *L'Avion*, September 1936, 8.
44. Colimateur, 8.
45. The title of this section is taken from Anon., "Good-Bye, Thompson Trophy, See You Again—We Hope!," *Contact*, September 12–19, 1936, 5.
46. Anon., "Detroyat Off for Capital," *San Pedro News-Pilot*, September 10, 1936, 11; Anon., "Detroyat Plans Cross-Nation Hop Next Year," *Albuquerque Journal*, September 11, 1936, 1; Anon., "Michel Détroyat rentre en France," *Le Petit Journal*, September 11, 1936, 2; Anon., "French Air Victor Welcomed," *Evening Star*, September 12, 1936, A-16; Anon., "L'Aviation—Michel Détroyat renonce à tenter le record Los Angeles-New-York," *Journal des débats politiques et littéraires*, September 11, 1936, 6; Anon., "Détroyat à Washington," *Le Petit Journal*, September 12, 1936, 5; Anon., "French Airman Received by Notables," *Sunday Star*, September 13, 1936, A-8; Anon., "Detroyats Envoy's Guests," *Sunday Star*, September 13, 1936, E-1; Desgranges, "Dernière heure," 2; Roger Peyronnet de Torres, "Nouvelles de l'aviation," *L'Intransigeant*, September 3, 1936, 4; Détroyat, *Tu seras pilote*, 163–64.
47. Anon., "Good-Bye, Thompson Trophy."
48. Anon., "Les victoires de Détroyat stimulent l'industrie américaine," *Le Petit Journal*, September 13, 1936, 8; Anon., "L'Aviation—après les victoires françaises en Californie—échange de télégrammes," *Journal des débats politiques et littéraires*, September 14, 1936, 4.
49. The title of this article is my translation of Lucien Dubech, "Aéronautique—Michel Détroyat fêté à l'Hôtel de Ville a reçu hier la Grande médaille d'or de la Ville de Paris," *L'Auto*, October 2, 1936, 3.

50. Anon., "Ainsi que l'aviateur Détroyat," *Le Petit Journal*, September 22, 1936, 3.
51. Anon., "Ainsi que l'aviateur Détroyat," 3; Desgranges, "Dernière heure," 2; Jacques Mortane, "Détroyat: L'homme qui a étonné les Américains," *Le Petit Journal*, September 23, 1936, 1.
52. Anon., "Échos—bien mérité," *L'Avion*, September 1936, 14; Anon., "Les faits du jour—petites informations," *L'Action française*, October 1, 1936, 2; Anon., "Aéronautique—le courrier de l'air," *L'Auto*, October 1, 1936, 3; R. B., "Michel Détroyat reçoit la médaille d'or de la Ville de Paris," *L'Action française*, October 2, 1936, 2; Dubech, "Aéronautique."
53. Anon., "Aéronautique—l'Aéro Club de France a fêté hier Michel Détroyat et les vainqueurs des épreuves aéronautiques de cette année," *L'Auto*, October 10, 1936, 3; Anon., "On a fêté Michel Détroyat et les vainqueurs des épreuves de l'année," *Le Petit Journal*, October 10, 1936, 8.
54. The title of this section is taken from Charles F. McReynolds, "Air Race Thrills and Threats," *Flying Aces*, December 1936, 94.
55. C. G. Grey, "Matters of the Moment—Detroyattaboy," *Aeroplane*, September 16, 1936, 346.
56. Anon., "The National Air Board Says," *Popular Aviation*, December 1936, 33–34.
57. Anon., "Editorials," 70; Anon., "National Air Board Says," 33–34; Charles F. McReynolds, "Air Race Thrills and Threats," *Flying Aces*, December 1936, 94.
58. McReynolds, "Air Race Thrills and Threats," 94 (emphasis in original). Here McReynolds is referring to the musical instrument rather than the World War II rocket launcher that's also known as a bazooka. In 2025 currency, the potential prize money in the 1937 edition of the NAR was worth about $2.3 million.
59. McReynolds, "Air Race Thrills and Threats," 94.
60. McReynolds, "Air Race Thrills and Threats," 94.
61. Anon., "Detroyat Off for Capital," 11; Anon., "Editorials," 70; Anon., "Thompson Trophy Race," 15; McReynolds, "Air Race Thrills and Threats," 94; R. C. Wood, "The Deutsch de la Meurthe Race," *Popular Aviation*, December 1936, 24.
62. The title of this section is my translation taken from Anon., "Cette semaine, en France et ailleurs—Michel Détroyat est remis en liberté," *Aviation française*, November 14, 1945, n.p.
63. Anon., "L'actualité—les 'National Air Races'—Jacqueline Cochran remporte le 'Bendix Trophy,'" *Les Ailes*, September 8, 1937, 3; Anon., "La technique—la grande épreuve—neufs engagements pour la Coupe Deutsch," *Les Ailes*, July 20, 1939, 7; Anon., "Le Weatherhead Trophy a été gagné à 930 km.-h.," *Les Ailes*, September 28, 1946, 1; Georges Houard, "L'actualité—d'une aile à l'autre—un renoncement après d'autres," *Les Ailes*, September 9, 1937, 3; Georges Houard, "L'actualité—d'une aile à l'autre—nouveau playdoyer pour la Coupe Deutsch," *Les Ailes*, September 15, 1938, 3; Encyclopedia of Cleveland History, "National Air Races," Case Western Reserve University, accessed May 19, 2025, https://case.edu/ech/articles/n/national-air-races.
64. Anon., "Dernière heure—Michel Détroyat 'super' chef pilote," *Le Petit Parisien*, March 2, 1937, 3; Anon., "L'actualité—Michel Détroyat, nationalisé," *Les Ailes*, March 4, 1937, 3; Anon., "Sur les terrains—les avions en essais . . .—les avions militaires," *Les Ailes*, December 23, 1937, 9; Anon., "Dernière heure—Détroyat et Guillaumet sont partis pour New-York," *Le Petit Parisien*, March 3, 1938, 3; Anon., "–," *L'Air*, April 1,

1938, 211; Anon., "Dernière heure—le paquebot 'Normandie' est rentré de New-York avec un jour de retard," *Le Petit Parisien*, April 7, 1938, 3; Anon., "Des avions américains?," *L'Air*, May 1, 1938, 269; Anon., "Informations," *L'Air*, May 20, 1938, 324; Anon., "Aviation militaire—la Fête de l'Air—Villacoublay 10 juillet 1938," *L'Aérophile*, August 1938, 170; Anon., "La technique—les avions en essais . . .—les avions militaires," *Les Ailes*, January 26, 1939, 7; Anon., "Air—le courier de l'air," *L'Auto*, February 5, 1939, 3; Anon., "Les dernières 24 heures," *Ce soir*, February 5, 1939, 3; Anon., "Bibliographie—le pilotage des avions modernes," *L'Air*, September 1, 1939, 545; Anon., "Le monde des ailes pendant la guerre—donnez-nous de vos nouvelles!," *Les Ailes*, October 26, 1939, 7; Anon., "Dans quelle arme est affecté . . . ," *L'Air*, December 1, 1939, 687; Anon., "Dans l'Armée de l'Air," *L'Air*, January 6, 1940, 10; Anon., "French Supply Officials Here on Champlain," *Brooklyn Daily Eagle*, May 27, 1940, 8; Maurice Blondel la Rougerie, "La présentation des prototypes à Villacoublay," *L'Aérophile* 45, no 12 (December 1937): 266; Jean Cuny and Gérard Beauchamp, *Curtiss Hawk 75* (*Collection Docavia*, 22) (Paris: Éditions Larivière, 1985), 87–92; Détroyat, *Pilote d'acrobatie*, 130.

65. Anon., "Au fil de l'air—Détroyat pilotera l'avion du Maréchal et de M. Pierre Laval," *L'Air*, January 1943, 23; Georges Février, "Pilote expert . . . Michel Détroyat a retrouvé des ailes," *L'Auto*, June 17, 1942, 1; Anon., "Detroyat, Speed Pilot, Wants to Aid Allies," *Evening Star*, July 13, 1944, A-20; Anon., "Cette semaine, en France et ailleurs—la première chambre civique a rendu son verdict—elle éloigne Michel Détroyat de Paris et de la Côte d'Azur et le frappe d'indignité nationale," *Aviation française*, January 16, 1946, n.p.; F. B., "Indignité nationale à vie pour Michel Détroyat, qui recrutait des pilotes français pour les Allemands," *L'Aurore*, January 15, 1946, 1, 2; René Grenier, "Détroyat est déclaré indigne et interdit de séjour," *Combat*, January 15, 1946, 2; Jean M. Mecker, "Pilotes d'essais," *Décollage*, November 7, 1946, n.p.; Dr. Pascal Ory, email to author, February 1, 2020.
66. Anon., "Detroyat, Speed Pilot," A-20; Anon., "Paris Test Pilot Abandons Nazis," *Plainfield Courier-News* (NJ), July 13, 1944, 13; Grenier, "Détroyat est déclaré indigne," 2.
67. Anon., "Détroyat raflait nos avions pour le Boche!," *L'Humanité*, October 24, 1944, 1; Anon., "Michel Détroyat et trois autres aviateurs passés à l'ennemi sont arrêtés," *Combat*, October 25, 1944, 1; Anon., "Et voici l'escadrille 'Saxonne' . . . ," *Franc-Tireur*, October 25, 1944, 1; Anon., "L'épuration—d'autres journalistes et des aviateurs," *L'Aurore*, October 25, 1944, 1, 2; Anon., "Michel Détroyat et trois autres," 1; Anon., "L'épuration—l'aviateur Michel Détroyat est arrêté," *Ce soir*, October 25, 1944, 2; Anon., "La justice bafouée—Michel Détroyat larbin de l'aviation allemande a bénéficié d'un non-lieu!," *L'Humanité*, November 9, 1945, 1, 2; Anon., "Michel Détroyat devant les juges," *Combat*, November 10, 1945, 1; F. B., "L'affaire d'Air-France—Rogner les ailes françaises," *L'Aurore*, November 30, 1944, 1, 2; Anon., "Cette semaine, en France et ailleurs—Michel Détroyat est remis en liberté," *Aviation française*, November 14, 1945, n.p.; F. B., "Indignité nationale," 1, 2.
68. Anon., "Cette semaine, en France et ailleurs—la première chambre civique a rendu son verdict—elle éloigne Michel Détroyat de Paris et de la Côte d'Azur et le frappe d'indignité nationale," *Aviation française*, January 16, 1946, n.p.; F. B., "Indignité nationale," 1, 2; Grenier, "Détroyat est déclaré indigne," 2; André Jean, "Un vilain oiseau—un

verdict de clémence pour Détroyat traître à sa patrie!," *Franc-Tireur*, January 15, 1946, 1; Mecker, "Pilotes d'essais," n.p.

69. Anon., "L'Actualité aéronautique—Michel Détroyat," *Aviation Magazine*, October 11, 1956, 3; Anon., "From All Quarters—Michel Detroyat," *Flight*, October 12, 1956, 601; Détroyat, *Pilote d'acrobatie*, 42–45; Raymond Saladin, "Souvenirs sur Michel Détroyat," *Aviation Magazine*, February 1, 1957, 15–17; Julien Dubois, "Michel Détroyat, l'As français, et son 'château' des Weppes," *La Voix du Nord*, December 22, 2024, 20, https://www.lavoixdunord.fr/art/region/michel-detroyat-l-as-francais-et-son-chateau-des-ia21b49775n2564479; Anon., "L'aviateur Michel Détroyat est mort," *Le Monde*, October 6, 1956, 7, https://www.lemonde.fr/archives/article/1956/10/06/l-aviateur-michel-detroyat-est-mort_2237388_1819218.html.

CHASING THE FUTURE

Why US Airports Seem Always Under Construction

Janet Bednarek

In the late 1950s, commercial aviation entered the "jet age." Planes became faster and air travelers—the so-called jet set—were the epitome of glamour. Images from the late 1950s through the 1960s showed well-dressed men and women enjoying gourmet food and abundant alcohol while being whisked away to exotic locations around the world.[1] These images, though, carefully avoided the airports at which passengers began and ended their journeys. Particularly in the United States, airports have long been seen as weak links in the air transportation system. At the dawn of the jet age, travelers frequently complained that airports were too crowded and often dirty. Before the invention of the jet bridge, passengers walked outside across the tarmac in all sorts of weather to climb a steep staircase to board their aircraft (and reversed the process upon reaching their destination). Amenities were few. Local officials, often eager to attract air travelers to their cities, responded to these critiques by beginning a seemingly never-ending cycle of airport redesign and construction.

"Pardon Our Progress": Those who have flown in the United States over the last forty or fifty years have all but certainly encountered signs at airports asking passengers to be patient during construction. At various times, a US air passenger would have arrived at the terminal to find projects underway to expand ticketing areas, add gates, and upgrade baggage claim areas. In the 1990s, passengers were greeted with signs promising new, expanded retail outlets and food options. After the 9/11 terrorist attacks, airport officials scrambled to insert enhanced security screening areas into existing spaces and enforce new rules that fundamentally changed the airport experience.

And especially at the airports serving the nation's largest cities, passengers experienced months (even years) of detours and temporary facilities as local officials constructed completely new, expanded, and hopefully, more elegant terminal facilities. For the last half-century and more, local airport officials have engaged in an incessant struggle to keep up with growth and changes in the air travel environment.

This chapter aims to explore three factors behind what appears to be an endless parade of airport construction (and sometimes deconstruction) projects. First, during the 1950s and 1960s, air travel grew at rates that generally outpaced even some of the most optimistic predictions. This placed local airport owners and managers in a constant state of having to "catch up" to the volume of air traffic. At the same time, these airports witnessed the dawn of the jet age and the need to redesign terminals to serve the new, larger aircraft. In the late 1970s, deregulation of US air travel led to another period of rapid growth in air traffic while also introducing added uncertainty to the airport landscape. As more airlines shifted to a "hub-and-spoke" model, cities competed against one another as airlines dangled the prospect of "hub status" to facilities throughout the country. Indeed, several cities did benefit from becoming hubs. However, what deregulation could give, it could also take away. Consolidation in the airline industry in the 1990s and early 2000s reduced the number of major hub airports, presenting some local officials with the issues associated with managing decline rather than growth.

Second, the security regime adopted after 9/11 challenged the AirMall concept, a feature introduced to the United States in the early 1990s aimed at increasing airport revenues through enhanced retail opportunities at the airport. Some airport terminal designs placed the new, expanded shopping options near gate areas (beyond what passed for security checkpoints pre-9/11), while others offered expanded shopping opportunities closer to the ticketing area (before the security checkpoints). However, the terrorist attacks of 9/11 challenged AirMall layouts, as heightened security measures soon ensured that only ticketed passengers would be allowed past greatly enhanced checkpoints, thus significantly reducing the number of potential shoppers, while the expectation of lengthy security procedures discouraged passengers from "wasting time" shopping before enduring long security checkpoint lines.

Finally, throughout the postwar period, ideas about what the "airport of the future" should look like changed frequently. From the 1950s-era "Terminal City" concept in New York to the "Aerotropolis" concept of the early twenty-first century, both domestic and international models depicting how one could design or redesign a futuristic airport repeatedly presented new target goals for airport owners and managers. As a result of these three factors, US airports have faced a variety of pressures that have encouraged them to continually chase the future.

THE CHALLENGE OF GROWTH (AND DECLINE) AND EQUIPMENT: PASSENGER NUMBERS, DEREGULATION AND THE JET AGE

Between 1950 and 1960, passenger numbers at US airports tripled from just over 19 million to just over 62 million. The numbers nearly tripled again between 1960 and 1970, when the number of passengers exceeded 169 million. Growth continued over the next twenty years as passenger numbers climbed to 465.5 million in 1990. And twenty years later, the number stood at 720 million. In 2019, the last full year before the COVID-19 pandemic, passenger numbers reached 925 million.[2] The remarkable growth in passenger traffic at US airports has far exceeded the overall growth in the US population. Between 1950 and 2010, for example, the US population more than doubled from 150.69 million to 309.35 million. During those same years, the number of passengers on US airlines soared from 19.220 million to 720.496 million, a factor of thirty-seven.

Reflecting on the first decade of rapid growth in post–World War II air travel, a 1960 *Time* article on the nation's airports concluded with a somewhat rosy statement about airport design from the head of the Federal Aviation Agency (FAA, changed to the Federal Aviation Administration after 1967), Elwood Quesada. He said that the new airport the federal government had recently built just outside Washington Dulles International Airport was designed to meet not just the needs of the 1960s but the 1970s as well. Airport designers, he opined, should think well into the future. "Not looking far enough ahead," he said, "is one of the errors we've been making through the history of commercial aviation." But now we have "forecast the requirements and are not indulging in building for today. We are building for ten years, twenty years, fifty years from now."[3]

Yet most contemporary forecasts of passenger growth proved inaccurate, challenging the ability to predict future needs. Atlanta's municipal airport, for example, underwent a major expansion in the early 1960s. It included new and expanded runways as well as an up-to-date terminal building that replaced a World War II–era converted hangar that had served as the city's initial postwar terminal. However, passenger numbers overwhelmed capacity as soon as the new airport terminal opened in 1961. Designed to handle six million passengers per year, in the first year of operation, it handled over nine million. Within three years, the city had to begin planning another major expansion of the airport, including additional terminal facilities.[4] To a greater or lesser degree, Atlanta's story would be repeated at airports around the country. Elwood Quesada may have hoped that local officials could plan and build airports for fifty years in the future, but the future often came far sooner and more suddenly than anyone had imagined.

The doubling and redoubling of passengers through the 1960s and 1970s overwhelmed relatively new facilities across the country, forcing local officials to scramble to increase capacity. Chicago's O'Hare airport, completed in 1963, exceeded the number of passengers expected by 1970 as early as 1965. Additionally, Los Angeles, San Francisco, New York, and Washington, DC, all built new or expanded airports by the early 1960s only to find that, by mid-decade, each of those airports faced capacity challenges.[5] To increase the handling capacity of existing facilities, airports and airlines experimented with new ways to handle ticketing and baggage check-in. Further, to accommodate the new, larger jets, airport terminals added long "finger concourses" stretching out from the main facility. While these provided more room for the jets, they meant longer walks for the passengers. At Atlanta, Miami, and Chicago's airports, for example, passengers found themselves having to walk as far as a half-mile from the ticketing area to the departure gate.[6]

Eero Saarinen, designer of the classic jet-age terminals at Dulles and JFK, proposed two different answers to move passengers more quickly and efficiently. At Dulles, he called for the use of mobile lounges. These large, bus-like vehicles moved passengers from the terminal directly to airplanes parked on the ramp.[7] At his TWA terminal at JFK, Saarinen planned for moving sidewalks. The TWA terminal when finally constructed, however, did not include the moving sidewalks, although, unlike the mobile lounges, these did become familiar features at many large airports.[8]

A number of cities explored the idea of dealing with the capacity issue by building completely new airports, however, the actual number of new facilities constructed proved quite small. Between the early 1960s (after Dulles opened) and the early 1970s, only Houston and Dallas-Fort Worth in Texas and Kansas City, Missouri, dedicated new major commercial airports. High costs, an economic downturn in the early 1970s, and local opposition due to environmental concerns (especially the persistent noise problem) all effectively worked to shelve most plans for completely new airports and delayed many plans for airport expansion.[9]

The capacity issue continued to challenge airport officials and airlines through the 1970s and became even more daunting after the passage of the Airline Deregulation Act in 1978, which ended extensive controls over the aviation landscape in the United States. Until 1978, the Civil Aeronautics Board (CAB), a regulatory agency created in 1938 to protect what Congress deemed an "infant" industry, tightly regulated airlines in the United States. The CAB had broad authority to regulate the entry and exit of airlines from air routes, set airfares, oversee the financial health of airlines, and generally protect airlines from competition. The means by which the CAB fulfilled its mandate varied over time, though it generally worked to restrict both the entry and exit of airlines from routes and to set fare levels that guaranteed a certain return on investment. It also carefully monitored mergers and acquisitions.[10]

This tightly regulated system had consequences not only for the airlines but for the nation's airports as well. The CAB determined which airline or airlines served which city. It restricted competition on flights between the nation's largest cities and also guaranteed flights to the nation's smaller cities. Cities wishing to expand air service had to woo not just the airlines but the CAB as well. Cities threatened with diminished service could plead their case to the CAB, which had the power to require an airline to serve specific locations. The CAB's mandate that even smaller cities enjoy the benefits of faster jet service contributed to the rapid switch from piston-engine aircraft to jets. That same policy also created the consequent need for longer runways at many airports to handle the new aircraft. Although both airlines and cities often complained, the CAB contributed to a very predictable, if not stress-free, environment.[11]

By the late 1960s, though, it became clear to many critics that the regulatory system no longer worked. They argued that it protected weaker airlines, promoted inefficiencies, and kept airline ticket prices unnecessarily high. Economists, including Alfred Kahn, who would later serve as chair of the CAB, conducted studies that unfavorably compared the nation's major airline companies with unregulated, intrastate carriers in California and Texas. According to Kahn, these smaller airlines managed to operate with greater efficiency and lower costs than the regulated carriers. He and others began to argue for a significant overhaul of the airline regulation structure.[12] Congress responded with the Airline Deregulation Act, which called for a gradual phasing out of the CAB's regulatory functions, including deciding on route entry and exit, fares, and mergers and acquisitions. The CAB officially ceased operations on December 31, 1985.

Deregulation brought a number of immediate challenges to local airport officials. First, it set off a sharp rise in the number of passengers from just over 200 million in the mid-1970s to 410 million in 1987, a boom that led to extensive terminal construction.[13] Further, deregulation freed airlines to set their own route structures, including the adoption of the hub-and-spoke system aimed at increasing load capacities by funneling all flights through a few major airports. The evolving hub-and-spoke system played an important part in the airport construction boom by promising the reward of increased passenger traffic to airports selected as hubs. The result was a level of intense competition between cities for airline service probably not seen since the early days of commercial aviation. On the other hand, deregulation also encouraged airport officials to rethink their lease arrangements with airlines. Many moved away from long-term leases to shorter-term agreements to secure more flexibility in attracting new airlines to their markets.[14]

Under these altered circumstances, airport improvement projects started or reached completion during the 1980s in cities across the country. As part of its pitch to host the Summer Olympics in 1984, Los Angeles added a new international terminal and made improvements to its domestic terminals. At the same time, Chicago secured approval for a major expansion at O'Hare; Boston started to modernize and expand Logan's Terminal C; the Dallas city council approved a three-year, $28 million improvement at Love Field; and Orlando dedicated a new international concourse that doubled the airport's capacity. Smaller cities, such as Milwaukee, Omaha, and Cedar Falls, Iowa, also participated in the airport improvement sweepstakes during the deregulation bonanza of the 1980s.[15]

Deregulation not only encouraged existing airlines to rapidly expand their route structure but also opened the way for new passenger airlines to enter the market. Under the legislation, the primary barrier to entry remained "fitness"—a CAB ruling that an airline was "fit, willing and able" to offer passenger airline service. The CAB retained the authority to determine fitness until the end of 1985. After that date, responsibility shifted to the Department of Transportation. In the meantime, in line with its emphasis on increased competition, the CAB liberalized its procedures for determining the fitness of an airline. Critics argued that this would jeopardize safety, but the CAB countered that no airline could afford to operate in an unsafe manner. As with the case of awarding new routes, the CAB operated on the side of unlimited entry and maximum competition.[16]

As a result of both deregulation and additional economic pressures, the 1980s witnessed a major shakeout in the airline industry. As noted, a few of the major carriers, including American, United, Delta, and TWA, developed the hub-and-spoke system that concentrated flights at their large hub airports and fed their systems from numerous smaller airports, putting these airlines in stronger competitive positions. Some smaller carriers, such as Western, Republic, Allegheny, and Piedmont, sought to mirror the larger carriers' strategy but had limited success; most ended up merging with other carriers. Another group of carriers followed a low-cost, low-fare strategy. These included new entrant People Express as well as Continental, Braniff, and Frontier. The most successful of this group was Dallas-based Southwest Airlines, which had begun as an intrastate, low-cost, low-fare carrier and continued to profit and grow. Newer and smaller commuter airlines also sought to find their niche in smaller, low-density markets. Their need for access to the larger hub airports, though, led to partnerships with the major carriers. By the late 1980s, the eight largest carriers essentially controlled forty-eight of the fifty commuter airlines.[17]

The rapid expansion of air routes along with waves of mergers, acquisitions, and bankruptcies not only had a profound effect on the airline industry, but they also had a significant impact on the nation's airports. Local airport managers particularly saw opportunities related to the new hub-and-spoke route structure. Though many airports sought hub status, the major airlines, especially the largest, tended to create and fortify their major hubs at what were already some of the nation's largest airports—Atlanta, Dallas-Fort Worth, Chicago, and Los Angeles, for example. However, by the early 1990s, the largest airlines often had multiple hubs. Delta had its primary hub in Atlanta but also operated hubs in New York, Miami, and Dallas-Fort Worth, as well as Cincinnati and Salt Lake City. American's main hub was Dallas-Fort Worth, but it also had hubs in Chicago, Miami, and New York, as well as Raleigh-Durham and Nashville. United had its primary hub in Chicago but also operated hubs in Los Angeles, San Francisco, and Washington, DC, as well as Denver and Seattle.[18] As previously noted, hubbing was not exclusive to the largest airlines. Piedmont established hubs in Charlotte, Baltimore, Raleigh-Durham, and Dayton, Ohio. Allegheny Airlines (soon to become USAir) had its major hub in Pittsburgh. Northwest operated its major hub in Minneapolis and had a hub in Memphis.[19] Thus, a number of cities enjoyed increased passenger flights at their airports as airlines built and expanded hub-and-spoke systems.

Becoming a major airline hub, however, often brought mixed blessings. On the one hand, hub status became a way for a city and its airport to enjoy increased visibility and air traffic. Further, expanding the airport to achieve hub status generally enjoyed the support of local business interests. On the other hand, local residents often objected, fearing diminished property values and quality of life due to increased aircraft noise. While aircraft had become less noisy since the early 1960s, they were still not quiet, and increased flights meant more constant sound. Moreover, the expanding hub-and-spoke system placed new pressures on airports that, according to a contemporary 1987 article, necessitated "serious redesign within existing facilities." While market changes happened quickly, major renovation projects could take years from planning to completion. Thus, the increase in passenger numbers added greater complexity to airport operations. Thomas J. Powers, manager of station operations for United at O'Hare, noted that if "an airline brings in forty flights at once, there are 160 possible connections for the people and the luggage on those flights." Further, as the article pointed out, "the mergers of recent years have meant sometimes awkward combinations of formerly separate carriers."[20]

The highly sought-after hub status could also prove a fleeting accomplishment, as the shakeout in the airline industry continued through the 1990s and into the early twenty-first century. At the same time airport managers in cities like Atlanta and Chicago struggled to keep up with growth and demand, other locations like Cincinnati and St. Louis found themselves with problems of contraction. Both cities had served as hubs for major airlines—Delta in Cincinnati and TWA in St. Louis—which dominated service to those cities. The authorities operating those airports pushed aggressive expansion plans in the 1990s and early 2000s with an eye toward maintaining and expanding their hub status. After TWA merged with American and Delta with Northwest, however, both airports lost their hub status. Instead of directing growth, managing the reality of declining traffic became a major challenge for airport officials in Cincinnati and St. Louis. The history of the Greater Cincinnati-Northern Kentucky International Airport, in particular, illustrates well the welcome problems and the unwanted hardships local airport managers faced in an often rapidly changing commercial aviation environment while chronicling the cyclical pattern of both construction and deconstruction at the airport.

HUBBING AND UN-HUBBING: THE CINCINNATI EXPERIENCE

The Greater Cincinnati-Northern Kentucky International Airport traces its origins to the late 1930s. In 1937, a catastrophic Ohio River flood put Cincinnati's Lunken Airport under several feet of water. Shortly thereafter, a group of Kentucky aviation boosters proposed the creation of a new airport on higher ground in Boone County, Kentucky, across the river from Cincinnati. The members of the Kenton County Airport Board (Kentucky law allowed an airport board in one county to own and operate an airport in another county) started work on the new facility but made little progress until after the outbreak of World War II.[21] In 1942, the Civil Aeronautics Administration awarded funds to develop the field, which Air Transport Command used during the war. As early as 1943, several airlines announced that they planned to move their operations from Lunken to the new facility after the war. The Kentucky boosters then proposed to name their new facility the Greater Cincinnati Airport, and on January 10, 1947, the airlines first utilized the field and its newly constructed terminal building.[22]

The new airport grew slowly during the 1940s and 1950s but entered the jet age on December 16, 1960, and experienced accelerated growth thereafter. Over the next decade, passenger air traffic doubled, prompting the construction of two new terminal buildings in 1974. An article in the local newspaper exclaimed that the new terminal facilities "should be an airline passenger's dream come true." The firm Heery & Heery from Atlanta, Georgia, designed the new terminals in what the article described as "an entirely new linear, low-level concept in airport terminal design, which now has become known internationally as the 'Cincinnati Concept.'" The author claimed that the new design would eliminate crowding and congestion in the baggage claim area as well as at the taxi stands. It would also eliminate "the long walk with heavy suitcases from the parking lot" and would be "one of the most innovative aviation projects since the Dulles Airport terminal near Washington, DC, completed in the early 1960s." The author concluded that the new three-terminal complex would allow Greater Cincinnati Airport to "hold its own with the world's finest for a long time." The 1974 article also stated that the new terminal complex gave the Cincinnati facility the capacity to handle eight million passengers—a total it actually would not reach until the 1990s. Within just a few years, deregulation and the advent of the hub-and-spoke system would challenge the airport's ability to "hold its own."[23]

In 1981, Delta Air Lines announced that it would use the Greater Cincinnati Airport as one of its hub facilities. Delta's president, David C.

Garrett Jr., stated, "It is the most significant increase in destination service we have ever made in one city in the history of our company." As a result, the airport that in 1974 thought it could "hold its own" witnessed the first in a series of expansion projects associated with Delta's growing operations at the airport. As part of its hubbing announcement, Delta stated it was spending "$5.5 million to add five boarding gates and make other modifications at its airport terminal to handle additional flights." Despite the fact that the 1974 expansion was supposed to allow for a capacity of eight million passengers, Delta's decision to create a hub at Cincinnati required the construction of a thirty-thousand-square-foot addition to its terminal into which, according to the article, it would "pack additional passenger waiting rooms, restrooms and concessions space."[24]

The 1981 expansion project was only the beginning. In 1983, the Kenton County Airport Board approved Delta's plans for an additional $38 million expansion.[25] In November 1985, Delta announced it would spend an additional $46 million to double the number of its gates at the airport. Construction on Concourse D began in April 1986. Months before the new facility opened in May 1987, on December 16, 1986, Delta added sixty daily departures, a total it would expand by adding an additional twenty-one flights within six months, coinciding with the opening of the new concourse. As part of this expansion, it also added nonstop service to Europe.[26]

Terminal expansion represented only part of the construction boom at the airport. By the early 1990s, Greater Cincinnati International Airport, as it was now known, ranked as one of the fastest-growing airports in the country. Expansion was dependent on not just more gates but on a new runway. As early as 1988, C. B. "Bud" Deters, chair of the Kenton County Airport Board, declared, "We do need this runway bad." Local opposition delayed construction for a short time, but airport officials held a ribbon-cutting ceremony for the new runway on January 8, 1991.[27] The FAA's air traffic manager for the Greater Cincinnati International Airport, San Juan Romero, declared that the airport would not need any new capital projects once the new runway was finished. He said of Delta's operations, "You could double what they're doing now, and we could handle it."[28] While the facility's "airside" might be able to handle additional expansion, completion of that new runway in early 1991 set the stage for the realization of a new master plan for the landside, including the construction of extensive new facilities for Delta and its regional partner, Comair.

No sooner had the new runway opened than Delta Air Lines broke ground on a $315 million airport expansion project. The project involved replacing Delta's original terminal (built as part of the 1974 expansion) with "a spectacular new 200,000-square-foot terminal." The new terminal was designed to connect both with the existing Concourse D (completed in 1986) and with a new Concourse E. Once completed, the number of gates Delta controlled at the airport would double to fifty. The construction project also included a new customs inspection facility; a high-speed, underground people-mover system to connect the new terminal with Concourse D and Concourse E; and moving sidewalks within the concourses, as well as additional ticket counters and a larger baggage claim area. A 1992 article noted that the construction project was "Delta's third major expansion at the airport since 1986." The article also claimed that the project would produce "the airport of the future—now."[29]

The partially completed new terminal opened in October 1993. Passengers found not only a vastly expanded terminal but also a new system for designating the terminals and gates. What had been Terminals B, C, and D (the A designation was dropped with the 1987 expansion to leave it open for any future construction) became Terminals 1, 2, and 3 (the latter being the new Delta facility); the concourses for Terminal 3 were renamed Concourse A and Concourse B (the newest concourse).[30] The following year the airport completed construction on a remote concourse, Concourse C, for Delta's regional partner, Comair.

No sooner had the new facilities opened than the Kenton County Airport announced it was working on a new master plan "to guide airport growth for twenty years." The plan included the "demolition of Terminals 1 and 2 and construction of a new terminal" as well as "construction of another north–south runway."[31] Over the next twenty years, the airport board did order the demolition of Terminals 1 and 2, and a new north–south runway opened in 2005, but little else went to plan as envisioned in 1994.

Since 2000, the number of passengers at Greater Cincinnati International Airport has fluctuated greatly, from a high of 11.2 million in 2005, when it was the twenty-second busiest airport in the United States, to a low of 2.7 million in 2014, when its ranking fell to fifty-fourth. Passenger numbers had declined after 2000 due to the 9/11 terrorist attack, while the 2005 number represented a recovery from that general downturn. From 2006 until 2013, though, the airport repeatedly witnessed often drastically reduced annual passenger numbers. Its recovery only began in 2014 with numbers steadily increasing through 2019, the last year before the impact of the COVID-19 pandemic.[32] While some of the losses in passenger traffic through 2019 mirrored national trends, most, particularly between 2006 and 2013, came as a direct result of decisions by Delta's corporate leadership.

After years of growth, the post-9/11 downturn and rising fuel prices forced Delta into bankruptcy in September 2005. It was not the only airline in financial trouble, as Northwest, United, and US Airways also filed.[33] Though Delta emerged from bankruptcy in 2007, its restructuring had already hit Greater Cincinnati International Airport hard, as it involved not only Delta flights at the airport but those of its regional carrier, Comair.[34] The situation became worse for Greater Cincinnati when Delta and Northwest Airlines merged in 2008. The merger resulted in the new Delta Air Lines cutting operations at two of its hubs, Memphis and Cincinnati.[35] Even before the merger was complete, in August 2008, Delta announced it would close Concourse C in early 2009 and move Comair operations to Concourses A and B, where Delta flight cuts had already opened up space.[36] The restructuring continued into 2009 and 2010. On March 16, 2010, Delta announced that it would close Concourse A and move all its operations into Concourse B.[37] Greater Cincinnati International Airport had fallen a long way from the days when it served as Delta's second-largest hub and ranked as the twenty-second busiest airport in the nation. Though Cincinnati remained a minor hub for Delta, between 2005 and 2010, passenger numbers plummeted from 11.2 million to 3.9 million. The numbers would continue to drop through 2013, when it ranked as the fifty-third busiest airport in the United States. Instead of managing growth, the Kenton County Airport Board had to shift to managing (and hopefully reversing) decline.

The Kenton County Airport Board announced further consolidations of airline operations in 2011. In June, the board decided to close Terminal 2 and move all operations from that terminal to Concourse A, which, as noted, had closed the year before and required a buy-out of Delta's leases on the gates. Airline operations had already ceased in 2007 in Terminal 1, the oldest of the three terminals, built in 1947. The consolidation plan required a $31 million remodeling of the mothballed concourse.[38] The board viewed the reopening of Concourse A as part of a plan to attract new airlines to the Cincinnati market. Candace McGraw, chief executive officer of the board, stated, "First and foremost, it gives us the ability to grow air service here. . . . We have eight gates in Terminal 2 right now, and we're reactivating sixteen in Concourse A."[39]

The Kenton County Airport Board was not the only one learning to manage decline. As noted, St. Louis Lambert International Airport lost its

TWA hub status. Additionally, Greater Pittsburgh International Airport ceased to serve as a US Airways hub. Airport management teams in St. Louis and Pittsburgh, in ways similar to airport leadership in Cincinnati, looked for ways to generate additional income. At Pittsburgh, the maintenance staff took over responsibility for maintaining the baggage systems and boarding gates for all airlines operating at the facility. The St. Louis airport director sought tenants for one of its empty terminal buildings, hoping that it might be converted to leased office space. In contrast, the board in Cincinnati could reflect on a significant bright spot—DHL, an international package and parcel express service, consolidated many of its operations at the airport in 2009. According to airport officials, the company's aircraft generated "forty percent of the airport's landing fee revenues."[40]

The remodeled Concourse A opened in May 2012, and by 2013, Greater Cincinnati International Airport was on the road to recovery. The focus had shifted, however, from transient passengers (those flying into Cincinnati to change planes) to local passengers. As Candace McGraw stated, "We have invested in serving the local traveling public and those investments are paying off. . . . We've placed an emphasis on diversifying our carriers, our routes and our fares and it has made our airport very appealing to the region's travelers. The airport's long-term success is directly connected to growing our local passenger base."[41]

At the same time, though, the airport's footprint in many ways continued to contract. In February 2016, the airport board announced it would demolish Terminals 1 and 2.[42] The following month, the board announced the demolition of Concourse C.[43] Further, while downsizing remained the primary theme, construction and upgrades to the remaining terminal and concourses continued. The airport witnessed a $6 million upgrade to Terminal 3 and its concourses during 2017 and 2018. The changes included "a floor-to-ceiling makeover in baggage claim that include[d] more energy-efficient lighting, new carpet and wall treatments." Crews also installed new carpeting in the tunnel connecting the terminal to the concourses as well as on the ticketing level of the terminal. The following year, construction began on a new rental car facility that would "improve access to the terminal and elevate the passenger experience," according to officials, who also declared the project as part of the airport's efforts to "build for the future."[44]

The long-term growth of passenger traffic as well as deregulation and the restructuring of the US commercial airline industry that came in its wake created myriad challenges for the nation's airport operators. The next great series of challenges came following the terrorist attacks of September 11, 2001.

SEPTEMBER 11 AND AVIATION'S "NEW NORMAL"

After the September 11, 2001, terrorist attacks, many began talking about a so-called new normal, a time stretching into the indefinite future during which many of our common experiences—attending sporting events and visiting museums, for example—would include the acceptance of certain new security measures due to an apparently perpetual vulnerability to international terrorism. This "new normal," however, became immediately and perhaps most obvious at the nation's airports. Within days of the attacks, US airline passengers found themselves in airports patrolled by uniformed and armed military personnel. Identification was scrutinized. Pat downs were frequent. While the most stringent of the security measures eventually faded, the days of arriving at the airport twenty minutes before your flight were gone. For the sake of greater security (real or perceived), Americans have since adjusted to this new normal at the airport.

That new normal not only challenged passengers' ideas about security at the airport; it also threatened the most recent major innovation at US airports—the AirMall concept, an improvement designed to enhance airport revenues, first seen in European airports. The AirMall concept reflected an international movement toward the privatization of airport operations to make them appealing to passengers. The British Airport Authority (BAA), the entity that had managed Great Britain's major airports since 1965 and that the government privatized in 1986, experimented with the new mall concept at Heathrow in order to bolster airport revenues. Duty-free shopping had long composed an important source of revenue for airlines at Heathrow, as elsewhere, but a new European Union-mandated ban on tax-free shopping prompted the BAA to expand and diversify retail opportunities at Heathrow before passengers reached customs. And it worked. Very quickly, fees from retail concessions provided 65 percent of the airport's revenue.[45]

In the United States, officials faced the challenge of not only increasing airport revenues but also dealing with an unintended consequence of deregulation. The new hub-and-spoke system worked well for airline revenues, but it created long wait times for air travelers booked on connecting flights at the new hub airports. US airport terminals had long housed a variety of shops and restaurants. In fact, in the early years, airport operators looked for any opportunity to generate revenue, including on-site swimming pools, tennis courts, oil wells, observation decks, and pay toilets. When affluent travelers predominated, airports often boasted of high-end restaurants and elegant cocktail lounges or nightclubs.[46] The shops and eateries, though, were fairly limited in numbers within the airports, and while you could get a haircut or a shoeshine and buy a newspaper or wait out a flight over cocktails, airports did not yet resemble shopping malls. That changed in the 1990s.

Deindustrialization hit both Pittsburgh, Pennsylvania, and its metropolitan region hard. Local leaders responded in the 1980s by adopting many strategies to spur new economic development, including a plan to rebuild the city's airport. The Allegheny County Airport Authority had long ago purchased land around the airport to deal with noise complaints and to provide for expansion.[47] As a result, by the time the county launched its improvement project, Greater Pittsburgh International Airport was second in total land area only to the Dallas-Fort Worth airport, having grown from five thousand acres to twelve thousand acres. Further, during the 1980s, Allegheny Air, the main carrier at the airport, grew through merger and acquisition into USAir, with Pittsburgh being one of its hub airports. The heavy hub-and-spoke traffic strained the capacity of the old, fifty-four-gate airport facility and provided the tipping point for the campaign to expand the airport and build a new terminal.[48]

The new airport terminal opened in September 1992. Much of the press the new facility received focused on the mall-like character of the food courts and stores located in the center of the X-shaped building. A new way of managing the shops also caught the attention of aviation observers. Previously, airport managers granted stores operating in US airport terminals what were essentially monopoly contracts; this enabled the stores to charge high prices because they lacked competition. The Allegheny Airport Authority, however, had contracted the management of the terminal to the BAA. Through Pittsburgh, BAA brought the European AirMall concept to the United States. BAA granted no monopoly concessions. Instead, it contracted with a number of franchises to provide food or other goods—three separate companies, for example, held newspaper concessions. Further, the concession contracts emphasized what BAA called "street pricing"—concessionaires were not to charge highly inflated prices for their goods compared to what they charged in their nonairport locations. BAA not only managed to fully rent all retail space before the terminal opened, but more than half of the companies opening shops at the Pittsburgh airport had never operated at an airport before. This provided Pittsburgh International with a unique and wider mix of retail options than any other airport in the United States.[49]

That distinction, however, soon vanished after BAA introduced its AirMall concept to Indianapolis in 1995 after taking over management of that city's airport system. A *New York Times* article announcing the contract emphasized that what travelers would notice most about the change in management would be "more name-brand stores and concessions at the airport."[50] Whether managed by BAA or not, airports all over the country soon responded to the Pittsburgh model. In 1997, for example, the Port Authority of New York and New Jersey completed a refurbishment of the main terminal at LaGuardia Airport. Though other improvements were also part of the project, most attention focused on the new mall, filled with shops and food vendors, on the second floor of the terminal in a new forty-five-foot wide, three-story atrium where a statue of Fiorello La Guardia had previously stood.[51]

Despite challenges, by the late 1990s, both hub and nonhub airports were turning to retail as a way to entice travelers to use their facilities. In many airports, based on the Pittsburgh example, the new design placed the concessions just beyond the security checkpoints. All departing passengers, therefore, passed through the shopping area on their way to the gates, while connecting passengers waiting on flights did not have to pass through security in order to access the shops.[52] Retailers soon saw the advantages of airport locations, as they discovered they could make far higher profits per square foot of retail space at the airport than at a traditional mall. However, both airport officials and retailers had to learn new lessons after 9/11. In contrast to the Pittsburgh model, the new terminal at Ronald Reagan Washington National Airport, which opened in 1997, placed its major shops before the security checkpoints in the National Hall—a concourse-level, glass-enclosed walkway between the two main terminals. That model worked well until 9/11, when the introduction of new, more stringent, and time-consuming security measures led to fewer passengers, once past security, exiting the secure area in order to shop. In the months after 9/11, companies with stores in both airports reported that their Pittsburgh stores were doing far better than their Washington stores.[53]

Yet by early 2003, airport retail sales seemed to be on the rebound generally. The security protocols put in place after 9/11 encouraged passengers to arrive at the airport hours before their flight time. Long security lines could take up much of the added time, but when they did not, passengers experienced increased waiting times before their flights. To pass the time, passengers shopped. As US air travelers grew accustomed to allowing for more time at the airport, they also began to spend more money on items such as food and books. Retailers who catered to business travelers increasingly dependent on their laptops and other electronic gear opened shops offering charging stations, fax machines, and modems. Airport hotel chains also provided new amenities, including low-cost workout rooms or fitness centers. As more families began to travel, more airports added play areas to keep youngsters happy as well.[54]

At the same time, the challenges to both address growing passenger numbers and maintain airport shopping revenues continued. In 2016, officials of the Metropolitan Washington Airports Authority, which manages both of Washington's major airports, announced a $1 billion improvement program at Ronald Reagan Washington National Airport. The largest part of the project involved the creation of a new terminal to handle commuter flights. When completed, the new terminal will replace Gate 35X, "a notorious choke point where travelers, in rain, sun or snow, are required to board shuttle busses to get to their planes." The planned improvements also included a change to the security checkpoints. As noted, after 9/11, enhanced security checkpoints at the entrances to the two main terminals (B and C) created a significant divide between the retail stores in the National Hall and at the passenger gates. In the redesign, the security checkpoints will move upstairs to the arrivals level. Although that will place National Hall and its restaurants and shops out of reach of nonpassengers, it will open the flow between Terminals B and C as well as the new commuter terminal and National Hall. Airport authorities believe that the redesign will result in greater revenues, as "passengers will have more time—and more places to eat and shop once they pass through security."[55]

Forecasting not just how many passengers might pass through a given airport in the future but also what those passengers might expect in the way of amenities has proven quite challenging. Several visions of the "airport of the future" have purported to provide answers only to find that the future turned out to be not exactly what was expected.

AIRPORTS OF THE FUTURE AND INTERNATIONAL COMPETITION

In the first decades of the twenty-first century, a number of articles have appeared declaring that some airport somewhere represents the "airport of the future." Not surprisingly, ideas about what might represent the "airport of the future" have changed over time. Since at least 2000, when a company called Skytrax announced the results of its first World Airport Awards, a great deal of press has focused on competitive rankings of international airports.[56] As with "airports of the future," the "world's best" honorific has generally been bestowed on airports in Asia, with Singapore's Changi Airport earning it for the eighth consecutive year in 2020. Other cities with top-ten airports in 2020 included Tokyo, Doha, Seoul, Munich, Hong Kong, and Amsterdam.[57] The seeming inability of US airports to compete in these international rankings has spurred a number of airport improvement projects including a massive rebuild of New York's LaGuardia Airport, for which ground was broken in 2016.[58] Repeatedly, since at least the 1950s, airport managers have worked to provide customers with what they hope will prove the model for "airports of the future."

One of the first models for the "airport of the future" appeared in New York in the 1950s. The Port Authority of New York and New Jersey introduced a new concept in airport design with the announcement of plans for the new Idlewild (later JFK) Airport in New York City. Port Authority planners envisioned an airport that could handle up to 140 planes at a time and up to 8.5 million passengers per year. Instead of building one massive terminal building, planners proposed a vast complex of terminals—ten in all—to serve both international and domestic travelers. "Terminal City" included an International Arrival building, two Airline Wing buildings, and seven additional terminals designed and built by individual airlines. The individual terminal buildings, the planners argued, would allow passengers to access their flights with a minimum amount of walking. They estimated that 85 percent of passengers would either originate or terminate their travels at the airport, thus requiring the use of only one terminal. Passengers using one airline but needing to change planes (an estimated 10 percent of all passengers) would also only need to use one terminal. Only an estimated 5 percent of passengers would need to transfer from one terminal to another. A ground transportation system would shuttle them as needed.[59]

The prediction that the multiple terminals would not result in passenger inconveniences was quickly proven false. As early as 1960, one article stated that there was an "interline problem of serious proportion" resulting in "frequent cases of baggage left behind [and] missed plane connections," with the misplaced baggage being the primary concern.[60] According to Nicolas Blum's history of the airport, missing bags were only the start of the facility's issues. Over the years, while the airport became (and remains) a key driver in the metropolitan economy, it also became known for its "jammed and confusing roads, epic flight delays, persistent crime, decaying terminals, smelly bathrooms, noise pollution, and abrasive employees."[61]

In the face of such criticism, in the early twenty-first century, the Port Authority abandoned the "Terminal City" concept, which had been seldom, if ever, replicated anywhere else. As Barry Abramowitz, the assistant director of the aviation capital program at the Port Authority, said of "Terminal City," "They had their logic, and they had their time. We're now past that." As a result, the airport launched a $9 billion construction program to replace the Terminal City layout with "a ring of mega terminals, diaphanous arenas with airfoil roof lines, connected to parking garages and the elevated AirTrain stations."[62] As one future vision faded, another took its place.

Beginning in the 1980s, officials in Denver sought to replace their original municipal airport, Stapleton International, with a new airport for the future. One futuristic characteristic was its sheer size—fifty-three square miles. It was not, however, the largest commercial airport built to date. Officials in Montreal had attempted to build the world's largest commercial airport, Mirabel, in the 1970s. At 151 square miles, Mirabel dwarfed anything built by that time. However, the Canadian airport failed to attract airlines and soon closed to commercial passenger traffic. Denver would also not long hold its title as, within four years of opening, the title of "world's largest airport" passed in 1999 to King Fahd International Airport in Saudi Arabia at nearly three hundred square miles. Though the size of Denver's airport captured a great deal of attention, the futuristic characteristic that made the airport famous—or infamous—was its "revolutionary" baggage handling system.

Denver's airport planners hoped to set their facility apart from all others not only in its capacity to expand from its initial five runways to twelve runways, from eighty-eight gates to over two hundred gates, and to accommodate up to two hundred million passengers per year, but also with a state-of-the-art, automated baggage handling system. Estimated to cost $200 million, Denver officials bragged that the new system would be the "largest and most sophisticated in the world." The fully automated system was supposed to move seven hundred bags a minute to their final destinations (plane or baggage claim) within ten minutes. From the first tests, however, the new system proved completely unworkable due to "misloaded bags, jammed carts, spilled luggage, and general chaos." The failure of the baggage system directly led to repeated delays in inaugurating operations at the new airport. The opening date was extended from October 1993 to February

1995. United Airlines, which had insisted on the new baggage handling system, used part of it to handle baggage for its outgoing flights but eventually abandoned the system entirely in 2005.[63]

Twenty-five years after first opening, Denver International Airport was again looking toward the future. United Airlines has invested in yet another new high-tech baggage system, which, according to 2020 reports, has managed to move twenty-two thousand bags on its busiest day while jamming only fifteen times. Other improvements aim at building out the gate capacity to allow for eighty million passengers by 2025 (compared to sixty-nine million in 2019). Wellington Webb, the city's first African American mayor, who oversaw most of the construction of the airport between 1991 and 1995, had his own take on the nature and future of airports: "The thing about airports is it's never done. It's never finished. . . . If you go to a city and the airport isn't under construction, that airport is dying."[64]

Starting in the 1990s, a number of individuals began writing about yet another vision of the airport of the future. In 1996, Roger Collis, a travel journalist for the *International Herald Tribune*, wrote about "SkyCity," the name given to a building connecting two of the terminals at the Arlanda Airport outside of Stockholm, Sweden.[65] He argued that "SkyCity has brought the city to the airport with a beguiling complex of hotels, restaurants, supermarkets, boutiques, bars, and conference and exhibition facilities." SkyCity also featured a number of services, including telecommunications, banking, health, travel, and fitness as well as a nondenominational church. Collis posited that "SkyCity is a paradigm of the airport of the future" and that soon people would travel not to cities but to airports, as the airport would become "a destination in its own right." According to Lars Sjolander, a vice president of the company that controlled the hotel and catering concessions at SkyCity, businesspersons from throughout Sweden often decided to hold their meetings at the airport. As he noted, "SkyCity is the meeting center of Sweden—typically, two executives coming in from Stockholm and two or three flying in from the provinces."[66]

Within a few years, however, that same Roger Collis published an article entitled "Airports of the Future Should Look Like the Ones of the Past." In that article, Collis wrote about the airports of the 1960s and 1970s that he remembered as being "user-friendly and human scale." While noting that airport managers throughout the world were working to increase airport capacity in the wake of burgeoning passenger traffic, he argued that they needed to reinvent the airport to bring back the human scale of the past. However, he envisioned that the new human scaling would apply primarily to business travelers (like himself), who should be able to enjoy "special check-ins, lounges, concierge services and 'fast-track' channels through security and immigration." Collis seemingly understood, however, that the frequent business traveler accustomed to such "fast-track" services might experience heightened frustration when traveling for leisure and finding themselves once again faced with long airport lines. The author also noted that airports would need to plan for a future in which an increasing number of passengers would be over sixty years of age and for whom long walks might be problematic. He envisioned a future airport in which technology would work to "personalize" the airport experience for each traveler, providing them with timely and helpful information and guidance.[67] In some ways, the future has arrived, as new technologies are attempting to "fast-track" passengers through airports. For example, in 2020, Delta Air Lines began experiments with facial recognition systems at America's busiest airport, Atlanta's Hartsfield-Jackson International.[68]

Perhaps the most influential of the most recent visions of the airport of the future has been that of the "aerotropolis." The brainchild of John D. Kasarda, emeritus professor of management and sociology at the University of North Carolina, the concept has proved more influential overseas than in the United States, though for a time, several US airport authorities explored adopting the planning model. In *Aerotropolis: The Way We'll Live Next*, coauthored with Greg Lindsay, Kasarda offered what he called his "simple definition" of the term: "An aerotropolis is basically an airport-integrated region, extending as far as sixty miles from the inner clusters of hotels, offices, distribution and logistics facilities." He went on to state that in the aerotropolis "the airport itself is really the nucleus of a range of 'New Economy' functions . . . [enhancing] competitiveness, job creation, and quality of life."[69]

Kasarda first began working out his aerotropolis concept in the early 1990s as part of a North Carolina state government effort to develop an underutilized airport in the Research Triangle into a major cargo hub. In 1991, Kasarda published a piece in *Urban Land* arguing for the economic development potential of a globally oriented air cargo facility. In response to the ideas in that article, the state of North Carolina created the Global TransPark Authority to turn Kasarda's concept into reality. The aerotropolis reflected Kasarda's belief that the United States had entered a "fifth developmental era" in which the engines of the earlier developmental eras—seaports, rivers and canals, railroads, automobiles, and trucks—would be supplanted with airports as "the primary generators of jobs and wealth." Though the

Global TransPark took far longer to develop than Kasarda had hoped (and did not live up to his expectations), Kasarda nonetheless continued to develop his ideas about the relationship between cities and their airports.[70]

Kasarda first used the term "aerotropolis" in 2000 in an Urban Land Institute publication. In that article, Kasarda detailed the type of development that had occurred without deliberate planning around a number of US airports, including those in Dallas-Fort Worth, Los Angeles, Atlanta, Chicago, and Washington, DC. However, when discussing the "rise of the aerotropolis," he shifted his attention to Asia, highlighting more deliberate planning in the Philippines, South Korea, and Hong Kong.[71]

In many ways, though, the aerotropolis concept has less to do with the airport itself than the areas around the airport. Kasarda has been most successful in promoting his ideas in Asia and the Middle East, where his aerotropolis concept has influenced decisions to construct entirely new airports and shaped development goals in surrounding areas.[72] In the United States, the concept has been more important for efforts to promote development just outside existing airports.[73] While it has influenced local debates about the use of "excess" land at various airports, in at least some cases, local airport managers have decided instead to expand airport operations on airport property rather than using it for more commercial or business purposes.[74]

Whether about the airport itself or its surrounding territory, visions of the airport of the future have evolved since the 1950s. Most have focused on improving the passenger experience at the airport—moving them through the facility faster while still providing them with ample amenities while there. Such visions have resulted in repeated updating and redesign of terminal facilities. Kasarda's ideas concentrated more on the economic development potential of airports that not only handle passengers but also serve as global cargo hubs. The construction activities around aerotropolis-minded airports are more likely to come in the form of warehouses, distribution centers, hotels, and office parks. Regardless of the particular vision, airports across the United States have repeatedly engaged in major construction projects in their ongoing quests to chase the future.

CONCLUSION

In 1947, Arthur C. Sylvester, the chief of the Planning Division of the Civil Aeronautics Administration, published an article in *Landscape Architecture Magazine* titled "Tomorrow's Landing Fields and Our Present Planning

Concepts: Future Airports for Commercial and Personal Aircraft." The article began with a rather prosaic statement: "Future airports for commercial and personal aircraft will be very much like the airports of today, except that they will be better designed and better equipped to accommodate airplanes and people." In that statement, he at least accurately represented the hopes and goals of airport planners in the postwar period. As has been shown, most airport projects since World War II have aimed at meeting the challenges of rising (or falling) numbers of passengers, larger aircraft, and connecting people and their baggage faster. In other ways, however, his predictions fell far from the mark. He particularly erred in his emphasis on seaplanes, which he viewed as becoming "more and more popular" and necessitating the construction of many more seaplane bases throughout the country. He also predicted that few airports would need longer and heavier runways, as only a few airports would need to handle "the large airplanes making transoceanic and transcontinental flights." Most aircraft used for commercial service, he predicted, would be designed to use existing runways. He gave as an example the forty-passenger Martin 202, which needed a runway of less than four thousand feet.[75] Just as technological advances rendered Sylvester's vision of the future obsolete, difficult to predict passenger numbers, larger jet airliners, changing federal aviation policies, new security concerns, and evolving visions of airport design have continually challenged airport managers, leading to seemingly endless rounds of airport construction projects aimed at creating the "airport of the future."

NOTES

1. For a description of how airlines created and used such images to promote air travel in the 1950s and 1960s, see David T. Courtwright, *Sky as Frontier: Adventure, Aviation, and Empire* (College Station: Texas A&M University Press, 2005), 133–50.
2. See "US Airlines (Passenger and Cargo)," Airlines for America, March 18, 2025, https://www.airlines.org/dataset/annual-results-u-s-airlines-2/. Although the chart might suggest uninterrupted growth until after 2005, there were several years in which passenger numbers declined over the previous year—1969–70, 1974–75, 1979–81, 1988–89, 1990–91, 2000–2002, and 2007–9. The decreased passenger numbers generally coincided with downturns in the US economy, though other factors also contributed. The number of passengers in the United States reached a peak in 2007 at nearly 770 million before falling in 2008 and again in 2009. The numbers began recovering in 2010 but would not recover to 2007 levels until 2015.
3. Elwood Quesada, "Airport Cities: Gateways to the Jet Age," *Time*, August 15, 1960, 68, 77. Even when finding ways to move passengers faster and more efficiently, moving

their baggage so that it arrives at the same place and at the same time as the passengers remains a seemingly unsolvable problem. Officials in Denver in the late 1980s and early 1990s sought the ultimate futuristic solution with an automatic bag handling system that instead proved a case study in trying to grasp the future too soon. (Kirk Johnson, "Denver Airport Saw the Future. It Didn't Work," *New York Times*, August 27, 2005, https://www.nytimes.com/2005/08/27/us/denver-airport-saw-the-future-it-didnt-work.html.) The answer to making sure your bags arrive at the same time as you do seemingly has not come with new futuristic technology but with more people utilizing carry-on bags, which also allow passengers to avoid checked baggage fees.

4. Betsy Braden and Paul Hagan, *A Dream Takes Flight: Hartsfield Atlanta International Airport and Aviation in Atlanta* (Athens: University of Georgia Press, 1989), 112–14, 125–26; Alastair Gordon, *Naked Airport: A Cultural Study of the World's Most Revolutionary Structure* (New York: Metropolitan Books, 2004), 217–18. For additional information on the difficulty in predicting future airport and air traffic growth, see Ian Kincaid, Michael Tretheway, Stéphane Gros, and David Lewis, *Addressing Uncertainty About Future Airport Activity Levels in Airport Decision Making* (Washington, DC: Transportation Research Board, Airport Cooperative Research Program Report 76, 2012).
5. For an overview of the airport expansion programs in these cities, see Robert H. Cook, "San Francisco Airport Expansion Started," *Aviation Week and Space Technology* 78 (June 24, 1963): 41, 43; Cook, "O'Hare Walking Distance Stirs Criticism," *Aviation Week and Space Technology* 79 (July 15, 1963): 45, 47; Cook, "Idlewild Sprawl Poses Transfer Problems," *Aviation Week and Space Technology* 79 (July 29, 1963): 33–34, 37; and Cook, "Atlanta, Miami Share Concepts, Problems," *Aviation Week and Space Technology* 79 (August 5, 1963): 47, 49.
6. For a sense of the ongoing capacity issue in the 1960s through the early 1970s, see Harold D. Watkins, "Airport Congestion Is Forcing New Wave of Expansion," *Aviation Week and Space Technology* 83 (October 25, 1965): 174–83; "Traffic Growth Swamps Airport Facilities," *Aviation Week and Space Technology* 85 (October 31, 1966): 145–59; and Harold D. Watkins, "Traffic Sparks Airport Needs," *Aviation Week and Space Technology* 98 (May 28, 1973): 66–74.
7. Dulles International Airport is replacing the futuristic airport mobile lounges with a futuristic underground AeroTrain. Lisa Rein, "Passenger Train Goes into Operation Tuesday at Dulles Airport," *Washington Post*, January 26, 2010, http://www.washingtonpost.com/wp-dyn/content/article/2010/01/25/AR2010012502837.html?noredirect=on.
8. Harriet Baskas, "A Short History of Airport Moving Walkways," *USA Today*, September 28, 2016, https://www.usatoday.com/story/travel/flights/2016/09/28/airport-moving-walkways-history/91187032/.
9. "Fiscal, Social Obstacles Slow Airport Advances," *Aviation Week and Space Technology* 95 (November 15, 1971): 35–36.
10. Mark F. Rose, Bruce E. Seely, and Paul F. Barrett, *The Best Transportation System in the World: Railroads, Trucks, Airlines, and American Public Policy in the Twentieth Century* (Columbus: Ohio State University Press, 2006), 76–83; Paul Stephen Dempsey and Andrew R. Goetz, *Airline Deregulation and Laissez-Faire Mythology* (Westport:

Quorum Books, 1992), 159–71; Richard H. K. Vietor, "Contrived Competition: Airline Regulation and Deregulation, 1925–1988," *Business History Review* 64 (Spring 1990): 68–74.

11. Vietor, "Contrived Competition," 68–74.
12. Rose, Seely, and Barrett, *Best Transportation System*, 83–96, 186–87; Vietor, "Contrived Competition," 74–83.
13. Carole A. Shifrin, "Official Hope Capacity Crisis Will Spur Expansion of Airports," *Aviation Week and Space Technology* 127 (November 8, 1987): 83, 87, 91.
14. Carole A. Shifrin, "Deregulation Bringing Airports More Interest in Own Destiny," *Aviation Week and Space Technology* 121 (November 12, 1984): 174–75.
15. "Airport Renovation, Expansion to Increase in 1985," *Aviation Week and Space Technology* 121 (November 12, 1984): 174–75.
16. Dempsy and Goetz, *Airline Deregulation*, 199–209.
17. Vietor, "Contrived Competition," 96–99.
18. Andrew R. Goetz and Christopher J. Sutton, "The Geography of Deregulation in the U.S. Airline Industry," *Annals of the Association of American Geographers* 87 (June 1997): 243.
19. Goetz and Sutton, "Geography of Deregulation," 245–46.
20. Martha M. Hamiliton, "Airports Being Revamped to Handle Increasing Traffic," *Cincinnati Enquirer*, May 31, 1987 (originally published in the *Washington Post*), 46.
21. Arnold Knauth et al., eds., *U.S. Aviation Reports, 1928* (Baltimore: United States Aviation Reports, Inc., 1928), 537–39.
22. "Detailed History," Greater Cincinnati Northern Kentucky International Airport, accessed May 2, 2012, http://www.cvgairport.com/about/history2.html; "U.S. Plans Airport for Covington: Aeronautics Bureau Submits Project," *Cincinnati Post*, September 28, 1940, 1; "City Loses Out on New Airport: Ky. Site OK'd $2,000,000 Allotted for Huge Field Near Covington," *Cincinnati Post*, October 1, 1942, 1; "Kenton Field Seen as New Air Hub," *Cincinnati Post*, June 8, 1943, 1; "Kenton Airport Offered to ATC, Ferrying Unit; Two Services May Use Field as Base; Army Confirms $100,000 Project at Lunken Cancelled," *Cincinnati Post*, March 4, 1944, 1; "Use of Airport to Be Offered," *Cincinnati Post*, June 7, 1944, 22; "Kenton Airport Nears Completion as Talk of New Field Here Fades," *Cincinnati Post*, August 24, 1944, 20.
23. Bob Brumfield, "Airports: Ours and Theirs," *Cincinnati Enquirer*, March 24, 1974, 146.
24. Wayne Buckhout, "Airline Expanding: City Lands Delta 'Hub,'" *Cincinnati Enquirer*, April 16, 1981, 1.
25. Greg Fields, "Board Approves New $38 Million Wing at Airport," *Cincinnati Enquirer*, April 23, 1983, 25.
26. "Detailed History"; Gregg Fields, "Delta Air to Build Concourse: Project Will Expand Cincinnati Gates to 22," *Cincinnati Enquirer*, November 2, 1985, 1; Mike Boyer, "Delta Expansion Gets Off the Ground," *Cincinnati Enquirer*, May 11, 1987, 17.
27. For a detailed discussion of the runway controversy, see Janet R. Daly Bednarek, *Airports, Cities, and the Jet Age: US Airports Since 1945* (New York: Palgrave Macmillan, 2016), 212–15; and Chris Graves, "Runway Opens into a New Era," *Cincinnati Enquirer*, January 9, 1991, 41.

28. Jeff Harrington, "Airport Ready to Fly When Delta Is," *Cincinnati Enquirer*, September 14, 1990, 19.
29. "Delta and Cincinnati: Partnership Continues," *Cincinnati Enquirer*, April 15, 1991, 17; Randy Mott, "Delta Unveils Expansion Plans," *Cincinnati Enquirer*, August 2, 1992, 18. See also James Ott, "Cincinnati Expansion Project Key to Delta, Comair Future," *Aviation Week and Space Technology* 139 (October 18, 1993): 51.
30. Boyer, "Delta Expansion"; Patrick Crowley, "Áirport '94," *Cincinnati Enquirer*, October 3, 1993, 1.
31. Patrick Crowley, "Airport Plans Non-Stop: 20-Year Proposal: Terminal, Runway," *Cincinnati Enquirer*, October 3, 1994, 1.
32. "Passenger Boarding (Enplanement) and All-Cargo Data for U.S. Airports," Federal Aviation Administration, accessed May 14, 2021, https://www.faa.gov/airports/planning_capacity/passenger_allcargo_stats/passenger.
33. Chris Isidore, "Delta Air Lines Files for Bankruptcy," *CNN Money*, September 15, 2005, https://money.cnn.com/2005/09/14/news/fortune500/delta/.
34. Aude Lagorce and Padraic Cassady, "Delta Air Lines Exits Bankruptcy," Marketwatch, April 30, 2007, https://www.marketwatch.com/story/delta-air-lines-emerges-from-bankruptcy.
35. Leslie Josephs, "'We Wanted to Go First.' Here's What Is Different in the Decade Since Delta's Merger with Northwest Upended the Airline Industry," April 7, 2018, https://www.cnbc.com/2018/04/07/a-decade-after-deltas-northwest-merger-upended-the-airline-industry.html.
36. Sharon Coolidge, "Concourse C's Descent," *Cincinnati Enquirer*, August 31, 2008, 1.
37. John Nolan, "Delta Consolidating Operations in Cincy," *Dayton Daily News*, March 17, 2010, 8.
38. "Cincinnati Airport to Close Terminal 2," *Dayton Daily News*, June 22, 2011, 8; Amanda Van Benschoten, "Airport Buys Old Comair HQ," *Cincinnati Enquirer*, July 19, 2011, A5.
39. Amanda Van Benschoten, "Coming In on Time," *Cincinnati Enquirer*, August 16, 2011, 5.
40. Jane L. Levere, "As They Lose Traffic, Once Bustling US Airports Have Space to Rent," *Hindustan Times*, July 10, 2012, https://www.hindustantimes.com/business/as-they-lose-traffic-once-bustling-us-airports-have-space-to-rent/story-WWRvLBzRYsPBre3cFb7JhP.html.
41. "News release," Greater Cincinnati Northern Kentucky International Airport, accessed February 10, 2020, https://www.cvgairport.com/about/news/2013/09/26/local-passenger-and-cargo-traffic-show-steady-increases.
42. Caitlin Koenig, "CVG Collecting Stories to Remember Terminals 1 and 2 Before Demolition," February 16, 2016, http://www.soapboxmedia.com/devnews/021616-cvg-terminals-1-2-history-project.aspx.
43. Jason Williams, "Concourse C at CVG Flies into History," *Cincinnati Enquirer*, March 5, 2016, A8.
44. "Terminal and Concourse Get a Makeover," Greater Cincinnati Northern Kentucky International Airport, accessed May 26, 2020, https://www.cvgairport.com/about/

news/2017/08/28/cvg-terminal-and-concourses-get-a-makeover; "CVG Continues Construction to Build for the Future/Strong Financial Ratings Support Improvements," Greater Cincinnati Northern Kentucky International Airport, accessed February 10, 2020, https://www.cvgairport.com/about/news/2019/03/01/cvg-continues-construction-to-build-for-future-strong-financial-ratings-support-improvements.

45. Marc Dierikx and Bram Bouwens, *Building Castles of the Air: Schiphol Amsterdam and the Development of Airport Infrastructure in Europe, 1916–1996* (The Hague: SDU Publishers, 1997), 252–53. The BAA model was also adopted by airports in Europe, including Schiphol Amsterdam in the Netherlands.

46. Gordon, *Naked Airport*, 140, 162, 166, 184. For examples of early examples of nonaviation revenue-producing activities at airports, see Janet R. Daly Bednarek, *America's Airports: Airfield Development, 1918–1947* (College Station: Texas A&M University Press, 2001), 79–85.

47. The Pittsburgh International Airport was at the heart of one of the most important court decisions regarding airport noise and who would be responsible for mitigating it. The Pittsburgh airport opened in 1952, and less than a year later, a nearby landowner, Thomas Griggs, sued over aircraft noise. When lower courts found the airport and its owner, Allegheny County, responsible, the county appealed all the way to the US Supreme Court. In 1962, in *Griggs v. Allegheny County*, the Supreme Court ruled in favor of Griggs, arguing that the county was liable for the damages caused by aircraft noise. As part of his argument in favor of Griggs, Justice William Douglas argued that just as a county would need to purchase enough land to make a bridge usable without damaging nearby properties, the county needed to purchase enough land to do the same for the airport. In the case of the Pittsburgh airport, he concluded, the county had not purchased enough land. See Bednarek, *Airports, Cities, and the Jet Age*, 165.

48. For a discussion of the Pittsburgh airport project and its connection to regional economic development initiatives, see Allen Dieterich-Ward, "From Satellite City to Burb of the 'Burgh: Deindustrialization and Community Identity in Steubenville, Ohio," in *After the Factory: Reinventing America's Industrial Small Cities*, ed. James J. Connolly (Lanham, MD: Lexington, 2010), 49–85; and Christopher P. Fotos, "Pittsburgh Expanding Capacity with Midfield Terminal Project," *Aviation Week and Space Technology* 130 (June 12, 1989): 329, 331.

49. Christopher P. Fotos, "Revolutionary Terminal Opens Era in Pittsburgh," *Aviation Week and Space Technology* 137 (October 5, 1992): 37–38; Edwin McDowell, "For Pittsburgh, a Model Airport at an Immodest Price," *New York Times*, November 8, 1992, https://www.nytimes.com/1992/11/08/business/for-pittsburgh-a-model-airport-at-an-immodest-price.html.

50. Adam Bryant, "Travel Advisory; A Full-Scale Mall at Indianapolis Airport," *New York Times*, November 12, 1995, https://www.nytimes.com/1995/11/12/travel/travel-advisory-a-full-scale-mall-at-indianapolis-airport.html.

51. Neil MacFarquhar, "La Guardia Sees Its Future in Smart, Small Shops," *New York Times*, July 13, 1997, https://www.nytimes.com/1997/07/13/nyregion/la-guardia-sees-its-future-in-smart-small-shops.html.

52. Fotos, "Revolutionary Terminal," 37–38; McDowell, "For Pittsburgh."

53. Jennifer Steinhauer, "It's a Mall . . . It's an Airport; . . . It's Both: The Latest Trend in Terminals," *New York Times*, June 10, 1998, https://www.nytimes.com/1998/06/10/business/it-s-a-mall-it-s-an-airport-it-s-both-the-latest-trend-in-terminals.html.
54. Betsy Wade, "Practical Traveler; Making Airports More Tolerable," *New York Times*, May 21, 2000, https://archive.nytimes.com/www.nytimes.com/library/travel/practical/pt000521.html; Kathleen Phalen Tomaselli, "Kids Can Fly High—Inside the Airport," *USA Today*, October 20, 2006, 9D.
55. Lori Aratani, "75 Years After It Opened, Reagan National Airport Is Getting an Upgrade," *Washington Post*, June 17, 2016, https://www.washingtonpost.com/local/trafficandcommuting/75-years-after-it-opened-reagan-national-airport-is-getting-an-upgrade/2016/06/17/55842f0a-3336-11e6-95c0-2a6873031302_story.html.
56. "World Airport Awards," Skytrax, accessed May 27, 2020, https://skytraxresearch.com/service/airport-of-the-year-awards/.
57. "The World's Best Airports During COVID-19," Skytrax, accessed May 27, 2020, https://www.worldairportawards.com/.
58. Julia Lauria-Blum, "Vintage Airport Made Anew: The Reinvention of LaGuardia Airport," *Metropolitan Airport News*, December 8, 2020, https://metroairportnews.com/vintage-airport-made-anew/.
59. "Idlewild to Get New Concept in Terminals," *Aviation Week* 62 (February 28, 1955): 87–88.
60. Glenn Garrison, "Idlewild Expansion Shows Gains, Problems: Decentralization Brings Trouble to Interline Passenger; Jetways, Conveyors Aid Ground Handling," *Aviation Week* 73 (August 29, 1960): 36.
61. See Nicholas Dagen Bloom, *The Metropolitan Airport: JFK International and Modern New York* (Philadelphia: University of Pennsylvania Press, 2015), 1–15.
62. David W. Dunlap, "J.F.K. Enters the Era of the Megaterminal," *New York Times*, March 19, 2020, https://www.nytimes.com/2000/03/19/realestate/jfk-enters-the-era-of-the-megaterminal.html.
63. Paul Stephen Dempsey, Andrew R. Goetz, Joseph S. Szyliowicz, *Denver International Airport: Lessons Learned* (New York: McGraw-Hill, 1997), 1, 18–21; Joe Rubino, "Denver International Airport at 25: From Boondoogle to Boon," *Denver Post*, March 1, 2020, https://www.denverpost.com/2020/03/01/denver-airport-25-years-boondoggle-anniversary/.
64. Quoted in Rubino, "Denver International Airport at 25," March 1, 2020.
65. "Stockholm Airport Sky City," Stockholm Airport, accessed May 28, 2020, https://www.airport-stockholm.com/skycity.php.
66. Roger Collis, "Airports of Future Skip Cities," *New York Times*, January 19, 1996. SkyCity seems to be a concept that continues to influence at least some airport designs. For example, as of 2020, the Hong Kong International Airport is developing its own "SkyCity" complex with retail, hotel, dining, and entertainment facilities aimed at transforming Hong Kong International "from the city's airport, to an Airport City." "Sky's the Limit: A New World-Class Destination at Hong Kong International Airport," accessed May 28, 2020, https://www.skycityhongkong.com/en.
67. Roger Collis, "The Frequent Traveler: Airports of the Future Should Look Like the Ones of the Past," *New York Times*, December 22, 2000.

68. Kelly Yamanouchi, "Delta Now Using Facial Recognition at Hartfield Jackson's International Terminal, Plans to Expand to Detroit," *Atlanta Journal Constitution*, November 29, 2018, https://www.ajc.com/blog/airport/delta-now-using-facial-recognition-hartsfield-jackson-international-terminal-plans-expand-technology-detroit/avJxkBSmoD4MBNQ6zaSuWL/.
69. Quoted in John D. Kasarda and Greg Lindsay, *Aerotropolis: The Way We'll Live Next* (New York: Farrar, Straus and Giroux, 2011), 174.
70. See John D. Kasarda, "An Industrial/Aviation Complex for the Future," *Urban Land*, August 1991, 16–20; Kasarda, "The Global TransPark," *Urban Land*, April 1998; and Kasarda and Lindsay, *Aerotropolis*, 170–73.
71. John D. Kasarda, "Aerotropolis: Airport-Driven Urban Development," in *Urban Land Institute: On the Future: Cities in the 21st Century* (Washington, DC: Urban Land Institute, 2000), 32–41.
72. See "About the Aerotropolis," Aerotropolis, accessed May 14, 2021, http://aerotropolis.com/airportcity/index.php/about/.
73. For example, see Chris Jennewein, "'Aerotropolis' Concept Proposed for Brown, Gillespie Fields," *Times of San Diego*, April 21, 2015, https://timesofsandiego.com/business/2015/04/21/aerotropolis-concept-proposed-for-brown-gillespie-fields/.
74. For example, see Harriet Baskas, "Aerotropolis: Are Airport Cities the Way of the Future?," *USA Today*, February 25, 2015, https://www.usatoday.com/story/travel/flights/2015/02/25/airport-cities/23943641/.
75. Arthur C. Sylvester, "Tomorrow's Landing Fields and Our Present Planning Concepts: Future Airports for Commercial and Personal Aircraft," *Landscape Architecture Magazine* 37 (April 1947): 94–97.

SELLING THE FIGHTER PILOT'S DREAM MACHINES

The F-15 and F-16 in the Public Eye

Michael W. Hankins

In 1973, McDonnell Douglas released a magazine advertisement featuring the F-15 Eagle. Calling it "The Fighter Pilot's Fighter," the ad copy emphasized that the Eagle was optimized for shooting down enemy aircraft in air-to-air combat. Just a few years later in 1976, another ad featured an image of the F-15 dropping a large number of bombs, proclaiming that the same exact fighter was among the most effective ground attack planes.[1] Another aircraft developed around the same time was the F-16 Fighting Falcon. Its promotional material likewise depicted a similar transition. Early depictions portrayed the plane as optimized for air-to-air combat in the sky, but later advertisements shifted to arguing that the F-16 was the best choice for bombing targets in support of ground troops.

This parallel messaging reveals much about the development of the airplanes and the institutions that produced them. Both the F-15 Eagle and the F-16 Fighting Falcon underwent similar evolutions. In both cases, a small group of fighter pilots, analysts, and engineers fought to create the ideal fighter pilot's dream machine, designing an aircraft to excel exclusively at air-to-air combat by maximizing maneuverability for the close-turning dogfight. These fighter advocates were at odds with other leaders in the US Air Force who sought to make the planes more versatile and capable of handling a variety of missions, including bombing.

This internal disagreement carried over into the public marketing materials for both aircraft. Press releases, official statements, company newsletters, industry coverage, marketing pamphlets, and advertisements all reflected the tension between presenting each plane as either the ultimate air-to-air fighter aircraft or a versatile jack-of-all-trades that could handle many types of missions. One reason for this confused messaging was the inherent conflicts that existed during the design phase. Contractors' profit motives encouraged shifting messages, as aircraft manufacturers sought to sell more airframes by marketing them as capable of performing more missions. Meanwhile, the military realized it was cheaper to modify existing planes to undertake more mission types rather than design totally new aircraft for each role.

In the bigger picture, however, the seeming confusion about the true purpose of these aircraft and how to talk about them reveals that this was a unique historical moment. New technologies had rendered the differences between fighter and attack platforms to be less distinct than in previous generations of aircraft. Of course, dedicated bomber and attack aircraft, such as the B-1 Lancer or the A-10 Thunderbolt II, still had important roles to fill, but the F-15 and F-16 proved that an aircraft could excel in air-to-air combat and ground attack. The first large-scale use of these aircraft in a major conventional war—Operation Desert Storm in 1991—blurred the line between tactical and strategic missions so much that the Air Force restructured itself in response.[2] Both the Eagle and the Fighting Falcon demonstrated that being a jack-of-all-trades no longer meant being a master of none.

AEROSPACE ADVERTISING AND THE EARLY COLD WAR AIR FORCE

The purpose of military advertising, promotion, and public relations campaigns is often confusing. After all, very few readers of aviation-themed magazines would be able to afford to purchase cutting-edge fighter aircraft, even if they were offered for sale to the public. Military aircraft advertisements are not principally intended to increase direct sales after the fashion of advertisements for other consumer products. Still, these ads serve several purposes. The most important goal is fostering general support and awareness for the concept of aerospace power as a key component—if not *the* key component—of a successful national defense. Civilian public support for air power, for the military-industrial complex, and for defense spending on aerospace technologies is necessary and beneficial for military contractors. Although individual consumers do not purchase these airplanes, those who do—members of Congress—must approve military budgets.

US representatives and senators are influenced by their staffs and by their constituents. In this sense, military aerospace advertising can build broad support for air power by establishing brand identities and, in some cases, generating "demand" for specific weapons platforms.

Many of these promotional materials are made for internal use. They outline the capabilities of aircraft in attractive ways for use by decision-makers in the military and government, or for distribution to journalists. These materials are also used for recruitment—both for contracting companies seeking to attract top engineering talent and for the military, which uses the allure of working with exciting new aircraft to encourage people to join the service. Finally, these advertisements can be used to sell other products by building awareness of a company's nonmilitary efforts. For example, McDonnell Douglas printed ads featuring the F-15 as a way to demonstrate their level of excellence in other programs, from civilian airliners to space stations to data management software.[3]

The F-15 and F-16 were born during an era in which the Air Force was in the midst of a cultural and doctrinal shift. Many service leaders thought fundamental change was needed after the Vietnam War. Military planners during the early Cold War were generally preoccupied with the dangers of a nuclear war against the Soviet Union. The Air Force, upon gaining its independence from the Army in 1947, had built its identity upon this scenario. Throughout the 1950s, the service's doctrine and equipment centered on strategic bombing operations—primarily using large bombers like the B-29 Superfortress, B-36 Peacemaker, B-47 Stratojet, and the iconic B-52 Stratofortress.

Most Air Force planners assumed that the Soviets would pursue a similar strategy of dropping nuclear weapons on the United States from large bomber aircraft, such as the Tu-95. This meant that the priority was defending against these Soviet bombers by flying toward them as fast as possible and delivering a guided missile. Designing planes to undertake traditional air-to-air dogfighting was not a major concern. A more important priority, US Air Force (USAF) strategists believed, was getting US bombers through enemy defenses. Thus, even tactical aircraft needed to be capable of delivering nuclear weapons quickly, which meant designing machines, including fighters, to be nuclear-capable and fast above all else. Agility was an afterthought. War planners and engineers were convinced that the era of dogfighting was over; fighter aircraft no longer needed to emphasize "turn and burn" close combat tactics but instead focused on flying as fast as possible. With the one exception, the F-86 Sabre (the development of which began in the closing days of World War II), fighters in the early Cold War era focused on high speed with little (if any) emphasis on maneuverability and dogfighting.[4]

The Air Force's "Century Series" fighters epitomized this idea. The F-100 Super Sabre, F-101 Voodoo, F-102 Delta Dagger, F-104 Starfighter, F-105 Thunderchief, and F-106 Delta Dagger were all ostensibly fighter aircraft, but they emphasized high-speed interception instead of maneuverability and were not optimized for air-to-air combat. The F-4 Phantom II, the premier fighter plane of the Vietnam War, was Navy-designed, but the Air Force (which bought more of them than the Navy) originally intended the plane to be part of the Century Series as the F-110 Spectre. Although the F-4 was more versatile than many of its predecessors, it also emphasized high-speed interception at the expense of air combat maneuverability.[5]

In 1961, then-incoming Secretary of Defense Robert McNamara directed the launch of a new fighter project to develop an aircraft suitable for use by the US Air Force, Navy, and Marine Corps. The "Tactical Fighter Experimental" program, or TFX, eventually resulted in the controversial F-111 aircraft. With a tandem seat and a large, heavy design that emphasized speed, the F-111 did not resemble the nimble dogfighters of previous eras. The Navy refused to buy it. Air Force Gen. Gabriel Disosway, who became commander of Tactical Air Command in 1965, hated the fact that the airplane had been given an "F" (or "fighter") designation, arguing it should have been called the A-111 or B-111 because it was better suited for attack and bomber roles as it lacked the capabilities of a true air-to-air fighter.[6]

Some air power analysts in and out of the service, including Navy test pilot Lt. Charles "Chuck" E. Myers Jr., considered the military's lack of air-to-air fighters unacceptable. "There were only two fighter airplanes in the United States inventory," he argued. "One was the Navy's F-8 and the other the Air Force's F-104. In the all-weather interceptor category we had F-101s, F-102s, F-106s, F-4Bs and F-4Cs." He concluded, "DOD was saying, '[The F-4 is] the greatest fighter in the world.' I was saying, 'It's not a fighter at all; it's an all-weather interceptor and there's a hell of a difference.'"[7] Lt. Gen. Arthur C. Agan agreed, arguing that "we *didn't* have fighters in development."[8]

DEFINING THE EAGLE

In the fall of 1964, Agan, in the role of director of plans, deputy chief of staff (DCS) for plans and operations at the Pentagon, commissioned a panel of former fighter pilots (including many famous aces) to study the then-contemporary state of tactical aviation. The study concluded that there was a need for a new fighter that emphasized maneuverability to defeat Russian fighters in air combat.[9] Agan worked to convince the incoming chief of staff of the Air Force, Gen. John P. McConnell, that an air-to-air fighter was necessary. McConnell agreed, as did Secretary of the Air Force Eugene M. Zuckert and Lt. Gen. James Ferguson, deputy chief of staff for research and development (DCS/R&D), who convinced Dr. Harold Brown, the director of defense research and engineering. In April 1965, Brown authorized the development of a new fighter, the F-X (for "fighter experimental"). These men were convinced that the Air Staff would not support a new aircraft that was optimized only for the air-to-air role, instead preferring multirole planes that could excel at ground attack as well.[10] Heinrich Weigand, scientific adviser to the director of development, disagreed; he alleged that the Air Staff preferred an airplane focused on air superiority and that the concession for multimission capabilities and ground attack was meant to appease the office of the secretary of defense.[11]

The F-X program quickly became mired in a debate about whether it should focus on the air-to-air role or serve as a multipurpose fighter-bomber and interceptor. Several factors pushed design efforts toward an air-to-air role. One factor was the Air Force's decision to purchase the Navy-designed A-7 Corsair II in 1965. This arose out of concerns beginning the previous year that several Air Force aircraft, especially the F-111, were too expensive to risk in anything less than an all-out nuclear conflict, and thus a low-cost alternative was needed. Debate raged in the service about acquiring either the A-7, a Navy plane that was effective in ground attack roles, or the Northrop F-5, which was more optimized for air-to-air combat. The decision to go with the A-7 gave fighter advocates ammunition to argue that the service had a gap in dogfighting capability. Another factor was studies of Soviet fighter capabilities, which in the summer of 1965 concluded that the Air Force needed a smaller, lightweight, more maneuverable airplane to counter emerging Soviet threats. Two years later, the public demonstrations of the MiG-25 and Su-15 spurred more concern that the US Air Force needed a more effective air-to-air capability.[12]

The third, and perhaps strongest factor that increased the Air Force's desire for a more dedicated dogfighting platform was the results of air-to-air combat then unfolding over the skies of Vietnam. US F-105s and F-4s struggled against smaller, more maneuverable MiG-17s. The first encounters against the North Vietnamese air force (Vietnam People's Air Force, VPAF) were a stark revelation. On April 3, 1965, MiGs attacked American aircraft for the first time during a bombing mission against Thanh Hoa Bridge. One VPAF plane damaged an F-8 while two other US aircraft were downed by ground fire. The next day, a larger formation of forty-eight F-105s escorted by F-100s attacked the same target. MiG-17s emerged from the mist and began a series of deadly dogfights. Three of the Thunderchiefs were shot down, although one of those was likely due to ground fire. The MiGs escaped.[13] This incident spurred several people in the Air Force to seriously pursue the development of a new fighter that could be optimized for air-to-air combat, and subsequent losses to VPAF only fueled that drive.

Despite these factors pushing the service toward a focus on air-to-air roles, in March 1966, when the Air Force awarded contracts for studies of a potential F-X to Boeing, Lockheed, and North American (with unfunded participation from Grumman and in-house contributions from McDonnell), guidance for those studies emphasized range and ground attack capabilities in addition to maneuverability. Ultimately, the Aeronautical Systems Division examined about five hundred potential designs and settled on a large, variable sweep wing design that resembled the TFX rather than the small, nimble dogfighter that fighter advocates wanted.[14]

Many USAF leaders were unhappy with this direction and called for further study in the hope of getting allies added to the mix. One was Maj. John Boyd, who joined the F-X program in September 1966. An F-86 Sabre pilot in the last months of the Korean War, Boyd had relatively little combat experience and no aerial combat victories, but he had nurtured a reputation (albeit a contested one) as an effective air-to-air pilot while an instructor at the Air Force Fighter Weapons School at Nellis Air Force Base, Nevada. More importantly, while pursuing an engineering degree from Georgia Tech, Boyd devised what he termed "energy maneuverability theory" (EMT), an idea centered around using equations from the field of thermodynamics to describe fighter aircraft maneuvers in terms of potential and kinetic energy. These mathematical constructs enabled fighter pilots to describe the type of agility and maneuverability performance they wanted from their aircraft in ways that could be understood and calculated by engineers. As historian Jacob Neufeld summarized, EMT "expressed in numbers what fighter pilots had been trying to say for years by moving their hands."[15] It also helped facilitate a move away from the speed- and altitude-based requirements of interceptors toward a maneuverability-based concept that could now be measured.

Boyd did not work alone. He collaborated with defense analyst Pierre Sprey, mathematician Tom Christie, and Chief of Advanced Tactical Systems in Research and Development Col. Robert Titus. Their efforts added to similar work from others further up the chain of command, especially Gen. Glenn A. Kent, who was the assistant for concept formulation to the DCS/R&D. These men, and others working with them, strove to eliminate excess requirements, making the plane smaller, lighter, and more maneuverable, with lower wing-loading and a focus on air-to-air combat.

At higher levels of leadership, Disosway, the head of Tactical Air Command, championed the air-to-air cause against others in the service who disagreed. "There were pressures from everybody you could think of to mess that airplane up," he said, "but we wanted to keep it pure air-to-air, knowing full well after a while that they would use it air-to-ground, but at least we didn't want it designed for that. It had to be designed for just air-to-air."[16]

What brought everyone together was competition with the Navy's fighter program, which was further along in development and had a clearer vision than the F-X. McConnell won many multirole advocates to his side by arguing that unity against the Navy was necessary, otherwise the USAF might be forced to buy another Navy aircraft. "We had a very difficult time in satisfying all the people who had to be satisfied as to what the F-X was going to be," McConnell testified to the Senate Armed Services Committee on May 28, 1968. "We finally decided—and I hope there is no one who still disagrees—that this aircraft is going to be an air superiority fighter." When asked if the plane would be used for ground attack missions, he retorted, "It would be over my dead body."[17]

On March 27, 1969, the DCS/R&D Lt. Gen. Marvin L. McNickle testified to the House of Representatives Committee on Armed Services that the F-15 was "an air superiority fighter to combat the MiGs," and that the goal of the program was "to design the best possible single-seat, twin-engine fighter for air-to-air combat." Testifying to the same committee on May 20, Gen. Roger Rhodarmer (assistant DCS/R&D) made it even more clear: "This aircraft will be designed as a single-purpose fighter-fighter. By that I mean, it is not a fighter-bomber, it is not designed to carry bombs. It is not a fighter-interceptor. It is an airplane designed to fight aircraft in air-to-air combat." He added, "We know what we want. . . . This aircraft is not saddled with a multipurpose role."[18]

Still, some disagreement seeped through. As Stuart Levin, writing in *Space/Aeronautics* magazine noted, "There's a superconsciousness (you can taste it in every conversation) that the plane must be optimized for the air-to-air dogfight," but he noted some ambiguity in that USAF "also asks (in muted tones) for air-to-ground strike capability." That added ground capability, Levin noted, "touches a raw nerve underlying USAF's loudly proclaimed identification of the F-15 as a pure dogfighter."[19]

Boyd and Sprey thought the Air Force had not gone far enough in optimizing the F-15 for the air-to-air mission; they considered it too heavy and insufficiently maneuverable. They wrote scathing memos asking the Air Force to strip the plane down further, but these went unheeded. Boyd and his associates thus began work on an idea for a new aircraft that would bear fruit years later.

Fairchild-Hiller, McDonnell, and North American turned in their proposals for the F-15 by July 1, 1969. The Air Force evaluated them according to eighty-seven different factors split into five categories: technical, operational, management, logistics, and cost. Each area had a different team of evaluators who scored the proposals separately. Thus, there was not any single overriding reason why one design was chosen over another, but McDonnell's entry scored highest in each individual category and had the lowest cost. Secretary of the Air Force Robert Seamans announced McDonnell as the winner on December 23, 1969.[20]

SELLING THE F-15

The first of McDonnell's twelve F-15 prototypes was ready to fly by the summer of 1972. The rollout of the airplane was accompanied by significant press, much of it touting the same single-minded focus on air-to-air combat that McConnell had expressed.

Although worried about the rising costs of the F-15 program, *Air Force Magazine*, in January 1972, hailed the aircraft as "unencumbered by the constraints of commonality and dual-role requirements" while focusing on whether the F-15 could defeat Soviet MiG fighters, especially the new MiG-25 Foxbat. Gen. John Meyer, Air Force vice chief of staff and one of the leading fighter aces of World War II, was not concerned. He said the F-15 "will outclimb, outmaneuver, and out-accelerate a MiG-21, a MiG-23, or any kind of MiG you might find in the next decade." At the time, some outlets reported that the MiG-25 could operate at speeds as high as Mach 3.8—significantly

Figure 7.1. Two F-15 Eagles from the 49th Tactical Fighter Wing return from a training mission in 1980 at Nellis Air Force Base, Nevada. Courtesy of the US Air Force.

faster than the SR-71 Blackbird. The Air Force, however, did not believe this at the time; the service was convinced the new MiG fighter's top speed was just slightly above Mach 3. (In reality, the aircraft's operational top speed was Mach 2.8, although it could perform a dash up to Mach 3.2 at the risk of damaging its engines.) In the same *Air Force Magazine* article, the director of the F-15 System Project Office, Brig. Gen. Benjamin Bellis, argued that such speeds were only useful if the MiGs wanted to run away, which they were welcome to do. Any actual air combat, he said, would happen at much slower speeds, and "in the real air-superiority battle environment, no known aircraft is more viable than the F-15."[21]

The rollout ceremony of the first F-15 prototype in June 1972 provided yet another chance for the press and the Air Force to publicly praise the F-15 while heralding its single-minded focus on air-to-air combat. *Flight International* magazine emphasized how different the Eagle was from the Century Series and Vietnam-era fighters that preceded it. Recalling the iconic aerial duels of the Korean War, the magazine proclaimed the F-15 "the first United States combat aircraft designed specifically for the air-superiority role since the F-86 Sabre . . . a throwback to an earlier age." Its advanced systems, the piece noted, were designed for "'eyeball-to-eyeball' combat," emphasizing its ability to defeat anything the Soviets could put in the air.[22] *Aviation Week and Space Technology* focused on the details of the flight tests but emphasized the air-superiority role and the F-15's focus on maneuverability, noting that "the prototype has been able to consistently outmaneuver the F-4 chase aircraft in turns."[23]

Early concept art for the aircraft likewise tended to underscore the air-to-air role as well by typically depicting the F-15 armed with air-to-air guided missiles, though not always. Some of the early art did point toward a ground attack role for the aircraft. Several of these pieces were used in magazine advertisements that repeated the messaging, calling the Eagle "The Fighter Pilot's Fighter," with accompanying copy that marketed the plane's alleged ability to defeat any aerial adversary in air combat.[24]

Airman magazine drove the point home in October 1972 in an article covering the test flights of the F-15 prototypes, which noted that when the Eagle becomes operational, "the Air Force will have an air superiority fighter geared to handle the entire spectrum of Soviet fighters. For the Eagle has remained what its supporters prayed it would be—a single purpose fighter dedicated to the air superiority mission."[25] Accompanied by lavish sketches from the famous aviation artist Keith Ferris, the article repeated familiar talking points that the F-15 was made for one purpose only: to defeat enemy aircraft in dogfights by emphasizing maneuverability and agility. This was in sharp contrast to the F-4 Phantom, which, as the piece repeatedly noted, was not designed for air combat. The article painted the F-15 as almost the opposite of the F-4 in an attempt to convince readers of the new aircraft's efficacy in air-to-air combat.

It must have come as a surprise, then, when only a few months later, in February 1973, *The Wall Street Journal* reported that "Air Force officials are calling the F15 [*sic*], designed primarily as a close-in dogfighter to best new Russian aircraft, 'another F4.'"[26] This sudden contradiction can likely be explained by the different audiences of *Airman* magazine compared to those of *The Wall Street Journal*. The latter's reference to the F-4 was intended as a compliment with the newspaper explaining to its readers that the F-4 was the "current front-line fighter of both the Navy and the Air Force, and one of the most successful planes ever built." Most coverage throughout the rest of 1973 continued to emphasize the air-to-air focus. For example, the Washington, DC, *Evening Star and Daily News* noted that the F-15 was "the first new dogfighter in nearly two decades"; and in March 1974, *Aviation Week and Space Technology* argued that the F-15 "represents for the Air Force a return to the doctrine that emphasizes close-in aerial combat using short-range weapons, a result of lessons learned in the skies over North Vietnam" and that its best weapon was its maneuverability.[27]

A sequel to that article in April 1974, however, hinted at a coming shift. Although the piece focused on the F-15 as a dogfighter and discussed maintenance in detail, it also noted the Eagle was designed to also have effective, simple, automated air-to-ground weapons delivery.[28] From this point on, the public discussion of the Eagle changed. The journal *NATO's Fifteen Nations* published a piece examining the possibility of NATO countries adopting the F-15 (which did not happen) and noted that the plane was "primarily conceived and designed as an Air Superiority Fighter . . . also capable to have a significant air-to-ground weapon load and delivery potential without bringing degradation to its basic Air Superiority mission."[29]

McDonnell Douglas confirmed this position in a November 1974 press release, which argued that "although designed specifically as an air superiority aircraft, the F-15 has proven to be equally suitable for air-to-ground missions without degradation of its primary role. It is able to carry a variety of air-to-air and air-to-ground weapons."[30] Somewhat earlier, the company had signaled this approach with the launch of a newsletter titled "Eagle Flight Leader" designed to promote the F-15. The majority of issues made little mention of ground attack but instead focused on the air-to-air role, in part by associating the aircraft with the colorful history of air-to-air combat pilots and planes. Famous aces such as Brig. Gen. Chuck Yeager and Lt. Gen. Michael Rogers flew the F-15 to report on its effectiveness, while another F-15 was painted with the nickname "Maloney's Pony" to honor World War II ace Lt. Tom Maloney. Other stories in the newsletters emphasized the F-15's performance in air-to-air simulations and its participation in air combat exercises such as Red Flag. The newsletter noted that F-15s were ordered to enter service with the 555th Tactical Fighter Squadron, famous for high-scoring aerial victories during the Vietnam War, which earned it the moniker "world's largest distributor of MiG parts." The photo of the announcement featured a background arrayed by the stars of MiG-kill markings, implying the Eagle was the inheritor of that role.[31] It was clearly important for the company to tie the F-15 to the long tradition of air-to-air combat history, although that did not remain the case.

Advertisements in 1976 began to shift toward emphasizing the F-15's versatility and effectiveness at ground attack bombing missions. One 1976 ad depicted an F-15 parked in front of a huge array of bombs, inset against a large photograph reminiscent of the iconic images of massive strategic bombers, displaying an F-15 dropping a large payload of ordnance. Counter to almost every depiction of the Eagle up to that point, the copy proclaimed, “This is the F-15 ground attack fighter. It doesn’t look any different from the F-15 air superiority fighter because it isn’t. Every F-15 ever made has built-in ground-attack capabilities that don’t have to be added on later. . . . Air-to-air or air-to-ground, it’s the same fighter.”[32]

By 1977, the British paper *Aviation News* wrote that the US Air Force’s F-15 were intended to be air-superiority fighters, “yet the manufacturers, McDonnell Douglas have built into this machine every possible potential to make it one of the most versatile aircraft yet built. Its predecessor, the F-4 Phantom has been adapted as a fighter, reconnaissance, ground attack, and naval aircraft . . . so should the Eagle.”[33]

Around this time, McDonnell Douglas began heavily promoting the F-15 as a multimission plane with significant ground attack capability. One pamphlet, “F-15A: Air-to-Surface,” claimed that “from its inception, the USAF F-15A was designed to provide both Air-to-Air superiority and Air-to-Surface capability.”[34] Another, “USAF F-15A Eagle: The Versatile Fighter,” claimed that “without compromise to air superiority, the F-15 was to have a secondary role of air-to-ground attack.” This pamphlet explained that the Eagle was adaptable for roles of interdiction, close air support, and tactical reconnaissance. It also introduced the idea of adapting the fighter to carry heavier bomb loads and, potentially, add a second crew member.[35]

In 1978, two other brochures, “Eagles for Tomorrow” and “The Free World’s New Standard” used similar language to describe the F-15’s capability as an air-to-ground and multimission plane; both went into significant detail about how the plane could perform in such roles and how the plane might be easily adapted for a wide variety of missions.[36]

A PURE FIGHTER

By the start of 1969, long before the F-15 had entered service, Boyd and Sprey had become frustrated with the Eagle. To them, the F-15 represented a missed opportunity: the Air Force bureaucracy had destroyed their vision for a true fighter—a simple, lightweight plane designed for close-quarters air-to-air combat. Myers recalled, “When I say, ‘We’re not happy with the F-15,’ I wouldn’t want people to think that I helped spawn *that* airplane, all I helped do was create the need for a new fighter airplane which we haven’t yet procured."[37] He said that the F-15 "should have been smaller and better. . . . That's what drove us to try again."[38]

Sprey led the effort to develop another aircraft. He gave a series of briefings at NASA and "all over the Pentagon . . . on behalf of an airplane that I called the F-X2 [or F-XX]."[39] Sprey's goal was to use Boyd's EMT concepts to design a "smaller, much more austere, and vastly higher performance airplane," one that's "a pure air-to-air fighter as opposed to the F-15 which by now is really a fighter-bomber in classical Air Force tradition."[40]

Maximizing maneuverability was key, he thought: "It is impossible to identify a level of maneuvering performance that is 'good enough.'" Achieving the necessary agility "can be accomplished *only* by rigorously eliminating every pound of weight associated with equipments [*sic*] and airframe specifications that are not absolutely essential to the mission of shooting down enemy aircraft—*then replacing that weight with more engine and more wing*."[41]

Calling themselves an "underground" group, Boyd, Sprey, Myers, and Christie soon found more allies. One was already present: Harry Hillaker, the chief of General Dynamics's preliminary design division in Fort Worth, Texas, who had met Boyd years earlier and had similar opinions about fighter design. By the late 1960s, the group had regular secret weekend meetings. Hillaker flew from Fort Worth to Washington, DC, on Friday nights, where he met with Boyd and Sprey in hotel rooms and worked on lightweight fighter (LWF) designs through the weekend. He then took the first Monday morning flight back to his job in Fort Worth.[42]

Another new member of the underground was test pilot Col. Everest Riccioni. He had flown fighters in World War II and held similar views as Boyd regarding the need for a small, lightweight dogfighter for air-to-air combat superiority.[43] Working closely with Boyd, Sprey, and Christie, Riccioni floated the idea of the group calling themselves "The Fighter Mafia," with himself as their "Godfather." Boyd still considered himself the leader.[44]

The group managed to get approval for $149,000 in funding for an EMT study, which they instead funneled to Northrop and General Dynamics to work on potential lightweight fighter designs while continuing to hold their secret hotel meetings. One of Boyd's associates who worked with the group recalled, "We just didn't want anyone knowing what we were doing. . . . This was totally illegal since we didn't provide the same opportunity to the other airframe manufacturers." Interviewed in 1987, Hillaker said of their process, "Under today's standards, I would probably be indicted."[45]

Figure 7.2. The YF-16, prototype of the F-16 Fighting Falcon, parked on a display ramp in 1973. Courtesy of the US Air Force.

General Dynamics Model 401 became the basis for the YF-16, and the Northrop 600 evolved into the YF-17. As Hillaker described, "The design objective of the original YF-16 was to maximize the usable maneuverability and agility of the aircraft"; to do so, "emphasis was placed on small size and low weight/cost, on advanced technologies, and on design/aerodynamic innovation."[46]

Early promotional material, including a pamphlet from General Dynamics dated September 1973, before the prototype was completed, confirms this emphasis. The company declared that the YF-16 was "a fighter plane in the classic sense of that term. It has been designed to achieve air superiority—to engage and then triumph over other aircraft in air-to-air combat. The man who commands such an aircraft has one primary mission—to fight, to maneuver the enemy into his sights and shoot him down."[47]

The YF-16 prototype was revealed publicly for the first time on December 13, 1973, at a rollout ceremony in Fort Worth, Texas, home of the plane's manufacturer, General Dynamics. The prototype was then shipped to Edwards Air Force Base in California for flight testing.[48] *Air Force Magazine*'s coverage of the rollout focused almost entirely on the technical details of the technologies demonstrated in the prototype while emphasizing the advantages of the low-cost lightweight fighter. However, General Dynamics's YF-16 Program Director Lyman Josephs was quoted about the purpose of the aircraft, saying, "In a dogfight, we believe, we will be able to handle anything that exists today or is on the drawing board." The article made no mention of multirole missions or ground attack capability.[49]

However, *Aviation Week and Space Technology* did, even before the first flight of the airplane. That publication's coverage of the rollout described that "although the prime design aim was to suit the airplane for the air-superiority role, company studies have also considered that it could handle a ground support mission and the capability exists for carrying a variety of bombs and rockets for this task." Josephs clarified that "we didn't make any compromises, and when we're designing an airplane for one mission, and it's small and simple, you can really understand the whole program." Yet the magazine also cited an unnamed source "close to the program" who stated, "It'll end up being a helluva good air-to-ground airplane and we're adding a few goodies so that we can demonstrate that sometime in the flight program. But that was all fallout."[50]

The YF-16 was not the only lightweight fighter prototype. Northrop had produced the YF-17. Both planes were intended to be "technology demonstrators" to evaluate specific new technologies. Beginning in January 1974, the Air Force Flight Test Center created a Joint Test Force to evaluate the prototypes. Led by Lt. Col. James R. Rider, the team coordinated the test plan with General Dynamics and Northrup, focusing broadly on maneuverability and acceleration as well as some specific performance tasks.[51] As of spring 1974, Air Force leaders still viewed the prototype program as a "technology demonstrator," not as a basis for procuring another new airplane. That soon changed.

James Schlesinger, who became the secretary of defense in July 1973, worked to convince the new air force chief of staff, Gen. George Brown, of the need to procure a lightweight fighter. In March 1974, Brown created a study group for the issue; it concluded that the Air Force should buy an operational version of the LWF as a complement to the F-15. However, the study also recommended that although this potential LWF should be "optimized for close-in air-to-air combat with a gun and close-in IR [heat-seeking] missiles," it should also possess "ground attack capability . . . greater than the F-4" and be capable of delivering nuclear weapons.[52] With this show of

Figure 7.3. A 1973 advertisement for the McDonnell Douglas F-15 Eagle emphasizes the aircraft's air-to-air capabilities. Courtesy of the Boeing Company.

Figure 7.4. This 1976 advertisement for the McDonnell Douglas F-15 Eagle notes the aircraft's ground attack capabilities. Courtesy of the Boeing Company.

support, on April 29, 1974, Schlesinger ordered that the prototype program was no longer a technology demonstrator but a competitive flyoff; the winner would go into production.[53]

Both aircraft performed well in test flights, although the YF-17 did not meet all of Northrup's predictions. Some of the pilots thought the YF-17 was easier to fly, as Rider recalled: "You had to fly the YF-16 all the time." But regarding the YF-17, he said, "You could put your daughter in it and it would go fast. It was a piece of cake!"[54]

On January 13, 1975, the Air Force announced that they had selected the YF-16. Secretary of the Air Force John McLucas insisted that the key factor deciding in favor of the YF-16 was performance. He argued that the YF-16 "had advantages in agility, in acceleration, in turn rate and endurance over the YF-17 . . . better visibility and better deceleration. . . . The YF-16 had lower drag and was a cleaner design."[55] Clearly, the performance characteristics that the Fighter Mafia valued, especially maneuverability, were the deciding factors.

Despite these early efforts and the intentions of the Fighter Mafia to make the ultimate air-to-air-only fighter plane, the Air Force and General Dynamics never truly saw the F-16 Fighting Falcon in quite the same way. Instead, even before the F-16 had been selected as the winner, they championed its versatility as a multirole plane capable of bombing missions. Promotional material from the manufacturer released during the 1974 competition presented the F-16 as an "air combat fighter" that used advanced technologies and techniques to maximize its ability as a maneuvering dogfighter. Yet the pamphlet also emphasized the versatility of the F-16, noting that it possessed a large ground strike capability that could be tailored for a variety of missions. The avionics systems also emphasized this versatility and ground attack capability.[56]

A MUTILATION OF CHARACTER

The F-16 Fighting Falcon prototype was the physical manifestation of the Fighter Mafia's ideal. However, after winning the competition in January 1975, the F-16 design went to the Air Force Configuration Control Committee, headed by former fighter pilot Gen. Alton Slay, to produce an operational version of the plane.[57]

The production version of the F-16 added almost one thousand pounds in structural and equipment changes and additional fuel storage. This included more pylons for ground attack ordnance, with the existing pylons strengthened to increase their weight limits. The loading capacity almost doubled, from 7,700 pounds to 15,200 in the production model.[58]

Despite the Fighter Mafia's objections, the Air Force added a ground-looking, all-weather, night-capable, medium-range radar to the F-16, the Westinghouse AN/APG-66. The company maintained that this system was "The Fighter Pilot's Radar," which would "allow the pilot to keep his head up and his hands on the throttle and stick throughout a dogfight engagement." With the flick of a switch, the radar provided ground mapping, improved with a Doppler beam, for both navigation and weapons delivery.[59]

Slay thought that the F-16's function as a complement to the F-15 dictated that it should be a multirole aircraft. Describing the new plane to the Senate in 1976, he argued, "The F-16 has a capability that the F-15 does not have, deliberately so. We did not choose to burden the F-15 radar with a significant air-to-ground capability. We have engineered the F-16 radar to have very good ground mapping [. . . and] to do an extremely good job of air-to-ground missions." He argued that the plane's excellent maneuverability was useful in roles beyond dogfighting: "We also found that the things that made [the F-16] good in an air-to-air role . . . were extremely good in [an] air-to-ground context." He concluded, "We got more than we paid for in having a multipurpose capable airplane."[60]

The move from creating a dedicated air-superiority fighter to a multirole aircraft played out in the press as well. In the weeks after the F-16 was selected in January 1975, many reporters, officials, politicians, and test evaluators emphasized that the Fighting Falcon was supposed to be a dedicated air combat fighter. One reporter covering the announcement emphasized that "the stress in design of the lightweight fighter has been for maximum maneuverability and handling in aerial dogfights."[61] Seven months later, this line had shifted. David Lewis, the chairman and CEO of General Dynamics, still emphasized the dogfighting aspect of the F-16 but added, "The versatile F-16 proved to have an exceptional air-to-ground capability with weapons delivery ranges far better than current operational aircraft."[62]

The Fighter Mafia and their allies fought against Slay's modifications. In 1975, Christie wrote a memo arguing that the changes made to the F-16 were "unacceptable." He said the "extensive air-to-ground capability of [the] proposed configuration compromises air-to-air capability."[63] Chuck Myers was infuriated. He sent a memo to Schlesinger's special assistant, Martin Hoffman, arguing that the changes made to the plane made it "a far cry from the austere FIGHTER" that the Fighter Mafia had envisioned.[64] He included a paper titled "F-16 (LWF/ACF) PROGRAM RESTORATION." It complained about the inclusion of ground attack and radar capability, then charged, "The expansion of mission spectrum is accomplished with an associated increases [*sic*] in weight, complexity, support burden, and a loss of air combat maneuvering capability, the one mission for which the original design had been optimized." The paper concluded, "This mutilation of the character of the LWF through the ACF missionization process is a management travesty which cannot go unchallenged."[65]

SELLING THE F-16

To promote the missionized production model of the F-16A, General Dynamics released an updated version of their earlier pamphlet to explain some of the changes that had been made. The pamphlet clarified that while maneuverability for the air-superiority role was the primary design consideration, "a natural fallout of this concept . . . is an outstanding strike mission capability," which enabled "delivery of a wide variety of guided and freefall bombs, dispensers, and air-to-ground guided missiles."[66] A press release from the company around this time called the F-16 "a replacement aircraft for the aging F-4 Phantom II fighters" and added that the Navy was considering the aircraft to meet its needs for a plane with both fighter and attack capabilities.[67]

General Dynamics clearly thought of the F-16 as a multirole platform even before full-scale production began; other press outlets continued reporting in a similar vein. *Aviation Week and Space Technology*, for example, noted that the prototype was not solely focused on air-to-air, as some of its advocates may have wanted, because of "the company's decision early in the program to provide the prototype with a tactical ground support capability, although it was ostensibly for a fighter technology program."[68]

One major reason for the shift in rhetoric toward an emphasis on the F-16's ground attack capabilities was the desire to generate foreign sales. In July 1975, *The New York Times* noted skepticism from some that the F-16 was not suited for a potential war against the Soviets in Europe. The plane was "a superb toy," one British fighter pilot told the paper, who explained that the Fighting Falcon's purpose was to "win dogfights and insure air superiority." Other unnamed specialists told the paper that NATO countries that decided to buy the F-16 "glossed over [its] deficiencies as a ground attack aircraft, and debate continues over what the proper role should be, especially in light of the kind of planes the Soviets are starting to put into service." Gen. John

Vogt, commander of Allied Air Forces Central Europe and of US Air Forces in Europe, agreed, telling the press, "One major, if not the major role is to provide a mass of fire power in support of the ground armies to turn off heavy Soviet armor in great quantities." The *Times* added that the newest Soviet aircraft—like the MiG-25, MiG-23, and Su-19 (the initial reporting name for the Su-24)—all had significant ground attack capability, implying that US and NATO forces should pursue the same.[69]

In March of 1976, the Royal Aeronautical Society's *Aerospace* magazine published its report on the YF-16 flight tests. It emphasized the air-to-air role, comparing the plane to the beloved air combat fighter of World War II, the P-51 Mustang. The magazine also compared it to the MiG-21, which had been more effective than expected in air-to-air combat against F-4s and F-105s in the Vietnam War. Despite this initial focus on air combat, the publication noted that the production model greatly increased its ground attack capability to make the plane more multirole capable, concluding, "We have found the YF-16 to be an excellent load carrier with the required flexibility in types of argument."[70]

Air Force Magazine's flight test report was written by the director of the F-16 Joint Test Force, Lt. Col. James Rider. He emphasized the air-to-air aspect of the fighter and its superior maneuverability but did acknowledge that "the production F-16 is designed for air-to-air and air-to-surface roles. The air-to-air capability will not be compromised in developing the air-to-surface capability." Rider noted that one of the important features of the F-16 was a lesson learned from Vietnam: the ability to switch from air-to-air mode to air-to-ground mode and back quickly, without looking down into the cockpit. The complicated array of radar controls and weapons control systems could all be automated to a single switch on the throttle.[71]

In December of 1976, *The New York Times* covered the F-16 in a very different way, emphasizing its role as a tank killer. According to the paper, Brig. Gen. James Abrahamson, director of the F-16 program, saw the F-16 "as an answer to both the more sophisticated Soviet fighters now deployed in central Europe and to Soviet tank superiority." The paper continued summarizing Abrahamson: "Tactically [the F-16's] role is between that of the F-15, designed to engage and defeat the most sophisticated Soviet fighters, and that of the A-10, a heavy, slower ground support aircraft of great fire power. The F-16 is also intended to supplement the F-111 and the F-4 in air-to-surface operations against hostile armor."[72]

This emphasis on air-to-ground and versatility was anathema to the wishes of the Fighter Mafia and their desire for a "pure" air-to-air fighter.

Figure 7.5. A 1978 advertisement for the General Dynamics F-16 Fighting Falcon highlights the multirole capabilities of the aircraft: that it excels in both air-to-air and air-to-ground missions. Courtesy of the Lockheed Martin Corporation.

To counter these arguments, in January 1977, General Dynamics released a presentation claiming that the idea the F-16 prototype had been ruined or compromised by the changes to the production model was a myth. The production model was actually quite close to the prototype, and in some ways was superior.[73] By this point, the company and the Air Force had fully embraced the idea of the F-16 as a multirole aircraft and plowed ahead with this as the main communications strategy in future promotional material.

The idea that the F-16 fit in between the F-15 and the A-10 was again emphasized in a General Dynamics Program Summary presented later in 1977, which officially referred to the plane not as an "air combat fighter" but as a "multirole fighter." The presentation emphasized the versatility of the F-16, noting that it was capable as a dogfighter but could also "deliver a larger air-to-surface payload over a greater distance than any fighter in its class." Infographics positioned the F-16, literally, between the F-15, F-111, and A-10, claiming it was capable of performing and complementing all of those aircraft on their missions.[74] A pamphlet from the same year also emphasized versatility, defining the plane as "capable of establishing superiority in air-to-air combat. In addition, it can carry exceptionally heavy loads of missiles and bombs for air-to-ground attack missions."[75]

General Dynamics published a new booklet in April 1977 branding the F-16 as a multirole fighter, emphasizing versatility and the ability to excel in ground attack as well as air-to-air combat.[76] Almost every press release from the contractor from 1977 on referred to the plane as the multirole fighter or the "multimission" fighter.[77] Magazine inserts began emphasizing the same. A 1978 advertisement featured the multirole capabilities of the plane, a trend that lasted into the 1980s, although this was not exclusively the case, as one 1988 ad still emphasized the air-to-air role of the plane.[78]

By the fall of 1978, the backstory had shifted to the point of insisting that the F-16 had been "designed as a 'multi-role fighter'"—almost the opposite of the Fighter Mafia's intentions. H. F. Rogers, the vice president of General Dynamics and director of the F-16 program, claimed that "the Air Force was looking for a new jet capable of both air-to-air and air-to-ground combat."[79]

DUAL ROLE FIGHTERS

The momentum taking both aircraft toward a multirole design was not only due to economic concerns or institutional momentum. The F-15 and F-16 were both designed at a time of significant technological change that began to blur the line between tactical and strategic roles. The period between the Vietnam War and the 1991 Gulf War can be considered a second interwar period. Like the first interwar period between the world wars, the 1970s and 1980s were a time of massive changes to US military technology, doctrine, and training. These changes allowed smaller tactical aircraft to become more successful at a wider array of mission types.[80]

Other technological improvements changed the way the Air Force considered and employed tactical aircraft. Improvements in radar technology and in guided missiles meant that missiles could lock and be fired from further away and from all angles rather than requiring a combatant to maneuver behind an enemy. The AIM-9L version of the Sidewinder missile was one significant development in that regard. New support systems such as the Air Force's E-3 Sentry AWACS (Airborne Early Warning and Control System) aircraft allowed for the identification of enemy aircraft at further ranges.[81] Massive improvements in computer processing power contributed to innovations in flight controls and cockpit displays. Compared to aircrews of previous generations of aircraft like the F-4 or F-86, computers were able to automate significant portions of the workload for F-15 and F-16 pilots, as well as give them more relevant information through an innovative Head-Up Display (HUD) that let them focus their view outside the aircraft rather than looking down at instruments or fumbling with complicated switches. Computer-assisted flight controls partnered with advances in radar and navigation technology, all of which allowed the aircraft to be more capable and versatile.[82]

Perhaps the most consequential and visible development was precision-guided munitions (PGMs). First debuted in small numbers in the final years of the Vietnam War, PGMs allowed aircraft to drop bombs on specific targets with significantly more accuracy using a variety of guidance mechanisms. Advancements in infrared targeting systems allowed strikes at night and in adverse weather conditions. Although these weapons were not perfect and were limited by the quality of intelligence information, PGMs allowed small groups of tactical aircraft (or single planes) to destroy targets that previously would have required large formations of strategic bombers and with less collateral damage.[83]

The end result of the technological and doctrinal changes that occurred throughout this second interwar period was that tactical and strategic roles for aircraft became less distinct. With PGMs, a small fighter like an F-16 could perform strategic bombing missions. After the combat experience of the Gulf War in 1991, the Air Force realized how significant these changes were and reorganized their major commands in response. The command that had defined the Air Force since its inception—Strategic Air Command—was disestablished, along with Tactical Air Command, to create the new Air Combat Command in 1992.[84]

Thus, both the F-15 and F-16 emerged during a time of transition and transformation, the extent of which was not completely evident at the time. In any case, by 1978, both the F-15 and F-16 were promoted by their manufacturers as multimission planes with significant ground attack capability. Air force leaders had another major concern about preparedness for potential conflict: The perception that the F-111 was getting too old. The F-111, a bomber and attack aircraft despite its "F" designation, was designed for high-speed flying at altitudes low enough to avoid detection by enemy radar. By the late 1970s, that aircraft was seen as incapable of handling advanced air defense threats. The Air Force procured an improved model, the F-111F, in 1978. That variant was significantly enhanced in 1982 when planners incorporated the AN/AVQ-26 Pave Tack pod into the F-111F's weapons bay. The pod, which used infrared sensors and a laser designator, allowed for the delivery of PGMs (albeit requiring difficult high-g maneuvering) and increased the accuracy of some unguided munitions. The new system increased the service life of the F-111, and it proved effective in both Operations El Dorado Canyon in 1986 and Desert Storm in 1991.[85] Despite the upgrades, concerns regarding the age of these aircraft prompted the commander of Tactical Air Command, Gen. Wilbur L. "Bill" Creech, to study alternatives for an "Enhanced Tactical Fighter" (ETF) to complement or even replace the F-111F.

The goal of the ETF was to devise a high-speed aircraft capable of undertaking low-altitude deep strikes against enemy ground targets without needing to rely on fighter escorts. Because there was a need for ground attack and an air-to-air component, the program became known as the "Dual Role Fighter." The Air Force solicited a proposal from McDonnell Douglas to modify the F-15 for this purpose. Creech met with the president of McDonnell Douglas while other Air Force leaders took similar steps to collaborate with the company. Creech and others outlined the exact air-to-ground weapons and avionics capabilities they wanted and concluded, "It's either go dual-role or get out of the F-15 business."[86]

McDonnell Douglas promoted a modified F-15 for exactly that role, producing new brochures proclaiming, "F-15 Eagle—the World's Best Dual Role Fighter for Today and Tomorrow."[87] This modified F-15 was not alone—General Dynamics, working with others in the Air Force who thought the F-16 was a better fit for the Dual Role Fighter, also sought a modified F-16 for this role. The result was the F-16XL, which used a larger delta wing to carry more air-to-ground weapons.

In 1981, the Air Force announced a comparative flight demonstration between the F-15E and the F-16XL. The planes, which had both originally been designed exclusively for air-to-air combat, were in a competitive flyoff to determine which was the better bomber. The Air Force announced the F-15E as the winner in 1984. The "Strike Eagle" went on to a long operational career while the F-16XL prototypes were sent to NASA for a successful career in flight testing.[88]

CONCLUSION

By the eve of the 1991 Gulf War, US air power had undergone a massive transformation since the end of the Vietnam War fifteen years earlier. The F-15 Eagle and the F-16 Fighting Falcon were only part of a larger shift in US military aviation, joining with other new planes such as the F-117 Nighthawk stealth attack aircraft, the A-10 Thunderbolt II, and the Navy's F-14 Tomcat and F/A-18 Hornet. These aircraft benefited from advances in computing, electronics, radar, engine design, and aeronautical engineering. Older aircraft supplemented the new generation, including F-4 Phantoms, F-111s, A-6 Intruders, and B-52 Stratofortresses, to name a few. Concurrent advances in precision-guided weapons, sensors, communication and control, training, and doctrine increased the combat capabilities of the collective fleet.

The fighter advocates who argued for cheaper, simpler, highly specialized air-to-air combat planes did so because they envisioned a large-scale, massive war with the Soviet Union that would have had high aircraft attrition rates. Those arguing against the fighter advocates, mostly the military and defense industry establishment, sought more versatile designs based on advanced technology. They, too, foresaw a similar type of large-scale conflict, albeit one in which technologically enhanced navigation, computing, precision guidance, and all-weather radar capabilities were advantageous. As with other military technologies, the way in which the F-15 Eagle and the F-16 Fighting Falcon were marketed reveals much about the development of the airplanes and the clash of cultures within the US Air Force and the defense industry.

Examining the design and public relations trajectories for both planes reveals similar, though slightly inverted, trends. The F-15 started as a multimission plane, with significant internal debate about its true purpose.

Fighter advocates came in, determined to make it optimized for an air-to-air role. Although they were largely successful (the operational F-15C was used primarily for air-to-air roles and had no air-to-ground capability), they thought their ideas had been compromised and instead worked on the F-16. The Fighter Mafia thought that the F-16 would fulfill their goals of being an air-to-air-only "pure" fighter, but this goal was almost immediately compromised, as the plane became advertised and later used as a multimission ground attack plane. Later, modified versions of both aircraft competed against each other for a contract as a ground attack "Dual Role Fighter."

These developments suggest some larger conclusions pertaining to the history of US airpower. First, while small groups of dedicated advocates can have a large influence in a major organization like the US Air Force, that influence has limits. In the case of the F-15 and F-16, the internal debates or even confusion about these aircraft carried over into the promotional and public relations campaigns for both aircraft. This blurred messaging was partly due to pure confusion but also prompted by the desire of contractors to sell more aircraft by justifying their planes as being useful in multiple roles—and the desire of the Air Force to have aircraft that could be versatile. It was more profitable for the companies, and cheaper for the military, to modify existing aircraft than to pursue developing entirely new planes. The further along in the development, production, and operational life cycles of each aircraft, the less influence the fighter advocates had in their promotional messaging.

The small group of fighter advocates was disruptive to the trends of the Air Force, but only to a point. The Fighter Mafia hoped to stop or reverse the trend of new aircraft becoming increasingly expensive. The F-16 itself was one of the only US planes that cost significantly less than the earlier aircraft of its type. However, the combination of Air Force planning preferences, doctrines, and the incentives of contractor businesses created a strong inertia. The F-16 was modified away from the Fighter Mafia's "pure" vision, and the trends they hoped to halt only continued afterward. The next generation of fighter aircraft, the F-22 Raptor and F-35 Lightning II, have seen dramatic increases in costs relative to previous fighters.

Second, the Air Force has sometimes been criticized for its preference for versatile, multirole planes instead of specialized aircraft that are optimized for a single mission. That preference became clear in the development of the Eagle and Fighting Falcon, as even when internal forces fought hard for a single-mission focus, that focus became blurred due to institutional inertia. However, although this emphasis on versatile, jack-of-all-trades aircraft has at times produced results that some find frustrating, such as the F-4 Phantom and F-111, in the case of the F-15 and F-16, the versatility approach worked. Both aircraft continued to serve well into the twenty-first century and have consistently performed exceptionally at a variety of missions, including air-to-air and various types of bombing and attack roles.

The decade of the 1970s was a historical moment in which technology had matured to a point where the Eagle and the Fighting Falcon could, in fact, excel and dominate in both air-to-air and air-to-ground roles in ways that previous generations (and perhaps future generations) could not. By designing for air-to-air combat effectiveness first, the Air Force had produced, unintentionally or not, planes that proved that being a jack-of-all-trades did not necessarily mean being a master of none.

NOTES

1. McDonnell Douglas magazine advertisements: "The USAF F-15 Eagle: The Fighter Pilot's Fighter," *Aviation Week and Space Technology*, September 10, 1973, 64; "This Is the F-15 Ground Attack Fighter," *Aviation Week and Space Technology*, May 24, 1976, 44. These and similar advertisements appeared in other contemporary publications.
2. See Brian Laslie, *The Air Force Way of War: U.S. Tactics and Training After Vietnam* (Lexington: University Press of Kentucky, 2015).
3. For more on the nature and evolution of aerospace advertising, see Megan Prelinger, *Another Science Fiction: Advertising the Space Race, 1957–1962* (New York: Blast, 2010); and Karen Miller, "'Air Power Is Peace Power': The Aircraft Industry's Campaign for Public and Political Support, 1943–1949," *Business History Review* 70 (Autumn 1996): 297–327.
4. Craig C. Hannah, *Striving for Air Superiority: The Tactical Air Command in Vietnam* (College Station: Texas A&M University Press, 2002), 23, 46; Earl H. Tilford Jr., *Crosswinds: The Air Force's Setup in Vietnam* (College Station: Texas A&M University Press, 1993), 24–28; Frederick H. Smith, "Current Practice in Air Defense," *Air University Review* 6 (Spring 1953): 31–39. See also Caroline F. Ziemke, "In the Shadow of the Giant: USAF Tactical Air Command in the Era of Strategic Bombing, 1945–1955" (PhD diss., Ohio State University, 1989).
5. See Glenn E. Bugos, *Engineering the F-4 Phantom II: Parts into Systems* (Annapolis: Naval Institute Press, 1996); and Michael Hankins, "The Phantom Menace: The F-4 in Air Combat in Vietnam" (master's thesis, University of North Texas, 2013).
6. Gen. Gabriel P. Disosway, Oral History Interview, October 4–6, 1977, USAF Historical Research Agency, K239.0512-974, 271 (hereafter cited as Disosway OHI); Tilford,

Crosswinds, 35. See also Robert Coulam, *Illusions of Choice: The F-111 and the Problem of Weapons Acquisition Reform* (Princeton: Princeton University Press, 1977).

7. Charles E. Myers, Oral History Interview by Jacob Neufeld, July 18, 1973, USAF Historical Research Agency, K239.0512–971, 2–11 (hereafter cited as Myers OHI).
8. Lt. Gen. Arthur C. Agan, Oral History Interview, April 19–22, 1976, USAF Historical Research Agency, K239.0512–900, 398 (hereafter cited as Agan OHI), emphasis in original.
9. Jacob Neufeld, "The F-15 Eagle: Origins and Development, 1964–1972," Office of Air Force History, November 1974, 7; Myers OHI, 31–32; Maj. Gen. John J. Burns, Oral History Interview, March 22, 1973, USAF Historical Research Agency, K239.0512–961, 1–2.
10. Neufeld, "F-15," 8–11.
11. Mr. Heinrich J. Weigand Oral History Program Interview #862, March 27, 1973, USAF Historical Research Agency, K239.0512–862, 1–6.
12. Michael W. Hankins, *Flying Camelot: The F-15, the F-16, and the Weaponization of Fighter Pilot Nostalgia* (Ithaca: Cornell University Press, 2021), 64–71, 82.
13. Chris Hobson, *Vietnam Air Losses: United States Air Force, Navy, and Marines Corps Fixed-Wing Aircraft Losses in Southeast Asia, 1961–1973* (Hinkley: Midland, 2001), 17–18; Hankins, *Flying Camelot*, 67–68.
14. Neufeld, "F-15," 17; James Stevenson, *McDonnell Douglas F-15 Eagle* (Fallbrook: Aero, 1978), 10.
15. Neufeld, "F-15," 19.
16. Disosway OHI, 295–96.
17. Quoted in Neufeld, "F-15," 26.
18. "Hearings on Military Posture and Legislation to Authorize Appropriations During the Fiscal Year 1970," House of Representatives Committee on Armed Services, HASC No. 91–14, March 27, 1969, and May 20, 1969, 2633, 3273–74.
19. Stuart Levin, "F-15: The Teething of a Dogfighter," *Space/Aeronautics* 52 (December 1969): 36.
20. Air Force Secretary Seamans, Press Conference, December 12, 1969, Smithsonian National Air and Space Museum (NASM) Archives, Fairchild Collection, box 396, folder 6, 7–8. This date must be an error, as other sources in this folder confirm the 23rd, as well as Jack Abercrombie and Mike de Garcia, "F-15 Aircraft Development," July 29, 2005, Greater St. Louis Air and Space Museum Collections, 1.
21. Edgar Ulsamer, "The Coming Cost Crunch of the F-15," *Air Force Magazine*, January 1972, 38–43. The article mistakenly refers to the Foxbat as the MiG-23. For information on the MiG-25's capabilities, see "Intelligence: Big-Mouth Belenko," *Time*, October 11, 1976, https://time.com/archive/6879753/intelligence-big-mouth-belenko/.
22. "F-15 Rolls Out at St. Louis," *Flight International*, July 6, 1972.
23. Donald E. Fink, "USAF to Evaluate F-15 This Week," *Aviation Week and Space Technology*, September 18, 1972.
24. Image series from Greater St. Louis Air and Space Museum Collections, D4C 63454 Jun-69, D4C 63455 June-69, D4C 75792, D4E 511033 Jul-3–69, D4E 511035 Jul-3–69, D4E 511036 Jul-3–69, D4E 511037 Jul-3–69, D4C-109737 Dec-27–73.

McDonnell Douglas magazine advertisements: "The USAF F-15, the Fighter Pilot's Fighter," *Aviation Week and Space Technology*, July 19, 1971, 68; "Our F-15 Is the Big News in Fighter Planes," *US News and World Report*, December 12, 1972; "USAF F-15 Eagle," 64.

25. John F. Gulick, "The Eagle Makes the Scene," *Airman*, October 1972, 25–30.
26. Richard J. Levine, "McDonnell Douglas's F15 Fighter Appears Headed for Big Air Force Production Run," *Wall Street Journal*, February 12, 1973.
27. "F-15 Gets Hedged Okay After Engine Trouble," *Evening Star and Daily News* (Washington, DC), March 1, 1973, F-3; Clark Martin, "F-15 Offers Superior Maneuverability," *Aviation Week and Space Technology*, March 25, 1974, 40.
28. Clark Martin, "Simplicity Is Stressed in F-15 Operations," *Aviation Week and Space Technology*, April 1, 1974, 50–53.
29. G. M. Bailly-Cowell, "NATO Central Europe Gets the F-15 Eagle," *NATO's Fifteen Nations*, April–May 1975.
30. McDonnell Douglas Corporation, "F-15 Eagle Air Superiority Fighter, Background Information," November 1974, NASM Archives, AM-251120–03.
31. McDonnell Aircraft Company, "Eagle Flight Leader" series, 1974–1977, NASM Archives, AM-251120–03.
32. McDonnell Douglas magazine advertisement: "This Is the F-15 Ground Attack Fighter," *Aviation Week and Space Technology*, May 24, 1976, 44.
33. "F-15A Eagle in Production," *Aviation News* 5 (April 29–May 12, 1977): 2.
34. McDonnell Douglas, "F-15A Eagle: Air to Surface," n.d., NASM Archives, AM-251128–01.
35. McDonnell Aircraft Company, "USAF F-15A Eagle: The Versatile Fighter," n.d., NASM Archives, AM-251120–02.
36. McDonnell Aircraft Company, "Eagles for Tomorrow," January 1978, NASM Archives, AM-251120–02; and McDonnell Aircraft Company, "The Free World's New Standard," September 1978, NASM Archives, AM-251120–02.
37. Myers OHI, 38 (emphasis in original).
38. Email from Charles Myers forwarded to Robert Coram, November 11, 2000, US Marine Corps Archives and Records Division, Robert Coram Papers, box 9, folder 3 (hereafter cited as Coram Papers).
39. Pierre Sprey, Oral History Interview, June 12, 1973, USAF Historical Research Agency, K239.0512–969, 39 (hereafter cited as Sprey OHI); Memo, Pierre Sprey to James Ferguson, July 18, 1968, Coram Papers, box 10, folder 4.
40. Sprey OHI, 39–40; Neufeld, "F-15," 64.
41. Pierre M. Sprey, "F-XX and VF-XX—Feasible High Performance, Low Cost Fighter Alternatives," staff study, Office of the Assistant Secretary of Defense (Systems Analysis), June 9, 1969, Coram Papers, box 7, folder 4, 1, 8 (emphasis in original).
42. Bill Minutaglio, "Tales of the Fighter Mafia," *Dallas Life Magazine*, May 3, 1987, 12–13.
43. Everest E. Riccioni, "The Air Superiority Fighter, a Modern Analysis," research report, FR 39919, Air War College, Air University, Maxwell Air Force Base, AL, April 1968, 43, 53–56, 104, 124–25, 150–55.

44. Robert Coram, *Boyd: The Fighter Pilot Who Changed the Art of War* (New York: Little, Brown, 2002), 240. See also Grant T. Hammond, *The Mind of War: John Boyd and American Security* (Washington, DC: Smithsonian Books, 2001), 83–88.
45. Email from Robert Drabrant to Robert Coram, November 8, 2000, Coram Papers, box 9, folder 3; Minutaglio, "Tales," 10.
46. Harry J. Hillaker, "YF-16 Design Concept and Philosophy," presentation to 23rd Israel Annual Conference on Aviation and Astronautics, February 11–12, 1981, Coram Papers, box 9, folder 4, 2.
47. General Dynamics, "YF-16: Lightweight Fighter Prototype Aircraft," September 1973, NASM Archives, AG-033110-01.
48. Wade A. Scrogham, *Combat Relevant Task: The Test and Evaluation of the Lightweight Fighter Prototypes* (Edwards Air Force Base: Air Force Test Center History Office, 2014), 10–13.
49. Edgar Ulsamer, "YF-16: On Time, on Track, on Budget," *Air Force Magazine*, January 1974.
50. Erwin Bulban, "YF-16 Stresses Advanced Technology," *Aviation Week and Space Technology*, January 7, 1974.
51. Scrogham, *Combat Relevant Task*, 13–19.
52. Daniel Mark Gillespie, "Mission Emphasis and the Determination of Needs for New Weapon Systems" (PhD diss., Massachusetts Institute of Technology, 2009), 263–68.
53. Scrogham, *Combat Relevant Task*, 24.
54. Scrogham, *Combat Relevant Task*, 33–34.
55. "News Briefing by Secretary of the Air Force, John L. McLucas at the Pentagon," January 13, 1975, box 21, folder "Lightweight Fighters (Navy & Air Force), 1974–75 (4)" of the Martin R. Hoffmann Papers, Gerald R. Ford Presidential Library (hereafter cited as Hoffmann Papers).
56. General Dynamics, "F-16: Air Combat Fighter," c. 1974, NASM Archives, AG-033100-01.
57. James Fallows, *National Defense* (New York: Random House, 1981), 105; Hammond, *Mind of War*, 97.
58. General Dynamics, "F-16 Program Summary," August 15, 1977, Aeronautical Systems Division 771456, NASM Archives, General Dynamics F-16 Fighting Falcon Series, Briefing Packets, AG-033100-03.
59. Westinghouse pamphlet, "AN/APG-68, the New Standard for Fighter Radar," n.d., NASM Archives, General Dynamics F-16 Fighting Falcon Series, Avionics Systems, AG-033100-02; Westinghouse Public Relations Release, "Westinghouse Starts Full-Scale Development of the F-16 Radar," n.d., NASM Archives, General Dynamics F-16 Fighting Falcon Series, Avionics Systems, AG-033100-02.
60. *Hearings Before the Committee on Armed Services*, US Senate, 94th Cong., 2nd Sess., S.2965, Part 6: Research and Development, February 25–26, March 2, 4, 9, 1976, 3739–3740; *Hearings Before the Committee on Armed Services*, US Senate, 94th Cong., 2nd Sess., S.2965, Part 9: Tactical Airpower, March 8–12, 1976, 4896.
61. "General Dynamics' F-16 Selected as Air Force's New Jet Fighter," *St. Louis Post-Dispatch* (St. Louis, MS), January 14, 1975.

62. Clyde H. Farnsworth, "Gen. Dynamics' 'Contract of the Century'" insert, "David S. Lewis Comments on Winning F-16 Contract," *St. Louis Post-Dispatch* (St. Louis, MS), July 29, 1975.
63. Memo from Robert J. Croteau to Mr. Sullivan through Mr. Christie, "F-16 DSARC II Position Recommendation," February 4, 1975, box 21, folder "Lightweight Fighters (Navy & Air Force), 1974–75 (5)," Hoffmann Papers, 1, 3.
64. Memo from Chuck Myers to Hoffman, February 21, 1975, box 21, folder "Lightweight Fighters (Navy & Air Force), 1974–75 (4)," Hoffman Papers.
65. Myers to Hoffman, "F-16 (LWF/ACF) PROGRAM RESTORATION," box 21, folder "Lightweight Fighters (Navy & Air Force), 1974–75 (4)," Hoffman Papers, 2–3.
66. General Dynamics, "F-16 Air Combat Fighter," September 1, 1975, NASM Archives, AG-033100-01.
67. General Dynamics, "General Dynamics F-16 Air Combat Fighter Program," c. 1975, NASM Archives, AG-033100-01.
68. "F-16 Gains Advantage in Market," *Aviation Week and Space Technology*, January 20, 1975.
69. "A 'Superb Toy' Made for Air Superiority," *New York Times*, July 27, 1975.
70. Neil R. Anderson, "Flying the YF-16—a Flight Test Report on the USAF Air Combat Fighter," *Aerospace*, March 1976.
71. James Rider, "YF-16 Pilot Report," *Air Force Magazine*, October 1976, 37.
72. Drew Middleton, "Air Force Is Pinning Big Hopes on F-16's," *New York Times*, December 7, 1976.
73. General Dynamics, "F-16 Prototype—Production," January 28, 1977, NASM Archives, AG-033100-03.
74. General Dynamics, "F-16 Program Summary," August 15, 1977, NASM Archives, AG-033100-03.
75. General Dynamics, "F-16 Multirole Fighter," May 1977, NASM Archives, AG-033100-04.
76. General Dynamics, "The F-16 Multirole Fighter," April 1, 1977, NASM Archives, AG-033100-04.
77. See collection of "General Dynamics News" releases, NASM Archives, AG-033100-09.
78. General Dynamics magazine advertisements: "Multirole F-16," *Aviation Week and Space Technology*, February 6, 1978, 213; "F-16 . . . Perfect Choice for CAS/BAI," *Aviation Week and Space Technology*, July 18, 1988, 42; "Why Enemy Pilots Don't Sleep Well," *Aviation Week and Space Technology*, January 11, 1988, 40.
79. Stephen Good, "F-16 Fighters Beginning to Roll Off Production Line," *Morning News—Sunday News Journal* (Wilmington, DE), October 15, 1978, D-18, originally for the *Dallas Times Herald*.
80. Benjamin S. Lambeth, *The Transformation of American Air Power* (Ithaca: Cornell University Press, 2000), 166–67. See also Laslie, *Air Force Way of War*.
81. C. R. Anderegg, *Sierra Hotel: Flying Air Force Fighters in the Decade After Vietnam* (Washington, DC: Air Force History and Museums Program, US Air Force, 2001), 158–59; Kenneth P. Werrell, *Chasing the Silver Bullet: U.S. Air Force Weapons Development from Vietnam to Desert Storm* (Washington, DC: Smithsonian Books, 2003), 187–205.

82. Steven A. Fino, *Tiger Check: Automating the US Air Force Fighter Pilot in Air-to-Air Combat, 1950–1980* (Baltimore: Johns Hopkins University Press, 2017), 214–31; Werrell, *Chasing the Silver Bullet*, 70, 86–89.
83. Lon O. Nordeen, *Air Warfare in the Missile Age* (Washington, DC: Smithsonian Institution Press, 2002), 227–32, 285–88; Werrell, *Chasing the Silver Bullet*, 137–55. See also Lambeth, *Transformation*.
84. Laslie, *Air Force Way of War*; Lambeth, *Transformation*.
85. Joseph T. Stanik, *El Dorado Canyon: Reagan's Undeclared War with Qaddafi* (Annapolis: Naval Institute Press, 20003), 155–57. See also Diane T. Putney, *Airpower Advantage: Planning the Gulf War Air Campaign, 1989–1991* (Washington, DC: Air Force History and Museums Program, 2004), 121, 260–61.
86. Albert Picirillo, *Elegance in Flight: A Comprehensive History of the F-16XL Experimental Prototype and Its Role in NASA Flight Research* (Washington, DC: NASA, 2014), 149–51.
87. McDonnell Douglas, "F-15 Eagle Air Force Tactical Fighter," n.d., NASM Archives, AM-251120-02.
88. Werrell, *Chasing the Silver Bullet*, 74–75. See also Picirillo, *Elegance*; and Edgar Ulsamer, "In Focus: The Dual-Role Eagle," *Air Force Magazine*, April 1, 1984.

CONTRIBUTORS

Marc J. Alsina earned his PhD in the History of Science and Technology at Johns Hopkins University in 2022. His dissertation, "Argentine Wings: The State, Popular Culture, and the Creation of a Technological Future in Argentina, 1910–1955," argues that aviation was central to the formulation of an Argentine technical identity that spurred industrialization and inspired a lasting dedication to technological work on the part of common people. He was a postdoctoral fellow in the Krieger School Society of Fellows in the Humanities at Johns Hopkins University and a research associate with the Smithsonian National Air and Space Museum until 2024.

Janet R. Daly Bednarek is a professor of history at the University of Dayton, where she teaches courses on urban history and the history of American aviation. Her work on airport history includes *America's Airports: Airfield Development, 1918–1947* (Texas A&M, 2001), *Cities Take Flight: A Centennial History of the American Municipal Airport* (American Public Works Association, 2004), and most recently *Airports, Cities, and the Jet Age: US Airports Since 1945* (Palgrave Macmillan, 2016). Her article "The Flying Machine in the Garden: Parks and Airports, 1918–1938" was selected for inclusion in *The Best American History Essays, 2007* (Palgrave, 2007).

Patrick Luiz Sullivan De Oliveira is currently an assistant professor of History at IE University in Madrid, Spain, and a research associate at the Smithsonian National Air and Space Museum. His book *Ascending Republic: The Ballooning Revival in Nineteenth-Century France* (MIT Press, 2025) explores how the balloon achieved an iconic status in France in the decades preceding the First World War and how ballooning became a rallying point for the conflicting social groups that composed the fledgling Third Republic—from republican savants to aristocratic sportsmen.

Marc Dierikx held a position as a senior researcher at the Huygens Institute of the Royal Netherlands Academy of Sciences in Amsterdam until his retirement in 2024. The author of some thirty books and other publications, he specialized in the history of air transportation and its relation to foreign policy. His latest work is *Holding Patterns: Air Transport and Foreign Policy in the Netherlands* (Brill, 2024).

RÉNALD FORTIER is Curator Emeritus at the Canada Aviation and Space Museum in Ottawa. During a curatorial career that extended from 1995 to 2021, he had the honor and pleasure to develop a number of exhibitions, both temporary and demi-permanent, and to add many important items, both big and small, to the world-class collection of that national museum. Dr. Fortier's main interests are the social and cultural aspects of the history of flight.

MICHAEL W. HANKINS is the curator for US Air Force, Navy, and Marine Corps post–World War II Aviation at the Smithsonian National Air and Space Museum and the author of *Flying Camelot: The F-15, the F-16, and the Weaponization of Fighter Pilot Nostalgia* from Cornell University Press. He is also an assistant editor of *From Balloons to Drones*, a scholarly web journal for the study of air power, and host of the *From Balloons to Drones* podcast. He is a former assistant professor of strategy at the USAF Air University eSchool of Graduate Professional Military Education and a former instructor of military history at the USAF Academy. Hankins completed his PhD in history at Kansas State University in 2018 and his master's in history from the University of North Texas in 2013.

SCOTT W. PALMER is currently a professor of history at the University of Texas, Arlington. A specialist in the interdisciplinary history of Russian technology, science, culture, and the arts, he is the author of *Dictatorship of the Air: Aviation Culture and the Fate of Modern Russia* (Cambridge University Press, 2006) and coeditor of *Science, Technology, Environment, and Medicine in Russia's Great War and Revolution* (Slavica Publishers, 2022) and *How History Is Made: A Student's Guide to the Reading, Writing, and Thinking in the Discipline* (Mavs Open Press, 2022). His lecture course "Flight Culture and the Human Experience" (https://spoke-network.org/courses/flightculture/) led him to conceive this volume.

JOHANNA RUSTLER is interested in women's and labor history in the First World War and the history from below. She will complete her PhD at the University of Aberdeen in 2024 with the thesis entitled "The Experiences of Employed Women and Girls in Britain during the First World War:

Continuity and Change in the Railway Industry." She is currently a senior research associate at the Historical Foundation of the Swiss Railways.

CAROLINE E. TAPP is the Social and Cultural History Curator in the Aeronautics Department at the Smithsonian National Air and Space Museum. Prior, she served as a Department of Defense public historian at the Naval History and Heritage Command and the 2021 Andrew W. Mellon Postdoctoral Curatorial Fellow at the American Philosophical Society Library and Museum. Tapp earned a PhD in American studies from the University of Texas at Austin and holds an MA in history and a BA in history and anthropology from Miami University (Ohio). Her forthcoming book reveals the interdisciplinary history of women who achieved careers as permanent US airline pilots from 1973 through 2001.

INDEX

Page numbers in italics refer to figures.

www.ingramcontent.com/pod-product-compliance
Lightning Source LLC
LaVergne TN
LVHW090730280825
819315LV00001B/2

* 9 7 8 1 6 4 8 4 3 3 0 7 8 *